Goddesses in South Asia

Goddesses in South Asia

Traditions and Transformations

Edited by

R. Mahalakshmi, Malavika Binny
and Megha Yadav

BLOOMSBURY
NEW DELHI • LONDON • OXFORD • NEW YORK • SYDNEY

BLOOMSBURY INDIA
Bloomsbury Publishing India Pvt. Ltd
Second Floor, LSC Building No. 4, DDA Complex, Pocket C – 6 & 7,
Vasant Kunj, New Delhi, 110070

BLOOMSBURY, BLOOMSBURY ACADEMIC INDIA and the
Diana logo are trademarks of Bloomsbury Publishing Plc

First published in India 2025
This edition published 2025

Bloomsbury Academic India
An imprint of Bloomsbury Publishing Plc

ISBN: HB: 978-93-61314-76-6; eBook: 978-93-61315-43-5
2 4 6 8 10 9 7 5 3 1

Typeset by Integra Software Services Pvt. Ltd.
Printed and bound in India by Replika Press Pvt. Ltd

To the real life goddesses—our grandmothers, mothers, daughters, sisters and sisters-in-arms

Contents

Images, Diagrams and Tables

Images/Figures

Diagrams

Tables

Acknowledgements

There are many who have provided support, encouragement and helped shape this volume, which has been a labour of love for us. First, the faculty and students at the Centre for Historical Studies, JNU, New Delhi, contributed to the holding of a conference on this theme, and enriched the deliberations through their participation. Scholars from different parts of the globe made presentations in the international conference held in May 2023, and this was the starting point for our volume. Our heartfelt thanks to Prof. Sree Padma, Bowdoin College, USA, for her kindness in delivering the inaugural address virtually, at a very late hour for her. Thanks are also due to Prof. Anamika Roy, University of Allahabad, Prayagraj, for being our valedictory speaker at the conference. The scholarship of these two scholars is well-known, and has informed our own premises and intellectual engagement with the study of goddess traditions.

The ten contributors to this volume have been patient every step of the way, despite our frequent correspondence and demands for immediate attention with regard to their chapters. This volume is as much the result of their efforts, and as editors we are thankful to them.

The Centre for Historical Studies, JNU, New Delhi, the Department of History, Kannur University, Kannur, and the Department of History, SRM University, Amaravati, provided the space for us to undertake our editorial responsibilities.

The History Collective (THC), an initiative to promote and provide a platform for excellence in historical research, has been supportive of this project from its inception. One of the editors, R. Mahalakshmi, was part of THC's project on temples in Telangana, and our thanks to the officials and staff at the Departments of Archaeology and Culture. A special thanks to Ms Shailaja Ramaiyer, Principal Secretary, Endowments, Government of Telangana, for permission to use photographs for the book cover.

Libraries and institutions that have afforded us the stimulation of an intellectual environment while allowing us the space to be immersed in our work, include the Centre for Advanced Study – CHS library at JNU, Government Ayurveda College, Tripunithura, Government Ayurveda College, Thiruvananthapuram, the India International Centre library, New Delhi, the Kate Hamburger Centre for Advanced Study *inherit.heritage in transformation*, Humboldt University, Faculty of Theology, Humboldt University, Department of History at SUNY Cortland and the SUNY University at Albany library.

The confidence of our publisher, Bloomsbury India, particularly Mr Chandra Sekhar, helped us carry the idea of the volume to fruition. The editorial support we gained from Karthiga and her team at Integra has been invaluable. Our gratitude. We are also deeply thankful to Trisha and Navoneel for spending many days and nights going through every line of the proofs.

As products of a glorious institution, we watch in dismay as our institutional edifices are being taken down through anti-intellectual policies, here and in other parts of South Asia, and indeed the world. Equally, we celebrate the resilience that is only possible when courage has been inculcated over generations. Our endeavour has been to demonstrate that power, by invoking the goddesses (and gods) in our everyday lives—the women and men who have spearheaded our intellectual lives and influenced the academic and the personal, by questioning, dissenting and presenting alternate ways of thinking about, and beyond, the world.

Introduction

R. Mahalakshmi, Malavika Binny and Megha Yadav

Goddesses are revered in several parts of the world, and although the names, forms and myths related to them may be different, the fact of their cultic existence is proof that in several societies the divine was conceptualized as feminine. A strong case has been made for regarding this phenomenon as the original concept of the divine, when no male/father figure was worshipped, either individually or attached to the goddess, and substantive archaeological evidence was brought to bear to support the proposition.[1] It was argued in a persuasive way.

> The main theme of Goddess symbolism is the mystery of birth and death and the renewal of life, not only human but all life on earth and indeed in the whole cosmos. Symbols and images cluster around the parthenogenetic (self-generating) Goddess and her basic functions as Giver of Life, Wielder of Death, and, not less importantly, as Regeneratrix, and around the Earth Mother, the Fertility Goddess young and old, rising and dying with plant life. She was the single source of all life who took her energy from the springs and wells, from the sun, moon and moist earth. This symbolic system represents cyclical, not linear, mythical time. In art this is manifested by the signs of dynamic motion: whirling and twisting spirals, winding and coiling snakes, circles, crescents, horns, sprouting seeds and shoots.[2]

The premise of goddess worship pre-dating that of gods in various cultures, and of this tradition continuing over millennia, has led to the perception that these were societies where women played an influential role. The reproductive powers of women, their monthly menstrual cycles, and their ability to nurture offspring through their bodies possibly paved the way for the veneration of the divine feminine. The mystery of human reproduction may have been understood in physiological terms, but its ideational and symbolic meaning would have persisted over time. Ironically, this occurred in contexts where women ceased to have any social recognition or agency in a real sense, as the growth of patriarchy in its myriad manifestations and institutional forms retained the divine feminine conceptually but transfigured her substantially. On the one hand, perhaps because of women's association with nature in terms of their reproductive capacity, they were given a secondary status; on the other, this was concomitant with culture and civilization being seen as male accomplishments. Male gods, their pantheons and their dominance in the religious terrain are attributed to this process of ideological formation. The triumph of patriarchy was also interpreted as 'the world historic defeat of women', which had ramifications in the religious sphere as well, with goddesses either marginalized or relegated to the roles of spouses and appendages of male gods. This understanding has informed the efforts of feminists around the world to retrieve and re-centre the goddess-centric belief system and transform it into a potent symbol for women's empowerment. For scholars of feminist persuasion or those influenced by feminism, goddess cults and the mythologies surrounding them are a window into the social world of gender, where women's imbrication in social institutions vis-à-vis men is mirrored in the divine realm. The hold of religion on the lives of 'thinking' humans – those immersed in language-mediated relationships and tied through their common beliefs and ideologies – arose from the social context. Power hierarchies, asymmetries of age, expertise and experience are as important in the creation and upholding of patriarchies as are economic factors, particularly in the form of control over material resources and the development of the notion of private property.[3]

A very interesting case where the academic interest in the goddess found a resonance among feminist collectives is in the archaeological site of Çatalhöyük, an important Neolithic settlement in the Konya plain of Anatolia in Turkey.[4] The numerous female figurines made of clay, and especially the imposing seated figure on a lion-flanked throne, led to the interpretation by the excavator of the site, James Mellaart, in the 1960s that the society producing these artefacts revered women as goddesses. Although subsequent excavations and interpretations have moved away from this viewpoint and postulated male and female deities being worshipped, with no singular cult of the goddess prevailing, this association continues to hold sway, particularly among the group known as Goddess feminists. At other sites of the Neolithic or of other periods – for instance, in Malta, New Zealand or India – the claiming of the female power embodied by the goddess has a resonance for feminists of various ilks.[5] The fascination for the goddess, thus, has moved (or possibly always was) beyond the academic desire to study the seemingly contradictory and complementary evolution and transmogrification of societies and cultures.

This volume is the outcome of a conference on Goddesses in South Asia held in the hybrid mode on 3–4 May 2023. This was part of the course 'Religion and Society', taught in the Centre for Historical Studies, JNU by one of the editors, R Mahalakshmi, over the past two decades. While organizing conferences and workshops to facilitate better discussion among scholars and enable students to be cognizant of issues and perspectives has always been the hallmark of education in JNU, there are serious challenges that have emerged in recent years. The first of these relates to the lack of funding, which has, of late, seemingly stemmed from non-academic concerns, causing serious academic damage. The second has a more immediate context and relates to the new modes and media of learning and teaching, which, while enabling for some sections, have left a significant number from underprivileged backgrounds lagging due to the digital divide. After the resumption of regular classes post-lockdown, we found as teachers that the sense of disorientation was very difficult for students (and, to some extent, teachers!) to shake off. Even in institutions such as JNU, where the academic curriculum is more fluid and involves discussion and reading as essential components, the personal losses and health issues suffered by so many made it difficult to find a purpose. In this atmosphere, it was felt that something to enthuse the community was needed, and what better way than to invoke the goddess. Scholars from across the country and the world responded with enthusiasm to the call, and the deliberations over two days brought to the fore rigorous textual, iconographic, and archaeological analysis within historical frames. The diversity of the traditions of the goddess in different regional historical contexts, and the sub-continental sharing of ideas and beliefs related to the divine feminine, expressed conceptually and through mythology, was the hallmark of the deliberations in the eighteen presentations made.

The volume brings together thirteen papers that were presented at the conference, organized into four parts. The first part attempts to frame issues that have concerned scholars and includes one essay that provides a broad overview of the goddess spectrum from religious, regional and local perspectives, drawing attention to the historical and anthropological studies as well as literary histories on the subject. The central argument is that goddess worship, like other cults or belief systems, has never been static; there have been assimilations, marginalizations and even complete revamping of traditions in different historical contexts. The fact that the goddess continues to elicit such strong feelings of devotion and admiration from academic and other quarters is rooted in this history of the transmogrification of her cultic persona and worship.

The second part brings together six important case studies that illuminate the conceptualization of the goddess as mother and in other forms. The earliest literary evidence, in the form of the sacred text *Ṛg Veda* (*c.* 1500–1000 BCE), is examined by Prerana Roy for its depiction of goddesses as mothers, protectors, lovers and beneficent deities. The cognate *Avesta* (*c.* 1200–1000 BCE), a product of a common cultural ethos as the *Ṛg Veda*, is scrutinized to unravel the shared conceptualizations and variant depictions of female divinities. Both texts studied are complex and layered, revealing a concern for the maintenance of cosmic order. In the Vedic tradition, terms of address or description for the goddess included *patnī*, *devapatnī* and *gñā*. Goddesses are invoked for the protection of the sacrifice or elements associated with it, such as the *barhi* grass; they are called *payasvatī*, brimming with milk, indicating their association with nourishment in the maternal sense. The *Avestan* goddesses are more often than not invoked to uphold morality and ensure the perpetuation of the patriarchal, patrilineal family. The concern with progeny, male progeny in particular, extends to childbirth, and goddesses in both traditions appear as the safe anchor for pregnant women. In both texts, the goddess is conceived in various ways, reflecting the social needs of her community of worshippers.

Jaina conceptions of the divine feminine are complex and incorporate theistic elements charged with philosophical content. What is particularly fascinating about the essay by Trisha is its focus on a text on prognostication, the *Aṅgavijjā* (*c.* first to sixth century CE), which brings two issues to the forefront. First, we see the Jaina engagement with the *joisa/jyotiṣa* knowledge system and, in this text, the belief in foretelling based on bodily marks and features. Second, there is the assimilation of theistic worship traditions, such as those of the *yakṣīs* and goddesses, indicating a shift in the patronage structures and contexts for the laity. While concepts such as *pañca parameṣṭhi* may have been difficult for the ordinary follower to comprehend, by introducing the notion of *lokapuruṣa* – the cosmic being – and incorporating the earlier great 'liberated' beings, including the *tīrthaṅkaras* at the highest level of this being, with the *devas*, then humans, and the lesser gods and goddesses, along with other aspects of creation being drawn into different levels on the body of that being, an attempt was made to appeal to popular needs. Knowledge of prognostication is personified in the form of the goddess *Aṅgavijjā*, who was created by none other than Mahāvīra, thereby legitimizing its status. Furthermore, several goddesses are mentioned, such as Hirī/Hrī, Sirī/Śrī, Lacchi/Lakṣmī, etc., and they are invariably associated with negative prognoses. This is related to the nature of Jaina ideas and the assimilative process by which known goddesses like Śrī are abstracted in their veneration, while other goddesses emerging from different sources became part of the Jaina tradition and acquired a more significant place. Mahiṣāsuramardinī, the epithet of the goddess Durgā who vanquished the demon Mahiṣa, is the subject of enquiry in Sneha Ganguly's chapter, which draws upon two important Puranic tellings of the myth. The *Devī Māhātmyam* (c. sixth century CE), found in the *Mārkaṇḍeya Purāṇa*, and the famous Śākta *Upapurāṇa*, the *Kālikā Purāṇa* (c. eleventh century CE), provide a vivid picture of the encounter between the goddess and the *asura* Mahiṣa. The comparison of the story of the origins of the goddess and the demon, their characteristics, encounters and the final triumph of the goddess indicates the accretion of elements that can be attributed to the tribal absorption and inclusion of several local cults and forms of worship within the Brahmanical sectarian pantheons. The iconographic canvas from different parts of the subcontinent accentuates this absorption.

Two other chapters focus on iconography with a view to discursively engage with representations and their signification. The images of the divine couple Śiva and Pārvatī from Kālañjara are placed in the context of the flourishing of Tantric Śaivism in central India. The influence of the Śaiva monastic organization in determining the nature of iconographic representation is also highlighted in Dolan Samanta's paper. Inscriptions attest to the Candella rulers having preceptors of the Pāśupata faith. Myths from the *Śiva Purāṇa* and *Liṅga Purāṇa* are used to foreground the gendered portrayal of the divine couple, their marriage and sexuality, which lend legitimacy to normative social ideas through their visual depiction in specific ways. Iconographic prescriptions for goddesses provided in the category of texts called the *Śilpa Śāstras* are the subject matter of Ashima Ahuja's chapter, with a specific focus on *Mayamatam* and *Mānasāra*. These prescriptive manuals, in their extant form, belong to a later period compared to the numerous temples that began dotting the many regional landscapes of the Indian subcontinent. Studies by various scholars have demonstrated that despite this apparent anomaly, the basic tenets of using a *tālamānam,* or system of measurement, and certain rules related to building and decorative techniques were known, indicating an oral tradition that would have been in vogue. The second interesting aspect is that, especially in the case of religious art and architecture, there were commonalities across regions despite the emergence of regional styles, lending to the view that the ideation was provided by the experts within those traditions, as the monuments and art were meant for a specific purpose. Ahuja's work focuses on how the texts presented the religious view – here, the Brahmanical one – on where to house which goddess within a settlement and within a demarcated sacred space, what forms of representation were prescribed when depicted by herself and with a male deity, and what meanings – social and cosmic – were conveyed through such characterization. Given the southern provenance of these texts, Ahuja analyses inscriptional references and the iconography of a few goddesses from the region.

The manifestations of the goddess as protectors and powerful beings are examined in four chapters. Using a cultural anthropological perspective, Arun Gupto reflects on humanity's quest for protection against natural and other forces, and how this quest manifests in the divine realm through the worship of goddesses such as Vārāhī in the Kathmandu Valley. The region experienced state formation in the mid-first millennium CE, and three important urban centres emerged that dominated the cultural landscape over the next thousand years, namely Kathmandu, Patan and Bhaktapur. Drawing a distinction between the Vārāhīs located on the outer perimeters of the city and those situated within the *mandiras* or temples, Gupto presents an illuminating discussion of the iconographic features and symbolic associations of the various goddesses. Based primarily on fieldwork, this chapter highlights the significance of the ethno-historical method in understanding the textual mutations that may occur in the ways people relate to divinities. The rigour of the historical method, particularly in drawing upon epigraphical sources, is demonstrated in Malini Adiga's chapter on Tantric goddesses in early medieval Karnataka. References to the goddess collective, as *mātṛgaṇa* and *saptamātṛ*, and to individual deities referred to by the generic names Bhagavatī or Śakti, were well known in the region for much of the first millennium CE, beginning with the fourth-century dynasty of the Kadambas. The Jaina *yakṣī* cult of Ambikā was known here from the seventh century, and it is believed that Jvālāmālinī may have originated here. In the case of the *yakṣī* Padmāvatī, known from at least the tenth century in the region, dynasties like the Gangas and Hoysalas a few centuries later laid claim to power and kingship thanks to her intervention. It is the two records at Kolar and Kukkanur attesting to Tantric worship, with descriptions of *cakra maṇḍalas* and Yōgēśvara-Yōginī practitioners, the *upacāras* to be followed, and the animal sacrifices to be provided for, that are most interesting. In the Kolaramma temple, datable to the eleventh century, Cāmuṇḍēśvari is enshrined in the *mūlasthāna* (sanctum sanctorum) and the other Saptamātṛkās were accorded a space, along with Yōgēśvarī. The other temple built a century later accords a special place to Jyeṣṭhādevi, who has the epithets Kāḷikā, Bhadrakāḷi, Mahākāḷī, Nīlā etc., whose worship in different forms could remove afflictions and establish power. The inclusion of Jyeṣṭhā, a reviled figure in the Puranic myths, as the central deity within Tantric Śaivism speaks to the nature of assimilations occurring within the Brahmanical traditions, and the reference to goddesses like Dēkamma signifies the appropriation of local cults into Brahmanism. Two striking elements brought out in this rich study are the intertwining of Kaula and Puranic traditions, and the institutionalized worship of young unmarried girls – the *kanyā pūjā*, which is still prevalent in some parts of the subcontinent especially during the Śarada Navarātri (autumn festival of nine nights/ the Dussehra), the most well known being the elaborate Newari celebration of it.

The textual celebration of the Tantric Guhyakālī and Kāmakalākālī in the *Mahākālasaṃhitā* forms the subject of Navoneel Ray's chapter. Believed to have been composed by one Ādinātha, possibly in the Mithila region, its first part – the *Guhyakālīkhaṇḍa* – was composed around the tenth century, while the second part – the *Kāmakalākālīkhaṇḍa* – belongs to the thirteenth, and its prominent attestation is found in seventeenth-century Nepal, thus revealing its complex and layered history as a text. Treating the *varṇas* as distinct and yet inclusive for the purpose of the ritual, Ray brings out the so-called transgressive elements as part of a strategy availed by the Karṇāṭa and Oiṇīvāra dynasties of Mithila to stake their power and use well-established Śākta precepts in the region to declare their control over realm and the people. Focusing on texts and visual sources, Megha Yadav draws our attention to the Buddhist deity Tārā, and particularly her association with the concept of *aṣṭamahābhaya* (eight great fears). There are several instances in the *Nikāya, Dhammapada* and other Pali texts where this concept is elaborated in its physical and social dimensions. Especially in the case of the physical, from the wilderness to mosquitoes, a range of fear-inducing physical distress were enumerated, and the remedy given was meditation on Buddha initially, and later the Mahāyāna tradition brought in various protective deities to be worshipped to allay these fears, the most prominent among these being Avalokiteśvara. It is very interesting that the *Lalitavistāra*, possibly composed in the fourth century CE, lists among the fears kings and gods along with *Nāgas, Yakṣas,* thieves, starvation etc. In western India, post-fiifth century CE, the number and list were standardized as follows: lions, snakes, elephants, evil spirits/demons, shipwrecks, captivity and slavery, the sword of the enemy ruler, and fire. Although mythology attributes her birth to Avalokiteśvara shedding tears of compassion, from which pool she emerged as a fully formed sixteen-year-old personification of *karuṇā*, Tārā became popular in her own right with an independent cult devoted to her emerging by the seventh century CE. An important point made by Yadav is the influence of the ideology of *bhakti* in Mahāyāna Buddhism, an almost completely ignored area in contemporary scholarship, which brought the worshipper to repose complete faith in the goddess Tārā as the refuge from the *aṣṭamahābhaya*. She draws attention to another relatively unexplored issue – the fifteenth-century Tibetan Buddhist attempts to refocus the worship of Tārā towards inner spiritual seeking, with the belief that the goddess alleviated the internal fears, rather than the literal, for instance, anger, envy, pride, greed etc.

Three chapters inform the discussion on contemporary iterations of the goddess, drawing upon historical conceptualizations and mythology. Communities have an intimate association with goddesses, and their characterization and characteristics flow from that relationship. Malavika Binny brings the intricate, complex and fluid conceptualizations of Māriyammaṉ through a study of folklore, rituals, songs and fieldwork in Kerala. Historically, the provenance of this goddess was within the *avarṇa* settlements of south India, and even today she continues to be very important among Dalit-Bahujan communities. However, over the past decades it appears that this goddess has become popular with the *savarṇas* as well, and temples on a grander scale in the typical Dravidian style, with Brahmin priests and Vedic/Sanskrit chanting, have been brought into her worship. That this is not a simple imposition or cult appropriation can be seen from the non-Brahmin, largely Vishwakarma, priests accepting the Brahmin's presence and rituals. Equally, the folk practices like walking on fire embers, which in Tamil is referred to euphemistically as *pū metikkal* (walking on flowers), or offering of blood sacrifices in the form of roosters and other animals, indicate the influence of the local cultic traditions. The enforced vegetarian diet of the goddess, due to Brahmanical influence, and the legal abolition of animal sacrifice, finds an interesting substitution in the form of gourds that are split with a heavy hand and instrument to enact the animal slaughter. Cross-dressing of the male priests and worshippers, the epithet of the goddess as Ardhanārīśvarī, and the mythological subversions of the Brahmanical lore indicate a complex process of absorption and assimilation that is a two-way process, which cannot be simplistically understood through concepts of Sanskritization or of 'great' and 'little' traditions.

The tragic death of a young woman named Roop Kanwar on the funeral pyre of her husband in 1987 in Rajasthan, India, symbolizing her chastity and duty as a *pativratā*, a custom glorified in literature and folklore as *sati*, is the subject of Twinkle Siwach's chapter. The myth of Sati, the consort of Śiva, who died rather than bear the insult meted out to her husband, has often been used to uphold the ideal wife within Brahmanical traditions.

Through a careful documentary description using various media such as newspaper reports, FIRs and interviews, the chapter explores how the woman, who ceased to be a living being in the eyes of her marital family upon the death of her husband, as well as in the eyes of a larger community of believers in the practice of *sati*, was transformed into a goddess in their perception. First brought under the purview of modern law in 1829 under William Bentinck, the governor-general of India, a new law was enacted in modern India, The Commission of Sati (Prevention) Act in 1987, in response to this incident. The rather crass response of the market is also highlighted, in terms of the posters and other items that were being sold both at the site of the *sati* and elsewhere. The response of women's groups, the state, law enforcement agencies and the spokesmen of tradition vividly brings out the conflicting views of women's identity as independent versus socially embedded beings, and the distorted connection that was drawn between woman and goddess.

Anisha Saxena highlights a different set of instances, which revolve around the goddess Durgā and the use of her iconography and characterization in the United States. The claims of the diasporic community about who could speak on behalf of the Hindu tradition, what could be the appropriate forms of representation of gods and goddesses, and the interesting interplay of the market and commodification of images (as also seen in Siwach's discussion) are some important issues raised here. In this context, the ascription of goddess identity and iconography to a public persona becomes a point of contention, as those who claimed to represent the keepers of the 'tradition' rejected it. This stands in contrast to the case of Roop Kanwar, who was 'made' into a sati goddess, where her death, endorsed by society, became her entry to eternal glory.

The chapters in this volume question simplistic and straitjacketed approaches to the goddess, who is never one-dimensional, with the same deity taking on different personas in texts and visuals, in regional and local contexts. The image chosen for the cover is of a Tantric goddess from Alampur, Telangana, worshipped today as Jogulāmbā. While her iconographic features are not definitive ascriptions of a specific goddess, they certainly draw on Brahmanical Tantric symbolism and Puranic mythology. Even though a Śaiva temple complex built by the Cālukyas of Badami in the seventh century is known from this site, and repeatedly received patronage from kings and others, and there is nothing in the written record to attest the same for Jogulāmbā's presence, the place is known as the seat of the goddess for her worshippers across the region, suggesting her prior cultic presence. Given that traditions are manifold, no single community can ever claim a definitive view on religious beliefs, as this would imply the negation of others' beliefs. The chapters in this volume attest that the conceptualization of the goddess is no exception.

Notes

1 Gimbutas, Marija. 1974. *The Language of the Goddess*. San Francisco: Harper and Row.

2 Ibid., xix.

3 Pioneers in the field of enquiry are: Engels, Frederick. 1902 (1884). *Origins of the Family, Private Property, and the State*. Chicago: Charles H. Kerr and Company. Beauvoir, Simone de. 1953 (1949). *The Second Sex*. London: Jonathan Cape. Lerner, Gerda. 1986. *The Creation of Patriarchy*. New York: Oxford University Press. Ortner, Sherry B. 1974. 'Is Female to Male as Nature Is to Culture'. In *Woman, Culture, and Society*, edited by M.Z. Rosaldo and L. Lamphere. Stanford: Stanford University Press, 68–87.

4 Rountree, Kathryn. 2007. 'Archaeologists and Goddess Feminists at Çatalhöyük: An Experiment in Multivocality'. *Journal of Feminist Studies in Religion*, 23 (2): 7–26.

5 Rountree, Kathryn. 2004. *Embracing the Witch and the Goddess: Feminist Ritual-Makers in New Zealand*. London: Routledge. Also see: Kohli, Seema (ed.), 2024. *Birthing the Goddess: The Feminine and the Idea of Birth*. Delhi: Aryan Books International. Dupuis, Stella (ed.), 2019. *Experiencing the Goddess: On the Trail of the Yoginis*. Delhi: Aryan Books International.

Part One

The Discursive Field

1

Framing the Goddess: Contexts, Methodologies and Concerns

R. Mahalakshmi

One of the most conspicuous elements in the religious life of the people of the Indian subcontinent has been the worship of the goddess. The work of Marija Gimbutas and other prehistorians, who believed that all societies first worshipped the mother principle and therefore goddesses were represented in the form of women and symbolized women's agency, paved the way for feminist scholars and theologians to explore the divine feminine in religion. Scholars like Rita Gross, Rosemary Reuther and Kathleen Erndl have regarded goddess worship as a symbol of empowerment or emancipation and have tried to explore the inclusion of theistic ideas and practices in androcentric religions.[1] Making a strong case for the anthropomorphization of the goddess and drawing upon Hindu ideas related to the divine feminine, Gross also evaluates how the presence of the goddess per se did not mean a non-patriarchal or anti-patriarchal religious society.[2] Even outside of the academic domain, although in several instances informed by it, there have been attempts to interpret and idolize some forms of the divine feminine, such as the publishing house Kali for Women, set up by feminists Urvashi Butalia and Ritu Menon in 1984, or more recently, Leena Manimekalai's film, *Kaali* (2022). The poster of the latter, which was to be screened as part of a project at Toronto Metropolitan University funded by the Aga Khan Foundation celebrating multiculturalism in Canada, elicited outrage in certain circles. The image on the poster was of the goddess Kālī smoking a cigarette and sparked a debate in India and abroad, with politicians, religio-political groups, and especially netizens among those accusing the director Leena Manimekalai of offending religious sentiments. What was this film about? Manimekalai described it as a 'performance documentary', imagining the goddess Kālī 'descending onto a queer female filmmaker' and viewing Canada – and its diverse people – through her eyes. Manimekalai says, 'She is a free spirit. She spits at patriarchy. She dismantles Hindutva (an ideology that seeks to transform secular India into a Hindu nation). She destroys capitalism. She embraces everyone with a thousand hands.' Kālī 'chooses love' and accepts a cigarette from 'working-class street dwellers'. The so-called offensive poster features the director dressed as the goddess Kālī, smoking, and holding aloft a rainbow flag, a symbol of the LGBTQ community.

The criticism of a personal take on the goddess by self-proclaimed keepers of religion is nothing new. M.F. Husain, the acclaimed painter, drew upon myths and tradition, and the goddess was often his muse. Satyajit Ray's Bangla film *Devi* (1960) also drew upon the goddess for inspiration, but from a critical perspective, where superstition and the reduction of women's agency in private and social life were represented. Husain and Ray had to face immense criticism, and Ray, in an interview, countered this by attacking the dogmatism that was sometimes an unfortunate part of religious consciousness.

It is from this vantage point – where the goddess provides a religious and symbolic anchor across communities and contexts – that we believe it is important to contextualize goddess worship, understand the impetus for its development in historical terms and explore the ways – disciplinary and methodological – that allow us to examine different dimensions of the divine feminine.

Devī in the Vedic, Puranic and Śākta Traditions

Textual and archaeological evidence have been analysed by numerous scholars to explore the ostensible long-standing continuity of goddess worship within the Brahmanical traditions across the vast Indian subcontinent. D.D. Kosambi, one of the first historians to highlight the significance of this phenomenon, argued that food-gathering communities were the ones who first venerated the 'mother goddess', and that 'god the father' could not have been conceived of before the pastoral period.[3] Methodologically, Kosambi's *Myth and Reality* drew attention to the transformation of religious ideas and cults over time and located these transformations within the broad historical contexts that were evolving. Broadly, he noted that in the sphere of religion, 'fossilized and stratified remnants of primitive observances, combined with caste and religion, hold a particular group together. The observances also located the coherent group relatively to others within a highly composite society. Change of status is reflected in, and acted till recently through some corresponding transformation in caste, sometimes by change in cult as well'. In other words, while there were contextual changes, there were significant continuities in the realm of beliefs and practices. N.N. Bhattacharya in his masterly study titled *Indian Mother Goddess* presented the view that the worship of goddesses emanated in social contexts where the fertility of the soil was appreciated, and that this reflected the importance of women in such societies. His hypothesis was that the worship of the mother goddess emerged in societies 'where agriculture developed considerably, without any intervening pastoral stage, mother right elements became the guiding forces of society'.[4] But he argued that this tradition was a pre-Vedic one, and may possibly be traced to the Neolithic and Chalcolithic cultures and Bronze Age civilization in India. Scholars have taken this argument forward, and particularly in the work of the latter there is an effective use of archaeological evidence from the Harappan civilization to posit a goddess-centric religion in those times.[5] For others, it is the rich literary corpus that provides evidence of continuity in goddess worship. V.S. Agrawala (1963), Pushpendra Kumar (1974), Stella Kramrisch (1978),[6] P.K. Agrawala (1983), J.N. Tiwari (1985)[7] and Tracy Pintchman (1994)[8] are some of the scholars who have studied the appearance of the divine feminine in the *Ṛg* and later *Vedas* and the continuity of these deities as seen in the post-Vedic and Puranic texts. Although there is an attempt in these works, in varying degrees, to foreground the historical contexts, the nature of the sources and the teleological perspectives render these problematic. More specific studies from the mid-twentieth century, such as those of Haripada Chakraborti and D.C. Sircar, draw our attention to multiple sources that may be used to reconstruct forms of the goddess in Śākta religion.[9] To a large extent, these scholars assume the historical context – religious developments were not linked to the nature of social transformations. It is in the materialist interpretation of the social milieu of the *Vedas*, or of Buddhism and other Śramaṇic traditions, or of Tantricism that a clear connection between religious traditions and the socio-economic and political contexts was established.[10] Such a methodology of linking religion with the historical context with regard to the study of goddess traditions is best exemplified in the essay by B.D. Chattopadhyaya that studied the evocation of goddesses in inscriptions from the mid-first millennium CE in areas where state formation was taking place for the first time.[11] Taking this argument forward, a recent work highlights the connection between the heroic goddess Durgā and kingship, in terms of its proclamation, imagery and praxis, in early India.[12]

The scholarship of David Kinsley and Thomas Coburn has also advanced the textual history of goddess worship significantly in interpretive terms, as its many facets, particularly the symbolic signification of tropes and motifs in mythological narratives, are brought out through a reflexive hermeneutic method.[13] Inspired by these efforts, but going significantly further, the writings of C. Mackenzie Brown and Tracy Pintchman, among others, as well as a recent edited volume by Michael Slouber, make important contributions to the field.[14]

Buddhist and Jaina Goddesses

Were conceptualizations of the goddess exclusive to the Brahmanical traditions, in the form of Vedic and Puranic religion? Starting from Kosambi, most scholars working on goddess worship have been cognizant of Buddhist and Jaina female deities, which, on closer examination, reveal that they are considerable in number and diverse in form. Figures such as Hāritī, the patron/stealer of children, appear in Buddhist mythology as being quelled by the Buddha because she was harassing the local population, indicative of patterns of appropriation of a local divinity, marginalizing her cult and asserting the superiority of Buddhism in the process.[15] It is with the works of Pushpendra Kumar (1992), Elisabeth Ann Benard (1994) and Miranda E. Shaw (2006) that full-fledged monographs devoted to Buddhist goddesses became available to the interested researcher.[16] These primarily focus on Buddhist textual traditions but judiciously use iconographic material to elucidate the evolution of goddess worship in Buddhism.

Benoytosh Bhattacharya, a pioneer, provided masterly critical editions of the *Sādhanamālā*, *Guhyasamāja Tantra,* and other Buddhist texts, paving the way for a better understanding of goddesses and their possible linkages with Brahmanical deities; interestingly, in the case of some, he argued that it was from Buddhism that the Brahmanical Śākta worship of the same deities emanated.[17] Decades later, Kumar's study of the evolution of Tārā with the emergence of Mahāyāna Buddhism, and the creation of a pantheon of Ādi Buddha, Dhyāni Buddhas, the Bodhisattvas, Śaktis and Ḍākinīs to accommodate the popularity of image worship and that of goddesses and spirits, was an important intervention.[18] Tārā, his work demonstrates, was well known as the most important female deity in the Buddhist pantheon by the Gupta period, evocatively conceptualized in mythology as born of a tear of Bodhisattva Avalokiteśvara. She was gradually worshipped in multiple forms as accompanying the Dhyāni Buddhas, differentiated by colour – white, blue, yellow, red and green – and still later, there were references to 24, a 100 and even 108 Tārās, signifying the symbolic richness attested by her philosophy. Believed to be the protector, especially of the seas (this may have been due to her name signifying 'carrying over'), she appears to have been the patron deity of merchants and traders along the west coast initially, and later became popular on the eastern coast, going up to Bihar and Nepal. Despite the wealth of detail here, Kumar's study does not go beyond textual description and relies on Bhattacharya for interpreting forms and symbolism of the goddess. Benard's study of Chinnamastā ushered in a more historically rooted analysis of the emergence of goddesses in Buddhism, delving into the iconographic descriptions as well as ritual and philosophical discussions in sacred texts, and unravelling the meanings accruing to the figures being worshipped.[19] Megha Yadav's important study of the first significant Buddhist goddess Prajñāpāramitā, as well as her contribution in this volume on Tārā, indicates that the field for investigation is rich and waiting to be explored further.[20]

While several scholars such as U.P. Shah, Shanti Lal Nagar, Sehdev Kumar and John Cort have described the iconography or worship of Jaina goddesses, an authoritative work focusing exclusively on Jaina goddesses is yet to be written. The focus on Ambikā by Maruti Nandan Prasad Tiwari suggests the immense possibilities for research on how non-theistic religions accommodated cultic worship, particularly of female deities; in the case of the Jainas, the early medieval context especially is significant in this respect.[21] Tiwari very rightly stresses the nature of patronage, limited royal backing, and extensive support from merchants and other professional groups in the early centuries of the development of Jainism, and suggests that the inclusion of figural worship, with a gradation beginning from the *tīrthaṅkaras* at the top and including, over time, *yakṣa* and *yakṣī* pairs, as well as the deeply philosophical and popular representation of goddesses as 'great knowledge', may be understood in terms of the changing social base of the religion. Virendra Singh Bithoo's detailed analysis of the sculptural representations of sixteen Mahāvidyās ('great knowledge' personified as goddesses) in the Dilwara temples – Vimala Vasahi (eleventh century CE) and Luna Vasahi (thirteenth century CE) – is an important effort in this regard. It not only highlights the figural representations and their symbolism but also brings up the issue raised by Tiwari regarding the social basis of religion, drawing attention to certain ideas and value systems that had gained currency when such a conceptualization emerged.[22] Anisha Saxena's research has brought attention to the historical transformation of the site of Osian in terms of religious orientation, particularly the re-configured Jaina goddess imagery there.[23] The mythology around Sacciyā Mātā/Saccikā Devī brings to the fore the issue of transformations and assimilations in religious traditions and also indicates the influence of the powerful merchant community of

Oswals, in addition to royal powers, in the making of this very important centre of goddess worship for Jainas and followers of Brahmanical religion.

Goddesses in Regional Traditions

It is with a focus on historical regions and the making of religious traditions that we see the most fascinating research emerging. Two major regions that have received significant attention in this regard are south India, with the Tamil Nadu region being the primary focus, and eastern India, with the locus around Bengal. Among the most illuminating works are those of David Dean Shulman (1980) and R. Nagaswamy (1981), which have placed goddess worship in the Tamil-speaking region within the larger religious developments taking place across a broad historical terrain.[24] Using a genre of literature that developed across the Tamil-speaking region, called the *sthalapurāṇa/talapurāṇam* in the medieval period, Shulman analyses the complex ways in which Brahmanical, regional and local cults, terminology and mythology become interlaced. In my own work, inspired partly by Shulman and mostly emerging from a personal feminist quest, I have focused on a variety of sources to unravel the worship of goddesses, situating their visibility and the apparent unitary conceptualization of the divine feminine despite the multiple forms and originary contexts in the state formation process. I have tried to bring in epigraphic and iconographic evidence to buttress discussions of the Sangam goddess Ko<u>r</u><u>r</u>avai, who metamorphosed into the Puranic Durgā and Pārvatī. The mythologies of the goddess, communities of worshippers and the gender dynamics that result in specific conceptualizations and mythopoeic imaginaries have been central concerns. Nagaswamy's focus on Śākta influences in the development of the Amma<u>n</u> cults in their multifarious forms has also greatly influenced my work on Ko<u>r</u><u>r</u>avai.

In the Bengal context, it is specifically in the work of Kunal Chakrabarti that the evolution of goddess worship during the habilitation of the Puranic Brahmanical tradition is examined. Chakrabarti refers to the *Upapurāṇas* as regional texts, composed in eastern India, which interwove the local traditions of goddess worship with the conceptualization of the great goddess, using philosophical concepts such as *prakṛti*, *mūlaprakṛti* and *śakti*. Chakrabarti seamlessly integrates ethnographic evidence with inscriptional and textual material to present a rich tapestry of the regional character of goddess worship in Bengal. Two recent works have admirably expanded the eastern Indian focus on goddess traditions. The first draws attention to the Nīlācala Hills in Assam, the seat of the goddess Kāmākhyā, and examines the development of the cult of the Mahāvidyās in eastern India through a study of Tantra and Śākta literature, juxtaposed with inscriptional and regional Puranic sources.[25] The second focuses on the transformation of the religious landscape in early Odisha, highlighting the marginalization of an important goddess *kṣetra* there and the emergence of a new kind of cultic hegemony within the broader religious landscape, rooted in the political and institutional transformations of the early medieval period.[26] Such studies are of great significance in demystifying a monolithic great Indian goddess tradition. Instead, they direct our attention towards the multiple forms of the divine feminine, exploring how she is conceived and worshipped in specific contexts that derive from ecological and historical cultures.

Goddesses in Islam and Christianity

Christianity and Islam were established in the Indian subcontinent in interesting ways, which, to the uninformed observer, appeared to militate against their essential character. Scholars have referred to such establishment through the framework of the 'vernacularization' of Islam and Christianity, which reveals a complex and intricate interweaving of ideas and practices into their fabric. Susan Bayly, in her seminal work *Saints, Goddesses and Kings*, drew our attention to the ambiguous relationship between communities of Muslims and Christians in south India and the diverse goddess cults, as well as the creation of cultic beliefs and worship that drew upon these existing forms of goddess worship.[27] For Bayly, the paradox was as follows:

> a society in which warlike Muslim and Christian saints, and indigenous divinities of blood and power came to be revered and worshipped by professing Christians, Muslims and Hindus. Everywhere in the south, 'people of the Book', self-professed adherents of the so-called convert religions, join their Hindu neighbours in ceremonial chariot processions modelled on those of the region's great Siva and Vishnu temples. In the region's pre-colonial states and kingdoms, Hindu and Muslim rulers stood as sponsors to the shrines and ceremonies of Christian Virgins and indigenous Tamil and Malayan' warrior goddesses; men of every origin and affiliation still fight fiercely over flags, banners and other tokens of ceremonial 'honour' and

> precedence, and cults of vegetarian abstinence flourish in close association with ferocious rites of blood-letting and supernaturally inspired ritual head-severing.[28]

These processes, it was demonstrated, were part of the historical context of medieval south India, in which communities actively engaged with the state within a power matrix, and caste became an important element of social ranking.[29] Thus, the communities who embraced religions, old and new, invented and reconfigured cultural practices to suit their situation. While the presence of Christianity and Islam may be identified in different historical regional contexts, the significance of trade in situating social groups professing Islam or Christianity has been identified as salient in facilitating this process. For instance, in the Tamil region, it is believed that the *Maraikkāyar*, a compound of *marakkalam* and *rāyar*, signified a ship owner from later Cōḻa times, and that they constituted a significant community that comprised the elite Muslims by the medieval period. It is in this context of the assimilation of Muslims, or later of Christians, within the medieval socio-political complex that the embracing of local cultic practices, especially those related to heroes and goddesses, is located.

The study by David Mosse advances the understanding of assimilation by directly incorporating caste into his examination of the evolution of Christianity in south India.[30] Mosse also advocates for looking beyond assimilation and vernacularization as frameworks through which we interpret, at least, Christianity in late medieval Tamil Nadu. The apparent bricolage of practices, ideas and cults within this religion, as it evolved in this region, was unified through a broader Christian theological framework. For instance, the veneration of *kaṉṉi*, 'sexually pure' young women who had died, often while protecting their chastity, was expressed in a twofold manner within Christian cultic belief in the Ramnad region. First, it involved the repudiation of sex and sin, particularly in the case of unmarried girls, which was celebrated in early Tamil culture as embodying a potent yet dangerous power not only associated with virginity but also with the chastity of women, semantically rendered as *aṇaṅku*.[31] The *kaṉṉi* concept also carried a Sanskritic symbolism, reflecting the virginity of the *kanyā*, as emphasized in the *Śāstras*. In Tamil traditions, the collective of mothers, known as Saptamātṛkā or Aṣṭamātṛkā in Brahmanical texts, were worshipped as *kaṉṉiyar*, signifying their unmarried (and virgin) status. This term was used as an invocation of Mary, the virgin mother, and the reference to women who had died by suicide as *kaṉṉi* conferred status upon them and their families.[32] Furthermore, as Mātā (Tamil, Ammā), Mary symbolized benevolence in her forms as Ārōkkiya Mātā (goddess of good health) and Aṭaikkala Mātā (goddess of refuge).[33] In the legendary origins of the *kaṉṉi*, encapsulated in ritual, there is an association with water or reservoirs and the forest or wilderness; these elements are traditionally linked with Durgā and Kālī.[34]

There are, thus, two processes that we can identify in terms of goddess worship in south Indian Christianity – the first is assimilation, and the second is contestation or reinvention of cults and practices. Methodologically, studies on the theme draw upon textual evidence, oral histories and fieldwork – the bedrock of anthropological studies of religion. Similar studies have been undertaken with regard to Islam. The history of religious processes in Bengal serves us with both models. The first, of assimilation, is exemplified by the revered protector of the mangrove forests of Bengal, Bonbibi of the Sunderbans, who is worshipped as both saint and goddess; her many names include Ma Bonbibi, Ma Fatima, Bon Devi and Pirani.[35] The worship of this figure among Muslims seems to have largely prevailed in the Sunderbans, Khulna, and North and South 24 Parganas.[36] Comparing this to the veneration of *pirs*, it has been argued that the more limited cultic significance of Bonbibi may be due to the fact that she is female and also that she is worshipped in the form of an idol. But like Satya Pir, a figure known from the late sixteenth century to be worshipped by Hindus and Muslims, what is striking is that it is the lowest social strata that seem to be the followers of Bonbibi's cult. An epic *Jahuranama* was composed by Munshi Mohammed Khater in the late 1800s that recounted the legend of Bonbibi as it prevailed in the folklore of the region. Born to the second wife of a devout Muslim, she was abandoned in the forest due to the machinations of her father's first wife. However, because of the blessings of the Prophet's daughter Fatima, she developed superhuman powers and vanquished the tyrants of the forest, Dakkin Ray and his mother Narayani. Here, the latter's Vaiṣṇava association is suggested, indicating some kind of contestation, in both religious and social terms. But it is not a simple conflict that we see here, for Dakkin Ray seeks advice from Gazi, who is a Pir and his friend, and later in the story Ray's mother Narayani, seeking truce, calls Bonbibi her sister.[37] Interestingly, Dakkin Ray takes on the form of a tiger in the course of the battle with Bonbibi, while we are told early on that during her infancy Bonbibi was brought up by a deer. Both instances show the close connection of the cult with the ecological culture that had evolved in the Sunderbans. The historical context of the expansion of Islam along the eastern frontier with the clearing of forests and spread of agriculture appears in the background of such mythmaking and cults.[38] It has been documented that the shrines of this goddess built by the local people who live in or access the forest are along tracks or pathways, and the worshippers believe their movement in the forests is secured by such locations for her places of worship.[39] It is in the iconography of Bonbibi that the element of assimilation through appropriation is best visible – she is shown seated on a tiger, or a half-human half-tiger image is placed near her.

In Tamil Nadu, we find a different kind of assimilation in the deification of a Muslim goddess within the holiest of holy shrines of the Vaiṣṇavas, Srirangam, as well as in three other shrines, namely Vandiyur, Melkote and Tirupati.[40] Venerated as Tulukka Nācciyār, legends describe her as the daughter of a Sultan who fell in love with the festival idol of Viṣṇu that was seized and taken to Delhi. Other versions refer to her as a local Muslim princess or personage and recount the love affair between her and Viṣṇu. Some of these legends, preserved in the later-day Srirangam chronicles called *Kōyiloḻuku*, draw attention to tribal communities in and around Tirupati and Melkote as part of their narratives. What is quite apparent is that, from the fourteenth century, the period of circulation of these legends, there are several interconnected religio-political processes occurring. The first relates to the consolidation of the Śrī Vaiṣṇava community with their many divergent ideas and practices encapsulated within the two broad frames of Vaṭakalai and Teṉkalai.[41] Secondly, the conquest of the Deccan and the extreme south by Malik Kafur, Alauddin Khalji's general, permeates the narrative. Thirdly, we find the invocation of Rāmānuja, the great eleventh- to twelfth-century philosopher credited with the theory of Viśiṣṭādvaita, in some of the Tulukka Nācciyār narratives. And lastly, the political context of Vijayanagara rule over the vast regions of southern Deccan and the Tamil south, from the fourteenth century, which expanded the agricultural frontiers through heavily forested areas, and in the course of this also forged linkages with forest communities who were assimilated into the state system is well documented.[42] We also find a substantial Muslim artisanal and trading community developing in urban centres and providing patronage to religious institutions. Tirupati Veṅkaṭeśvara, Mēlkōṭe Nārāyaṇasvāmi and Vaṇṭiyūr Vijayarāghava Perumāḷ temples were some important recipients of donations in post-Vijayanagara times.

On the other hand, we have religious contestations suggested in the imaginary of the goddess, as, for instance, in the conceptualization of Mangalacandi from the sixteenth century onwards in Bengal, where there is a play on the word Mangala, referring to a *daitya* as well as to Mongol, an apparent reference to the Mughals.[43] The narrative is similar to the Puranic tellings of Durgā and her vanquishing of the *asura* Mahiṣa, but the socio-political context is revealed in the nomenclature of the protagonists and the ecological setting of the conflict.

Folk Goddesses

It is from ethnographic surveys undertaken by missionaries, Indologists and administrators that we find the earliest studies of goddesses in different parts of the country. Bartholomäus Ziegenbalg (1713), W.T. Elmore (1915) and Henry Whitehead (1921) undertook surveys of local and village deities in south India and pointed out the numerous goddesses worshipped for various purposes, including protection from disease, and the boon of children and good husbands.[44] All of these focused on myths and oral histories, with an important element being the recording of ritual practices. Some interesting features noted by these scholars were: sacrificial offerings of fowl, goat, sheep and buffalo; self-mutilation practices such as piercing needles through the skin or tongue; walking on embers; etc. It is only in the 1960s and 1970s that historical sources were plumbed to buttress the rich anthropological data that is available to us. Studies on Nandā Devī, Śītalā Mātā, Aṅkāḷa Paramēcuvarī and other goddesses have shown us the apparent contradictions in the conceptualization of the goddesses, the connections between the Brahmanical, Buddhist or Jaina goddesses and these village deities, and the development of institutional worship and practices. On a recent field visit (February 2025) to Tharangambadi, Ziegenbalg's base in Tamil Nadu, we documented the annual *viḻā* of the goddess of the Mīṉavar/ fisherfolk, where the brahmanical *alaṅkāram*/ decoration of the *utsava mūrti*/ bronze processional deity was undertaken over ten days, along with the local ritual and worship of the image, richly decorated with a saree and flowers. The daily *prasādam*/ food offering is yam powder gruel mixed with raw chopped onions, green chillies and lime. The culmination of the festival is the *Mayāṉa Koḷḷai* or the night long procession through the village, to the crematorium and back, by the community priest. The ritual traditionally involved making an image of soil from an ant-hill, stuffed with entrails and bones of animals. The ancient Tamil Sangam practices, the historical transmutations of rituals, and the Brahmanical influences can be clearly identified. Pox goddesses like Māriyammaṉ, it has been argued, while linked with disease, were also rooted in the indigenous understanding of affliction, healing and well-being, and the religious and medical practices were often rooted in and mediated by Dalit Bahujan communities.[45] Sree Padma's work on the *grāmadevatā* in Andhra Pradesh effectively analyses practices such as *satī* – women who gave up their lives on the death of their husbands and who were then deified – and *pērantalu,* or auspicious women who, for different reasons, lost their lives before their husbands. These women were deified as goddesses, but the narratives clearly indicate that these cults were predicated on historical women whose life stories do not allow for easy divine associations. The narratives of such 'goddesses' are in the hands of performers, and due to the rapid transformation of the localities and regions, there are reinventions that simulate the textual and mediatized myths and imageries of the goddesses in different regions. In this regard, efforts at documentation and translation, such as in the context of the Tamil *Aṇṇaṉmār Katai* or the Kannada ballad of Cāmuṇḍeśvarī, vividly demonstrate the complex and complicated processes through which the divine feminine is anchored in her locality as well as in the form of a transcendental Sanskritic deity.[46]

Contemporary Prosopographies of the Goddess

While the *grāmadevatās*, as well as goddesses at a regional or sectarian level, have undergone several iterations in terms of their conceptualization and mythologies in various historical contexts, there are conspicuous instances of goddesses being invented in modern and contemporary times. The best example from the early twentieth century is given by Whitehead who has photos of a 'Plague Ammā' temple, dedicated to the redeemer of the deadly colonial disease.[47] Even better is the story of a goddess created by popular cinema – Santoṣī Mā (1975), although her invention may be traced to a decade earlier when shrines to this goddess were known in Jodhpur, Rajasthan.[48] The saga of a long-suffering woman who finally became a goddess, she was unknown by this name until perhaps a decade earlier in Jodhpur, Rajasthan. Her more common name was Lāl Sāgar kī Mātā, and she was worshipped with goat and other sacrifices. Santoṣī Mā on the other hand was projected as a *sāttvik* goddess – she was offered chickpeas/ *chanā* and jaggery.[49] The phenomenal rise of this cult has been linked to the disenfranchised immigrant women in the nameless north Indian urban sprawl that they now inhabited, who through religious rituals called *vratas*, known earlier in Brahmanical traditions but simplified in this new media, were allured by the promise of a better life. As recently as the Covid pandemic, the worship of Corona/Koronā Mātā who vanquished Coroṇāsura who was a creative addition to the goddess tradition, with temples being constructed to her in different parts of the country.[50]

All goddesses (and gods and other beings, including humans) have prosopographies, and the connections and continuities in their representation cannot belie the socially imbricated aspects of their lives, whether in their invocation, mythology or iconography. Kancha Ilaiah, in his polemical yet valid critique of Hinduism, raises the issue of Dalit-

Bahujan goddesses not being the same as Hindu goddesses, citing examples such as Pochamma, Kattamaisamma and Polimeramma, who are rooted in the land and connected to the productive cycles of the communities that worship them. Mainly aniconic, their temples are often open spaces, with small shrines under trees or along irrigation bunds.[51] However, through history, it is these very goddesses who became assimilated into larger religious streams, whether Brahmanical, Buddhist, Jaina, or even Islamic or Christian. That communities resisted the goddess's newly carved spaces, mythology and iconization of the aniconic is evident in the numerous local goddesses who continued to flourish as they were. A poem by Thamizhachi Thangapandian, a Tamil poet, brings forth one instance of such resistance – the goddess Vanapetchi, the ancient denizen of the forest, moving into the contemporary urban landscape at a time of out-migration from rural areas. The forcefully moved goddess does not want to be confined in the migrant imaginary, within four walls, Sanskritized, sanitized. She longs for the open verdant landscape that is her home. Here, the transformation of the goddess, even in contemporary times, is evocatively brought out, as she not only loses her space but also her identity, even as the people who venerate her themselves gain new identities and therefore seek to bestow a new one upon her. The goddess, thus, keeps moving.

Notes

1 Gross, Rita M. 1978. 'Hindu Female Deities as a Resource for the Contemporary Rediscovery of the Goddess'. *Journal of the American Academy of Religion*, 46 (3): 269–91; Reuther, Rosemary. 1983. *Sexism and God-Talk: Toward a Feminist Theology*. Boston: Beacon Press; Hiltebeitel, Alf, and Erndl, Kathleen (ed.), 2001. *Is the Goddess a Feminist? The Politics of South Asian Goddesses*. New York: NYU Press.

2 Gross, Rita M. 1993. *Buddhism after Patriarchy: A Feminist History, Analysis, and Reconstruction of Buddhism*. Albany: SUNY.

3 Kosambi, D.D. 1962. *Myth and Reality*. Bombay: Popular Prakashan. 1.

4 Bhattacharya, N.N. 1971. *Indian Mother Goddess*. Calcutta: Indian Studies: Past and Present. 9.

5 Gatwood, Lynn. 1985. *Devī and the Spouse Goddess: Women, Sexuality and Marriage in India*. Delhi: Manohar; Atre, Subhangana. 1987. *The Archetypal Mother: A Systemic Approach to Harappan Religion*. Delhi: Ravish Pubs.

6 Kramrisch, Stella. 1978. 'The Indian Great Goddess'. *History of Religions*, 14 (4): 235–65.

7 Tiwari, J.N. 1985. *Goddess Cults in Ancient India*. Delhi: Sundeep Prakashan.
8 Pintchman, Tracy. 1994. *The Rise of the Goddess in the Hindu Tradition*. Albany: SUNY.
9 Chakraborti, Haripada, *The Śākta Tāntrik Cult in India*; Sircar, D.C. (ed.), 1960. *The Śakti Cult and Tārā*. Kolkata: University of Calcutta; Sircar, D.C. 1948. *The Śākta Pīṭhas*. Delhi: Motilal Banarsidass.
10 The works of Kosambi and Bhattacharya have been cited above, which tried to co-relate cultic worship to socio-economic contexts. Also see, Bhattacharya, N.N. 1974. *History of the Śākta Religion*. Delhi: Munshiram Manoharlal. Around the same time, for the most influential works that contextualized early Indian religions in general, see, Sharma, R.S. 1973. 'Material Milieu of the Birth of Buddhism'. In *Material Culture and Social Formations in Ancient India*, edited by R.S. Sharma. Delhi: Macmillan, 117–34; Sharma, R.S. 1974. 'Material Milieu of Tantricism'. In *Indian Society: Historical Probings, In Memory of D.D. Kosambi*, edited by R.S. Sharma. Delhi: PPH, 175–89.
11 Chattopadhyaya, B.D. 2008 (2003). '"Reappearance" of the Goddess, or the Brāhmaṇical Mode of Appropriation: Some Early Epigraphic Evidence Bearing on Goddess Cults'. In *Studying Early India*, B.D. Chattopadhyaya. Ranikhet: Permanent Black, 172–90.
12 Sarkar, Bihani. 2017. *Heroic Shāktism: The Cult of Durgā in Ancient Indian Kingship*. UK: Oxford University Press.
13 Kinsley, David R. 1986. *Hindu Goddesses: Visions of the Divine Feminine in the Hindu Religious Tradition*. Berkeley and Los Angeles: University of California Press. Coburn, Thomas B. 1984. *Devi-Mahatmya: The Crystallization of the Goddess*. Delhi: Motilal Banarsidass; *Encountering the Goddess: A Translation of the Devi-Mahatmya and a Study of Its Interpretation*. Delhi: Sri Satguru Pubs., 1991.
14 Brown, Cheever Mackenzie. 1990. *The Triumph of the Goddess: The Canonical Models and Theological Visions of the Devī Bhāgavata Purāṇa*. Albany: SUNY; Pintchman, Tracy. 1994. *The Rise of the Goddess in the Hindu Tradition*. Albany: SUNY; Pintchman, Tracy. 2001. *Seeking Mahadevi: Constructing the Identities of the Hindu Great Goddess*. Albany: SUNY; Slouber, Michael (ed.), 2021. *A Garland of Forgotten Goddesses: Tales of the Feminine Divine from India and Beyond*. Oakland: University of California Press.
15 Kosambi, *Myth and Reality*.
16 Benard, Elisabeth Ann. 1994. *Chinnamastā: The Aweful Buddhist and Hindu Tantric Goddess*. Delhi: Motilal Banarsidass; Shaw, Miranda E. 2006. *Buddhist Goddesses of India*. New Jersey: Princeton University Press. 318.
17 Bhattacharya, Benoytosh.
18 Kumar, Pushpendra. 1992. *Tārā: The Supreme Goddess*. Varanasi: Bharatiya Vidya Prakashan.

19 Benard, Elisabeth Ann. 1994. *Chinnamastā: The Aweful Buddhist and Hindu Tantric Goddess*. Delhi: Motilal Banarsidass.

20 See, Yadav, Megha. 2020. 'Prajñāpāramitā: The Making of the First Buddhist Goddess'. In Mahalakshmi, R., *Art and History: Texts, Contexts and Visual Representations in Ancient and Early Medieval India*. India: Bloomsbury, 109–30.

21 Tiwari, Maruti Nandan Prasad. 1989. *Ambikā in Jaina Art and Literature*. New Delhi: Bharatiya Jnanpith.

22 Bithoo, Virendra Singh. 2020. 'Representation of Sixteen Mahavidya in the Dilwara Jaina Temple'. In Mahalakshmi, R., *Art and History: Texts, Contexts and Visual Representations in Ancient and Early Medieval India*. India: Bloomsbury, 131–48.

23 Saxena, Anisha. 2014. Landscapes, Memory and History: Claims and Conflicts in the Constitution of Sacred Geographies in Western India. Unpublished PhD Thesis: Centre for Historical Studies, JNU, New Delhi. Chapter 2.

24 Shulman, David Dean. 1980. *Tamil Temple Myths: Sacrifice and Divine Marriage in the South Indian Śaiva Tradition*. Princeton: Princeton University Press; Nagaswamy, R. 1981. *Tantric Cult of South India*. Delhi: Agam Kala Prakashan.

25 Shin, Jae-Eun. 2018. *Change, Continuity and Complexity: The Mahāvidyās in East Indian Śākta Traditions*. Delhi: Manohar.

26 Mishra, Umakanta. 2020. 'From *Virajā Tīrtha* to "Allegorical" *Nābhi Gayā*: Exploring the Changing Religious Landscape of Jajpur (Sixth to Fourteenth Centuries CE)'. In Mahalakshmi, R., *Art and History: Texts, Contexts and Visual Representations in Ancient and Early Medieval India*. India: Bloomsbury, 173–207.

27 Bayly, Susan. 1989. *Saints, Goddesses and Kings: Muslims and Christians in South Indian Society*. Cambridge: Cambridge University Press.

28 Ibid., ix.

29 Ibid., 1.

30 Mosse, David. 1994. 'Catholic Saints and the Hindu Village Pantheon in Rural Tamil Nadu, India'. *Man*, 29 (2): 301–32; *The Saint in the Banyan Tree: Christianity and Caste Society in India*.

31 Scholars have debated over the need to interpret this term in a nuanced manner; it seems however that the broad social and cultural framing of its occurrence does indicate this primary meaning and association. See, Hart, George L. 1975. *The Poems of Tamil: Their Milieu and Their Sanskrit Counterparts*. Berkeley: University of California Press.

32 Mosse, 'Catholic Saints', 309–10. The deification of married women as *sati* and of unmarried women as *kaṉṉi* is known across south India. The earliest detailed documentation of this was in Rev. Whitehead's field survey of village deities. See, Whitehead, Rev. Henry. 1999. *The Village Gods of South India*, New Delhi: Asian Educational Services. 1921. For a remarkable field survey in the Telugu-speaking areas, see, Padma, Sree.

2013. *Vicissitudes of the Goddess: Reconstructions of the Gramadevatas in India's Religious Traditions.* New York: Oxford University Press.

33 Mosse, 'Catholic Saints', 311.

34 Ibid., 316–17. For the early Tamil associations, see, Mahalakshmi, *The Making of the Goddess.*

35 Uddin, Sufia. 2012. 'Beyond National Borders and Religious Boundaries: Muslim and Hindu Veneration of Bonbibi'. In Schmalz, Mathew N. and Gottschalk, Peter, *Engaging South Asian Religions: Boundaries, Appropriations and Resistances.* Albany: SUNY, 61, 65.

36 Ibid., 65.

37 The seventeenth-century epic poem *Ray Mangala* composed by Krishnaram Das narrates how the Gazi was considered an intruder initially by Dakkin Ray, and how later they came together. See, Eaton, Richard M., *The Rise of Islam and the Bengal Frontier*, 270.

38 Uddin, Sufia, 'Beyond National Borders', 74.

39 Jalais, Annu. 2010. *Forest of Tigers: People, Politics and Environment in the Sunderbans.* Delhi: Routledge. 69.

40 Datta, Ranjeeta. 2003. 'The Politics of Religious Identity: A Muslim Goddess in the Srivaisnava Community of South India'. *Studies in History*, 19 (2): 157–84.

41 Narayanan, Vasudha. 2007. '"With the Earth as a Lamp and the Sun as the Flame": Lighting Devotion in South India'. *International Journal of Hindu Studies*, 11 (3): 227–53; Raman, Srilata. 2007. *Self-Surrender (prapatti) to God in Shrivaishnavism: Tamil Cats or Sanskrit Monkeys?* London and NY: Routledge; Datta, Ranjeeta. 2014. *From Hagiographies to Biographies: Rāmānuja in Tradition and History.* Delhi: Oxford University Press; Jagannathan, Bharati. 2015. *Approaching the Divine: The Integration of Āḻvār Bhakti in Śrīvaiṣṇavism.* Delhi: Primus.

42 See, Stein, Burton. 1989. *Vijayanagara.* Cambridge: Cambridge University Press; Karashima, Noboru. 1992. *Towards a New Formation: South Indian Society under Vijayanagar Rule.* Delhi: Oxford University Press.

43 Chatterjee, Kumkum. 2013. 'Mughals, Monsters and the Goddess in Bengal'. *Modern Asian Studies*, 47 (5): 1435–87.

44 Ziegenbalg, B. 1869. *Genealogy of the South Indian Gods, A Manual of Mythology and Religion of the People of Southern India*, Madras: Higginbotham and Co.; Elmore, W.T. 1915. *Dravidian Gods in Modern Hinduism: A Study of the Local and Village Deities of Southern India*, Hamilton: W.T. Elmore; Whitehead, Rev. Henry. 1921. *Village Gods of South India.* London: Oxford University Press.

45 Binny, Malavika. 2023. 'Towards an Iconography of Disease: Exploring the Gendered Worlds of the Goddesses of Epidemics'. *Studies in History*, 39 (1): 12–28.

46 Beck, Brenda. 2024. *Land of the Golden River: The Medieval Tamil Folk Epic of Poṉṉivala Nāḍu*. Canada: Friesen Press; Simmons, Caleb. 2022. *Singing the Goddess into Place: Locality, Myth, and Social Change in Chamundi of the Hill, a Kannada Folk Ballad*. Albany: SUNY.

47 Whitehead, ibid., Plate XI, XII, 76–7.

48 Hawley, John S., and Wulff, Donna Marie (eds.), 1996. *Devī: Goddesses of India*. Los Angeles and Berkeley: University of California Press. 3; Lutgendorf, Philip B. 2005. 'Who Wants to Be a Goddess? Jai Santoshi Maa Revisited'. *Chakra: Journal of Indian Religions*, 3: 72–112.

49 Das, Veena. 1981. 'The Mythological Film and Its Framework of Meaning: An Analysis of Jai Santoshi Ma'. *India International Centre Quarterly*, 8 (1): 43–56.

50 Yadav, Megha. 2022. 'Disease, Demon, and the Deity: Case of Corona Mātā and Coronāsur in India'. *Religions*, 13 (11): 1011. https://doi.org/10.3390/rel13111011.

51 Ilaiah, Kancha. 1996. *Why I Am Not a Hindu: A Sudra Critique of Hindutva Philosophy, Culture and Political Economy*. Kolkata: Samya. 90–7.

Part Two

Of Mothers and Others: Textual and Iconographical Conceptualisations of the Goddess

2

Mothers, Wives, Lovers and Beyond: Goddesses in the *Ṛg Veda* and the *Avesta*

Prerana Roy

There are a number of goddesses who appear in the *Ṛg Veda* (*RV*, henceforth) and the *Avesta*, and many of them are connected to and invoked in the context of motherhood, wifehood, caregiving and beyond. A close examination reveals that the Indo-Aryan and Indo-Iranian language cultures, represented by the *RV* and the *Avesta* respectively, had a common origin, and that a comparative study of religious beliefs, myths and conceptual frames in these texts has uncovered interesting similarities and differences. Names of divinities and, to some extent, their characterization demonstrate affinities, although in a fundamental binary categorization, the two texts favouring opposite sides. For instance, the *RV* prioritizes the *devas* as their gods, as opposed to the *asuras* or demonic beings, while the Ahura in the *Avesta* is invested with godhood and Daeva with demonic power. There are a number of goddesses mentioned in both textual traditions. Given their cultural cognitive commonalities, the association of goddesses with issues of domesticity, concerns around childbirth, and the formation of the household and the family reveals interesting aspects of the historical contexts and social worlds of the two texts. This chapter seeks to identify such concerns and analyse the conceptualization of the goddesses in this regard.

Texts and Contexts

Broadly dated somewhere between *c.* 1500 BCE and 1000 BCE, the hymns of the RV invoke and praise various deities, primarily in the context of ritual. These hymns retained their ritual importance and were transmitted orally for several millennia, during which poets continued incorporating changes and additions. Thus, despite assigning a date to the actual composition of the hymns in the text, the compositional span of the *RV* stretches over several centuries.[1] A continuation of an early elite tradition, the *RV* mostly represents the religious practices of only the upper strata of society, showing linkages to the political economy that was developing.

The *Avesta* generally refers to the oldest scriptures of the Zoroastrians, the term apparently derived from the Pahlavi (Middle Persian) term *apastak*, 'the foundation text', as distinguished from *Zend*, which means 'commentary, exposition'.[2] A crucial source for the teachings of Zarathustra, a prophet, this varied compilation of holy works (the *Avesta*), dating from different periods and belonging to different literary genres, also possibly means 'The Injunction (of Zarathustra)'; and is supposed to have been composed in two stages: 'Old' or 'Gathic' Avestan (featuring similarity to the language of the *RV*) and 'Young' Avestan (*Avn.*, henceforth).[3] The old Gathic *Avn* parts of the *Avesta*, the 17 *Gathas*, survive in this dialect and are believed to be compositions of the Prophet. Though only this part of the *Avesta* is directly attributed to him, the whole text is generally understood to be inspired by the Prophet's teachings. Further, almost all the Younger *Avn* texts are preserved with the understanding that they were all directly revealed to him by God. The dates of Zarathustra, as commonly understood, are 1200–1000 BCE, and his compositions belong to a time when writing was still unknown to the Iranians; even many centuries later, writing was considered appropriate only for non-religious purposes. Religious works were passed down orally; and it was not until probably the fifth century CE that these were committed to writing, and the oldest extant manuscript of the *Avn* is dated to 1323 CE.[4]

Under the Sassanians (fifth–sixth century CE), a composite body of *Avn* texts was compiled and codified, grouped into twenty-one *nasks* (books). The 'Great' *Avesta* contained all the texts already described, along with several other fragmentary portions, including the life and legends of the Prophet, doctrinal expositions, apocalyptic works, books pertaining to law, cosmogony and scholastic science. Copies were presumably placed in the libraries of the fire temples; but very few survived the ravages of time and dynasties, and only a quarter or fifth of the entire canon of the *Avesta* from Sassanian times exists. One could presume that they survived due to constant devotional use, both memorized and recorded in manuscripts, which were frequently written down by priests in their own homes. Around the fourth century CE, the *Avesta* was translated into Pahlavi, and commentaries were added to them.[5]

The extant *Avesta* is divided into five groups, the first of which is the *Yasna*, including the *Gathas*. Zarathustra's Gathas (Sanskrit cognate: *gāthā*) are short verse texts, recorded primarily in the form of utterances addressed by the Prophet to Ahura Mazda, the supreme deity, conveying visions of God and His purposes, as well as prophecies of things to come.

The *Gathas* were piously preserved by being made part of the liturgy of the *Yasna*, the ritual 'act of worship', which was solemnized daily. They were arranged formally in five groups and were set before and after the Yasna *Haptanhaiti*, the 'worship of the seven sections', and are understood to have been composed to accompany the traditional offerings to fire (*Avn. atar*) and water (*Avn. ardvi*). The *Yasna* liturgy was extended over the centuries and eventually expanded to seventy-two sections.

The second group is the *Visparat/ Visperad* (worship of all the Masters), a ritual text of twenty-three chapters, and it is recited in rituals and ceremonies related to *Gahambar* or seasonal festivals.[6] The third is the *Vendīdād/ Videvdāt* (*Avn. Vidaevadata*/ 'against the Daevas' – laws of those who fight against demons), mainly the priestly code and ecclesiastical law books, which are a mixed collection of prose texts in late Younger *Avn.*, probably compiled during the Parthian period. Most of these texts are concerned with laws of purity as a means of combating the forces of evil. The fourth group consists of the twenty-one *Yasts*, which bear features of epic literature and contains invocatory hymns and poems, as well as vivid descriptions of heroic episodes and legends. Finally, there is the *Khurdeh/ Khorda* or Little *Avesta*, understood to be a collection of select verses from the aforementioned texts. Together with some Middle Persian ones, these form a book of common prayer. Later, this collection became the daily prayer book of the Zoroastrian laity, dedicated to different gods such as the sun (*Avn. havar*), light (*Avn. mithra*), moon (*Avn. mah*), water (*Avn. ardvi*) and fire (*Avn. atar*).[7]

Goddesses in the *Garbha/ Gṛha*

The importance of maintaining a family within a household, which is sanctified with different kinds of sacrifices and offerings, underscores the repeated concern in the texts to maintain the *ṛta* (the divine cosmic and social order) by bringing more progeny, preferably sons, in both religious traditions. Conformity to the ritual and social principles ensuring the maintenance of this order or *ṛta* is ensured, primarily in the social sphere, by the three Ādityas: Mitra, Varuṇa and Aryaman. Representing the different principles that define social relations, these gods share their broader roles in ensuring and maintaining the natural as well as the social world in accordance with the *ṛta*; and we see goddesses too being largely propitiated for this purpose. Attributes associated with goddesses include the earth being defined as *ṛtajña*, that is, she who knows *ṛta* (*RV* 5.43.6). In another instance (*RV* 5.5.6), the two twilights, Uṣas and Savitar, are identified as mothers of *ṛta*. Aditi, another goddess of the *RV* pantheon, also figures along with Mitra and Varuṇa as protectors of *ṛta* (*RV* 6.51.3).[8]

One useful way of exploring how the textual world of both traditions upheld the *ṛta* is by examining the social roles attributed to the goddesses and, by extension, to the gods as well. Certain epithets, such as *gṛhapati*, literally meaning 'head of the household', are commonly associated with Agni, most likely due to the significance of the domestic fire.[9] A term typically used for Agni (e.g., *RV* 5.4.1) is *viśpati*, possibly meaning 'chief of the clan', though it is occasionally extended to other deities, such as Indra (e.g. *RV* 3.40.3). Agni's connection with Uṣas provides insight into the possibility that Uṣas is his *patnī*, or wife (*RV* 7.6.5); in another instance, he is represented as her lover, *jāra* (*RV* 7.9.1). Sinīvālī is addressed as the 'sister of the Gods with broad braids', tasked with providing children to the family, as well as a *viśpatnī* (mistress of the clan). Alongside Guṅgū, Sinīvālī, Rākā, Sarasvatī, Indrāṇī and Varuṇānī, she is invoked for the well-being of the family.[10] The goddesses are referred to as *gñā*, literally 'women', and as *patnīs* or *devapatnīs* – wives, or more specifically, the wives of gods (e.g. *RV* 5.46.8). Ideals of a good wife, subservient within the structure and attached to a male deity, emerge prominently. The constant associations of Agni with matters surrounding the hearth of the household also vividly illustrate the ideas gradually becoming entrenched around domesticity. References to Rodasī, who is consistently depicted as a companion or lover but not specifically as a wife, reveal another dimension of social organization that exists beyond or alongside the household.[11]

Very interestingly, Agni is in several places attributed with feminine qualities to facilitate this process. In one instance (*RV* 5.15.4), he is compared to a nourishing mother, and elsewhere (*RV* 5.25.7), it is suggested that his generosity is comparable to that of the *mahiṣī*, i.e., the wife of the *rājā*. The primary male gods, in many instances, bring the goddesses to the sacrifice – the core ritual practice visible in the *RV* – which can be seen in the close connection between Agni and the goddesses. In one instance, Agni is requested to intercede on behalf of the performers of the sacrifice with Aditi (*RV* 4.12.4). Elsewhere, he is requested to bring the *devas* with their *patnīs* or wives (*RV* 3.6.9) to the sacrifice. Uṣas and Naktā, the dawn and night goddesses respectively, are represented as bringing the *yajña* or the sacrifice to the mortal plane (e.g. *RV* 5.41.7). We also have invocations of goddesses in the hymns addressed to Agni, which mention the 'divine doors', possibly of the sacrificial space, identified as *devīs*, that are opened to facilitate interactions between the divine and the mortal realm (*RV* 2.3.5). Hymns addressed to Agni establish a connection between goddesses and the sacrificial grass or *barhis*. For instance, Sarasvatī, Ilā and Bhāratī – the goddesses with whom Agni is occasionally identified – are invoked for the protection of the *barhis* (*RV* 2.3.8). In one instance, Bhāratī with the Bhāratīs, Ilā with the *devās*, and Sarasvatī with the Sārasvats are invited to sit on the *barhis* (*RV* 3.4.8, 7.2.8). Elsewhere, prayers are offered to Agni to ensure that he brings Sarasvatī, Āpaḥ and Aditi along with a host of other deities (*RV* 7.9.5, 7.10.4). The bond between the sacrificial fire and the goddesses is hinted at in other ways as well. What we seem to see is a process of narrowing the gap between the sacrificial or 'godly' plane and the everyday mortal spaces like the household, with the goddesses, in a manner of speaking, playing critical roles in facilitating that process with active intervention from the male divinities.

Again, with regard to the sacrifice, Uṣas and Naktā, dawn and night respectively, visualized as two female weavers who are *Payasvatī* (full of milk) and as goddesses who weave the thread of the *yajña* (RV 2.3.6). Elsewhere, they, along with Varuṇa, Mitra and Indra with the Maruts (storm gods, usually visualized as a troop of identically armed and clothed young men who share common attributes), are requested to come to the sacrifice (*RV* 3.4.6). In an instance (*RV* 7.2.6), they are referred to as divine women (*divya yoṣaṇās*), as cows full of milk, and as much-invoked generous deities (*maghonī*). But the question that arises is why the gods are insistent on, and are almost changing their identities to, make goddesses a part of the *yajña* or sacrifice. Since the sacrifice was an important ritual component of the householder's life, does the involvement of these goddesses suggest the importance of the feminine/women in the household? What are the implications of their being brought to the sacrifice on the mortal plane by their male gods and not independently? Could this be understood as a continuous process of male figures controlling, coordinating and facilitating the goddesses, including the rivers, to legitimize and facilitate the patrilineal patriarchal household? Although there cannot be simplistic explanations for these allusions, it is quite revealing that the goddesses are, on the one hand, important for the upholding of the *RV* social institutions, and, on the other, their roles are diminished through association with the male gods.

Coming to the *Avn* tradition, the household and family are again very central concerns, and goddesses are once more significant as legitimating agents of social norms. For instance, the goddess Aśi is portrayed as a strong advocate of female morality. She laments women who abort their children, cheat on their husbands, or lie to their husbands about their children's paternity (*Yt* 17.10.58). Naturally, then, the begetting of children is seen as a battle against evil spirits, and sexuality is viewed in the context of a religious duty, albeit as a pious act only within the confines of marriage. We may also see the concern for progeny as tied to the need for social labour, meaning more workers in a growing economy.

The *Aśi Yast* says (17.10-11):

> *O Ashi Vanguhi! have their ladies that sit on their beds, waiting for them... adorning themselves, ...,with square bored ear-rings and a necklace of gold: 'When will our lord come? when shall we enjoy in our bodies the joys of love?' O Ashi Vanguhi! have daughters that sit ...,thin is their waist, beautiful is their body, long are their fingers; they are as fair of shape as those who look on can wish.*

At first glance, this is a very evocative composition that suggests women are waiting for sexual union with their husbands; the operative parts relate to the women waiting for their husbands, the objectification of their bodies, and the invocation of the goddess to enable this. Other hymns indicate that giving birth to children to continue the lineage and spread the faith had a major religious purpose – to further the kingdom of Ahura Mazdā and disable the powers of Angra Mainyu. The Zarathushtri wife was not only expected to bear children but specifically to bear 'male children', 'a troop of male children'.[12] Having a son is a blessing bestowed by the benevolent spirits upon the righteous; this gift is denied to a woman who does not follow the proper rituals.[13] There is a clear chastizing of the men and women who did not procreate by the goddesses.[14] The *Avesta* declares that a married man is far above him who is unmarried; he who has children is far above him who has no offspring.[15] Thus, to be without children is the greatest calamity that can befall a family. Moreover, childlessness is perceived as a curse sent by the good spirits against the impious.[16] The *Ābān Yast* (Yast of the Waters) is devoted to the great goddess of the waters, Anāhitā, and it is she who is prayed to for the purification 'of the seed in males, the womb in females, the milk in females' breasts'. She is the one who is venerated by 'maids of barren wombs' for children and a husband, and by young pregnant women for an easy delivery.[17]

In the *RV*, goddesses are invoked in connection with childbirth (e.g. *RV* 2.32.8), and some of them are Guṅgu, Sinīvālī, Rākā, Sarasvatī, Indrāṇī and Varuṇānī, who are invoked for *prajā,* or offspring. There are more specific prayers for valorous male offspring (*vīra*), such as *RV* 2.32.4, where Rākā is invoked for a valorous son, as well as prayers addressing the need for protection. Dyaus and Pṛthivī, for instance, are considered distinguished, as the *devas* are their sons (e.g. *RV* 7.53.1), and they are, like Uṣas, connected with *ṛta* (e.g. *RV* 4.56.7). They are also associated with prosperity, typified by the imagery of being full of *ghee* and milk (*RV* 6.70.1, 2). Additionally, there are depictions of motherhood, as in *RV* II.38.5, where the mother sets out the best (*jyeṣṭhaṃ*) portion of the sacrifice for her son, or in the comparison of the soma-pressing stones to 'playful (boys) jostling their mother' (*RV* X.94.14).[18]

The *RV* verse describing Aditi's pregnancy contains recurrent appeals for help from the three Ādityas: Mitra, Varuṇa, and Aryaman, who are primarily invoked for the maintenance of social order.[19] There are references to joint offerings to Agni and goddesses such as Ilā (*RV* 5.4.4), who, in another variant, is referred to as his mother (*RV* 3.28.3). References to the importance of maintaining a family within a household, sanctified with different kinds of sacrifices and offerings, re-emphasize the quest to maintain the *ṛta,* or the world order, by bringing forth more progeny, preferably sons, which seems to be a favourite theme across both literary traditions. One of the most prominent examples in the *RV* is hymn X.184.2, wherein the goddesses Sinīvālī and Sarasvatī are invoked to 'place' the embryo in the expectant mother. The Aśvins are also called upon to 'place the embryo', which they have 'churned out of the two golden kindling sticks, which is to be born in the tenth month'.[20] The constant symbolic overlaps between the changing and evolving roles of Agni, the hearth, and sacrificial fires within the household, and wombs – which gods are carving out of (again) 'fire kindling sticks'—seem to re-emphasize the importance of, as well as the bridging of the gap between, the cosmos and the human realm, where pregnancies are mystified and ritualized owing to the value of progeny, against the background of a social order transitioning from the early Vedic to the later Vedic society.

Another extremely interesting reference comes up in *RV* 1.164.33, where the Sun calls Heaven his own father, while the Earth is called his mother and his *bandhu*. The Sun interestingly adds that his womb is within the 'two open cups' (Heaven and Earth), wherein his father placed the child (himself, the Sun) from his daughter (Dawn). This sets one of the most important imageries related to birth in the text.[21]

The nurturing nature of Ilā is occasionally conceptualized in terms of milch cows or *dhenu*. In a prayer to Agni, she is envisioned as sitting with ghee in her hand (*ghṛtahastā*, *RV* 7.16.8), which symbolizes the need to invoke these goddesses for ease in the delivery of children. Sarasvatī, for instance, is invoked as *ghṛtācī*, with connotations of ghee, including smoothness, flowing, prosperity, and lustre (*RV* 5.43.11). Interestingly, childbirth rituals in different parts of South Asia reveal that mothers in the pregnancy and postpartum phases are given ghee in copious amounts for easier childbirth and better lactation.

Goddesses in All Forms: From Caregivers to Warriors

Within the world of motherhood and childbirth in the *RV*, mothers are given different characteristics. In *RV* 5.1.4, they are referred to as the two Uṣas (literally, dawn), which may be an allusion to the ritual junctures at dawn and dusk, sanctified by calling upon fire, the emblem of light.[22] We find other aspects of kinship and caregiving elsewhere as well. For instance, Agni's sister and mother (implicitly equated with the dawn and the earth, respectively) are represented as coming with *ghṛta* (ghee), one of the major components of sacrificial offerings (*RV* 2.5.6). Uṣas is compared to a *dhenu* (milch cow) whom Agni approaches (*RV* 5.1.1). In other instances, he is represented as living among the eternal mothers (*RV* 4.6.6). The multiple mothers of Agni also figure in more enigmatic statements about seven young women with a common womb receiving Agni as their embryo (*RV* 3.1.6). Scholars have argued here for an early echo of the notion of the Saptamātṛkās, but one needs to be cautious. It is possible that this allusion suggests the practice of several women raising a child in a household consisting of multiple members, with seven, usually considered an auspicious number, is used to denote the multiple mothers. In a similarly interesting symbolism, Agni is represented as being produced by ten sisters (*daśa svasṛ*, e.g., *RV* 3.29.13), alluding to the ten fingers of the hand that are used to work the fire sticks and produce the flame.

In another instance (*RV* 4.5.10), Agni is connected with Pṛṣṇi, also equated with the earth, and represented as a bovine mother, whose milk Agni tastes. There are other references to Uṣas in the hymns addressed to Agni. In one instance (*RV* 4.5.13), Uṣas are conceived of as multiple deities and as mothers of immortality, as well as Agni's other mothers. In fact, one of Agni's regular epithets is Apām Napāt (i.e. the offspring of the waters, e.g. *RV* 5.41.10). In what is perhaps an oblique reference to this bond, he is supposed to be 'found' in their midst by the sisters (*RV* 3.1.3). In another instance, he is represented as the embryo of both waters and plants (*oṣadhi*, once again grammatically feminine, *RV* 3.1.13). In some cases, Apām Napāt is conceived of as a child (*śiśu*) who places the embryo (*garbha*) in the waters and is then reborn from them (*RV* 2.35.13). That the relationship between the *garbha* and the *jani* (woman, wife, mother) is envisaged in dynamic terms is evident from an analogy where the latter is conceived of as running towards the former (*RV* 4.19.5). Elsewhere (*RV* 7.5.2), Agni is represented as playing a more dynamic, if not dominant, role vis-à-vis specific categories of water: he is the leader (*netā*) of the *sindhus* or flowing streams and a *vṛṣabha* or bull as far as *stiya* (i.e. stagnant water) is concerned. References to rivers, constantly along with birth myths, are also understood by scholars as the breaking of the water during childbirth. One needs to constantly keep in mind that the significance of these divine models of family interactions is to be understood as a relationship between the cosmos and the world in terms of the 'up above/here below' or macrocosm/microcosm theory. It is this which seems to underlie the extreme anxieties behind choosing the 'ideal wife' expecting her to emulate these goddesses who are taking care of the world order. So, while the goddesses are taking care of the world order or *ṛta* as well as holding up social conventions, the wives are expected to do the same within the household or the human realm, for the family. Simultaneously, the legitimation conferred on such relations by their sacralization in public rituals like marriage would have empowered the married couple, and particularly the householder, who could identify himself, explicitly or implicitly, with those who claimed access to power beyond the domestic sphere.

The myths surrounding the birth of Uṣas (the goddess of dawn), Indra and Agni are very interesting. Uṣas's birth is intriguingly defined in terms of the presence of a father, either Sūrya, the Sun, or the sky (e.g. *RV* 5.79.2). The myth of Indra's birth is narrated in a situation of conflict, wherein there is an environment riddled with tension over the destruction of the mother's womb or the son coming out to kill his father, Tvaṣṭar.[23] It is an obvious contrast to the more fluid narratives of birth associated with Agni. The birth of Agni is often attributed to two mothers (*mātrs*, e.g. *RV* 5.11.3, 7.3.9), a reference to the two pieces of wood that were rubbed together to produce the sacrificial fire, implicitly assuming that Agni is latent in the fire sticks or *araṇi,* just as the *garbha* (embryo) is latent in the *garbhiṇī* (literally, 'she who has or bears the embryo', *RV* 3.28.2). The power inherent in the wood is occasionally hinted at through epithets used for the fire sticks. The possibility of two mothers is deliberately reinforced, as, for instance, in references to heaven and earth as young women (*yuvatī*, *RV* 6.49.2). In one instance (*RV* 3.29.1), the *araṇi* is referred to as *viśpatnī* (i.e. the female head of the *viś*, the basic social unit recognized in the text). Other birth narratives depict more complex situations of fire being generated from the waters, as well as fire being produced from heaven and earth, whose gender identities are often blurred. The earth, once again, can be conceived as both mother and wife. Uṣas, likewise, is both sister and, perhaps, mother, as well as wife or lover.

Agni has other parents as well, including heaven and earth (Dyaus and Pṛthivī, e.g., *RV* 3.25.1). Agni is conceived of as lighting up both heaven and earth (*RV* 3.25.3), and the relationship is one of close bond – they are *subandhu* (*RV* 3.1.3). In other instances, we have explicit mention of Dyaus and Pṛthivī supporting Agni (*RV* 7.7.5).

Adding to this whole scenario, the spot where the sacrificial fire is kindled is almost invariably represented in phrases suggestive of birth. The space is frequently designated as a *yoni* (literally 'womb', e.g. *RV* 2.9.1, 4.1.11, 5.21.4, 7.4.5). This is occasionally conceived of as a golden womb, *hiraṇya yoni* (*RV* 2.35.10). The *yoni* is represented as the abode of *ṛta*, the ideal social and cosmic order (e.g. *RV* 6.16.35), in many instances, 'churned out of the two golden kindling sticks' by the Aśvins themselves (*RV* X.184.3), or *sukṛtasya yoni* (all that is well done, *RV* 3.29.8). This feminine imagery is occasionally elaborated upon. The *yoni* being prepared for Agni is compared with the wife (*jāyā*) who dresses up for her husband (*pati*) (*RV* 4.3.2). Elsewhere, the location of the sacrificial fire is equated with the *nābhi* (navel) (*RV* 4.10.8), in some cases explicitly that of the earth (*pṛthivī*, feminine, *RV* 3.29.4). This reminds us of the wedding rituals within the Vedas, where *muñja* or grass is made to touch the navel of the bride to enhance her fertility. Anyhow, in both instances just stated, we see that birth is defined in terms of the mother–son bond, which is both recognized and rendered visible through such imagery. In other cases, Agni himself is identified as the *nābhi* or navel of *ṛta* in one instance (*RV* 3.17.4) and of the *yajña* or sacrifice in another (*RV* 6.7.2).

Some verses (e.g. *RV* 5.41.19) are hopeful that the deities will accept the offerings being made. Here, it is hoped that Ilā, visualized as the mother of the herd, *yuthasya mātā*, and Urvaśi in heaven, along with all the rivers, will accept the offerings. We also sometimes encounter notions of a hostile goddess, and, following those, prayers to assuage such hostility (e.g. *RV* 5.42.16) addressed to the earth mother, *mātā pṛthivī*, to ensure that she does not hold any ill-feelings, or *durmati,* against the invoker.[24]

There are also more specific prayers for protection from disease (e.g. *RV* 7.50.4, where flowing waters in general and rivers in particular are invoked as a measure against a kind of disease affecting the foot). There are general invocations to Nirṛti, the goddess of destruction, who is requested to contain or restrict aging (*jarā*, *RV* 5.41.17), revealing the anxieties around aging and looking up to a goddess, particularly, for bestowing and preserving youth and lustre. Other specific prayers to goddesses relate to acquiring wealth. Rākā, for instance, is asked to provide *vasu,* among other things (e.g. *RV* 2.32.5). Elsewhere, she is also invoked as the provider of a thousand nourishments (*RV* 2.32.5). In another instance (*RV* 5.41.8), the deified cow (*go*) is requested to come rapidly with gifts. While this might suggest a direct reference to the cow, the term *dhenu* (milch cow) is occasionally assigned to other feminized elements. We have a prayer offered to the *sapta dhenu* (the seven cows, possibly the seven rivers) for wealth (*RV* 5.43.1). In the same context (*RV* 5.43.2), Dyaus and Pṛthivī are addressed as father and mother and invoked for wealth. More specifically, we have prayers for food addressed to Uṣas and Naktā (*RV* 2.30.5).

Taming the Goddesses/ Rivers

We have a large number of references to goddesses embodied as the waters and rivers, and to conflicts between Indra and a number of goddesses. Indra, for example, destroyed the cart/chariot of Uṣas with his *vajra*, or thunderbolt (*RV* 2.15.6). In other instances, we have goddesses who tremble, either from fear of Indra or, more specifically, when he destroys Vṛtra, his enemy in the text, often regarded as drought (*RV* 5.32.9, 2.11.9). Could it have been symbolic of some sort of struggle? That such goddesses 'needed to have been trembling' before a primary masculine figure in these texts? Was it one of the many ways of transforming the independent and sometimes even hostile goddesses into more malleable, nourishing figures? These questions arise against the background of goddesses in the hymns addressed to Indra as markedly different from those that we find in the verses addressed to Agni.

More vivid imagery occurs in the hymn addressed to the rivers Vipāś and Śutudrī, the Beas and the Sutlej respectively, constructed in the form of a dialogue between the rivers and the sage Viśvāmitra (*RV* 3.33), who is trying to calm them down by appealing to them as sisters and by claiming kinship in order to achieve a safe crossing. They are compared with swift mares and cattle and are represented as rushing to the sea as if on chariots. We also have *Vāc*, the goddess of speech, being restrained by the male gods, which substantiates the argument about major entities being 'won over' and 'possessed' by the male gods within the pantheon.

Anxieties around Abortion and Stillbirth

Abortion and miscarriages/stillbirths were great sources of contamination and meant that the woman had borne dead flesh within her womb.

Abortion was prohibited and regarded as murder. There are detailed injunctions regarding the prosecution of people for this crime. If the woman received help in getting an abortion from any person in the form of drugs, all stakeholders were considered equally guilty. The man is exhorted to take care of the woman and child and bring up the child until the age of seven.[25] The goddess *Aśi Vanguhi* 'wails' about the courtesan 'who destroys her fruit' and calls to ostracize her for the 'crime'.

> The *Vendīdād* says – *'And if the damsel, from dread of the people, shall destroy the fruit in her womb, the sin and the murder is on both the father and herself'; 'If a man come near unto a damsel... and she conceives by him, and he replies, "Go then to the old woman and apply to her that she may procure the miscarriage"; And the damsel goes to the old woman... and the old woman brings her some banga (bang/ mang, a narcotic made from hempseed), or shaēta (gold, probably some yellow plant or liquor), or ghnāna [that which kills (the fruit in the womb)]; or fraspāta (that which expels [the fruit] so that it perishes) or some other of the things that produce miscarriage; and [the man says], "Cause, thy fruit to perish!" and she causes her fruit to perish; the sin is on the head of all three, the man, the damsel, and the old woman.'*
>
> (*Vnd*: 15.12-15.14)

The *Vnd.* treats stillbirth as well, with extreme prescriptions. A mother delivering a stillborn is required to drink bull's urine (*gomez*), mixed with ashes, to 'wash over the grave in her womb' because she is considered 'unclean' due to contact with a dead creature. She is deemed so 'impure' that only cooked meat, bread and wine are prescribed for her to eat, all of them without any water. Only after three days can she purify herself with gomez and water, become 'clean', and then consume water.[26]

The *Vnd.* has multiple mentions of the requirement to keep a fire burning throughout the tenure of a woman's pregnancy, and especially during the first three days and nights after the delivery of a child, to render harmful forces unable to harm the child.[27] One cannot help but draw parallels with how fire begins to serve as both a meditative and protective entity across traditions, particularly within the realms of the household.

We see the *RV* reflecting a similar fear of or attitudes towards abortion when we have reference to 'The ill-intentioned ones without insight, causing Aditi to abort'.[28] Verse X.162 prays to deflect the dangers of miscarriage or harm to the embryo through the different stages of pregnancy, praying for the banishing of the one who takes the guise of either a brother, husband or lover and who plans to attack or 'smite the offspring' by prying apart the mother's thighs, lying between the married couple or licking within the womb. A similar concern arises with Indra's birth when his request to come out or be birthed from her side (rather than from the womb) makes the mother concerned that it might lead to a miscarriage.[29]

Menstruation Mayhems

We have a number of verses that are extremely anxious about notions of purity and impurity. The texts under study are almost obsessed with menstruation and menstruating blood. Here again, we see goddesses invoked to protect the womb against 'polluting agents'. Indrāṇī and Varuṇānī, as well as other *patnīs* of the *devas,* such as Agnāyī (associated with Agni), Aśvinī (associated with the Aśvins), Rāt, and Rodasī, are requested to come during the *ṛtu,* which literally translates to 'season' (a term generally understood to designate either menstruation or the post-menstrual period of women or *jani, RV* 5.46.8, which is regarded as especially fertile).

We have specific references in the *Vnd.* too, to rigid precautions at the onset of menstruation, to prevent contamination of the good creation of Ahura Mazda. These range from the woman being asked to withdraw from the family and sit apart in a designated place, so that her gaze doesn't fall on a sacred fire, the exact distance being measured by the number of paces from the water, ritual twigs (*baresma*), or other followers, to serving food to her in specific utensils, and to the requirement that anyone who had physical contact with her must purify themselves with bull's urine (*gomez*) and water.[30] We are able to draw parallels with the *RV* wherein we have references to the destructive power of virginal blood that gets spilled on the wedding night. Two passages in the *RV* elaborate on this, wherein the husband, who wishes to avoid the immediate destruction of his person and seeks a long life in the companionship of his wife, must give the *śāmulyam* (blood-stained cloth) of the first night after the wedding to the priest, who has the responsibility to discard it.

Shared Worlds, Different Milieus

What we have here, after sifting through the two traditions, is that the composers of the *Avesta* and *RV* shared worldly and domestic concerns, with goddesses appearing as facilitators and protectors of the established social order, although in limited ways, especially in the *RV*. The extent to which the existence or absence of goddesses in religious traditions serves as a proxy for women's 'real' power is a contentious issue, and one needs to continuously engage with the debates that attempt to understand societies with a strong belief in gods, which may not always be sympathetic towards women in everyday interactions; or conversely, how cultures need not always be patriarchal if goddesses are not prominent. The microcosmic and mimetic trends of the changing nature of goddesses are starkly apparent in both traditions, albeit with different textures. A case in point would be when Hambly attributes the changing and assimilative nature of the *Avn.* goddesses to the possibility that 'they may have had to fight harder in conquering their future homelands than other Indo-European contemporaries'.[31] In the Vedic realm too, as we move towards the later hymns, the situation is marked by increasing complexities; goddesses are sharply stripped of their individual status and relegated to subordinate positions as wives, lovers, mothers and more—possibly to better suit the trends of incipient state formation, which is most starkly visible in the later Vedic hymns. We have discussed multiple examples wherein goddesses, and by extension the gods too, are evolving their roles at a microcosmic level, with roles within the household becoming increasingly important in the incipient state societal structure.

The chapter raises a few questions to ponder. Are there any other ways we might approach and examine the gendered aspects of religious traditions and their ramifications? The issues raised about the social roles of the goddesses and the same being expected of/from wives, the anxieties around birth, and issues around purity/impurity, etc., need to be seen against the background of a transitioning society where pastoral clans were shifting to a more settled society. This transition to a new social formation was very closely connected to the issues of labour – social and domestic.[32] The ideal wife was very important in the process of such a transition. It is important to recall Gerda Lerner's argument that the 'deification of the feminine' is not because of the inherent nature of being female, but because of their ability to procreate.[33] Could we also try to relocate the position of the goddesses in the social planes and categories they functioned within, especially when there are so many references to the need for goddesses and women in ritual? Rather than see the goddess as 'less prominent', could we identify their position as more fluid/functional? The gaining of social acceptance for the early frameworks of an idealized household, with evolving ideas of a householder and his wife, was visible in the creation of ritual worlds, which had broad acceptability, in terms of both the ritual participants and the social categories of people of the times. The conceptualization of the goddesses in the *Avn.* and *RV* reflects such a historical context.

Notes

1 Jamison, Stephanie W., Joel P. Brereton (tr.). 2014. *The Rigveda – The Earliest Religious Poetry of India*. Oxford: Oxford University Press. 5–6; Mahalakshmi, R. 2018. 'Gods, Rituals and Religious Ideas: An Exploration of the Avesta and the Ṛgveda'. *Studies in People's History*, 5 (2): 131; Shrimali, K. M. 2022. *The Religious Enterprise: Studies in Early Indian Religions*. Delhi: Aakar Books. 125–6; Emmerick, Ronald E., and Macuch, M. (eds.), 2009. *The Literature of Pre-Islamic Iran*, Companion Volume I to *A History of Persian Literature* Volume XVII, London: I. B. Tauris & Co Ltd. 1–6.

2 Mirza, H.K. 1971. 'On Avesta, Pahlavi and Persian Sources'. In *Indian Civilization: The First Phase Problems of a Sourcebook*, edited by S.C. Malik Simla: Indian Institute of Advanced Study, 285–9; Emmerick, and Macuch, eds. *The Literature of Pre-Islamic Iran*, 1–65.

3 Boyce, Mary. Ed., Tr., 1984. *Textual Sources for the Study of Zoroastrianism*. Chicago: The University of Chicago Press. 1.

4 Mahalakshmi, 'Gods, Rituals and Religious Ideas'; Boyce, Ed., Tr., *Textual Sources for the Study of Zoroastrianism*; Mirza, 'On Avesta, Pahlavi and Persian Sources'.

5 Boyce, Ed. Tr. *Textual Sources for the Study of Zoroastrianism*; Mirza, 'On Avesta, Pahlavi and Persian Sources'.

6 Mirza., 'On Avesta, Pahlavi and Persian Sources', 286; Mahalakshmi, 'Gods, Rituals and Religious Ideas', 130; the term 'Gahambar' is 'the Middle Persian term for six of the seven obligatory Zoroastrian holy days. These appear to have been ancient seasonal festivals, refounded to honour Ahura Mazda and the six great Amesha Spentas, together with the seven creations … . The seventh festival is called in Middle Persian No Roz, "New Day", and is the greatest holy day, prefiguring annually the future 'New Day' of eternal bliss'. In Boyce, Ed. Tr., Textual Sources for the Study of Zoroastrianism, 3, 18.

7 Boyce, Ed. Tr., *Textual Sources for the Study of Zoroastrianism*; Mirza, 'On Avesta, Pahlavi and Persian Sources'.

8 Roy, K. 2002. 'Goddesses in the Ṛgveda'. In *Invoking Goddesses: Gender Politics in Indian Religion*, edited by Nilima Chitgopekar. Delhi: Shakti Books, 55.

9 *RV* I.12.6, 15.12, 36.5, 60.4, 66.9, 68.10, V.8.1; VIII.31.5–6, among other verses.

10 *RV* 2.32.6–8.

11 *RV* I.64.9; I.72.4; I. 102.7; I.167, among other verses.

12 Tīr Yast, (VI.15) – 'Here he calls for people to assemble, here he asks, saying: "Who now will offer me the libations with the Haoma and the holy meat ? To whom shall I give wealth of male children, a troop of male children, and the purification of his own soul?"' In Darmesteter (tr.).

1883. The Sīrōzahs, Yasts, and Nyāyis, Part II, The Zend Avesta, Oxford: Clarendon Press, 98.

13 *Mihir Yast* (XVI.65, Invoking the god Mithra) – 'Who is swift amongst the swift, liberal amongst the liberal, strong amongst the strong, a chief of assembly amongst the chiefs of assemblies; increase-giving, fatness-giving, cattle-giving, sovereignty- giving, son-giving, cheerfulness -giving, and bliss-giving'.; Yasna (X.15) – 'I renounce with vehemence the murderous woman's emptiness, … she herself, deceived therein, shall perish. And when she sits at home, and wrongly eats of H(a)oma's offering, priest's mother will that never make her, nor give her holy/ many sons!' in L. H. Mills (*tr.*). 1962 (1887). The Yasna, Visparad. Āfrīnagān, Gāhs, and Miscellaneous Fragments, Part III, *The Zend Avesta*, Delhi: Motilal Banarsidass Publishers, 242–3.

14 *Aśi Yast*, (XVII.57–59) – 'The first wailing of the great Ashi Vanguhi is her wailing about the courtezan who destroys her fruit: "Stand thou not near her, sit thou not on her bed!" – "What shall I do? Shall I go back to the heavens? Shall I sink into the earth?"'; 'The second wailing of the great Ashi Vanguhi is her wailing about the courtezan who brings forth a child conceived of a stranger and presents it to her husband: "What shall I do? Shall I go back to the heavens? Shall I sink into the earth?"'; 'This is the third wailing of the great Ashi Vanguhi: "This is the worst deed that men and tyrants do, namely, when they deprive maids, that have been barren for a long time, of marrying and bringing forth children. What shall I do? Shall I go back to the heavens? Shall I sink into the earth?"'. In Darmesteter (tr.). 1883. The Sīrōzahs, Yasts, and Nyāyis, Part II, The Zend Avesta, Clarendon Press, Oxford, 281.

15 *Vendīdād*. (4.47) – 'Verily I say it unto thee, O Spitama Zarathustra! the man who has a wife is far above him who begets no sons; he who keeps a house is far above him who has none; he who has children is far above the childless man.' In Darmesteter (tr.). 1880. The Vendīdād, Part I, *The Zend Avesta*, Oxford: Clarendon Press, 46.

16 *Yasna* (11.3) – ' … Childless be thou, shorn of offspring, evil-famed, and slander followed … '. In Mills (tr.). 1962 (1887). The Yasna, Visparad. Āfrīnagān, Gāhs, and Miscellaneous Fragments, Part III, *The Zend Avesta*, Delhi: Motilal Banarsidass Publishers, 245.

17 bān *Yast* (5.5) – 'This river of mine purifies the seed in males, the womb in females, the milk in females' breasts'; Ābān *Yast* (5.87) – 'The maids of barren womb, longing for a lord, will beg of thee a strong husband; Women, on the point of bringing forth, will beg of thee a good delivery.' in Darmesteter (tr.). 1883. The Sīrōzahs, *Yasts*, and Nyāyis, Part II, *The Zend Avesta*, Oxford: Clarendon Press, 55, 74.

18 *Jyeṣṭham mātā sūnave bhāgamādhādanvasya ketamiṣitaṁ savitrā* – (*RV*-2.38.5cd), in Muller, Vol. II, 115.

19 Jamison, Brereton (tr.) The Rigveda, 2014, p. 1658. Following '*mahi trīṇāmavo astu dyukṣam mitrasyāryamṇaḥ, durādharṣaṁ varuṇasya.*

nahi teṣāmamā cana nādhvasu vāraṇeṣu, īśe ripur aghaśaṁsaḥ. yasmai putrāso aditeḥ pra jīvase martyāy,| jyotir yacchantyajasram' – (*RV* X.185.1–3), in Sontakke, N.S., and C.G.Kashhkar (ed.), Ṛgveda Saṁhitā with the Commentary of Sāyanācarya, Vol. IV, Vaidika Saṁśodhana Maṇḍalā, Poona, 1946, 882.

20 Jamison, Brereton (tr.) *The Rigveda*, 2014, 1657–8.

21 Jamison, Brereton (tr.) *The Rigveda*, 2014, 358.

22 Roy, 'Goddesses in the Ṛgveda', 45–6.

23 West, M.L. 2007. *Indo-European Poetry and Myth*, 149; Jamison, 2014, 39.

24 We also have similar offerings to Anahita, the Avestan goddess, and concerns over whether she'll accept it or not.

25 *Vendīdād*.(15.12–15.14), 12 (38).

26 *Vnd*. Fargard V.VIII.45(135–158); In Darmesteter (tr.). 1880. *The Vendīdād*, Part I, *The Zend Avesta*, Oxford: Clarendon Press, 6.

27 Darmesteter (tr.). 1880. The Vendīdād, Part I, *The Zend Avesta*, Oxford: Clarendon Press, xciii.

28 *RV* – (7.18.8) – 'The ill-intentioned ones without insight, causing Aditi to abort, diverted (the course of) the (river) Paruṣṇī'. In Jamison, Brereton (tr.). 2014. *The Rigveda – The Earliest Religious Poetry of India*. Oxford: Oxford University Press. 904.

29 *RV* – (10.162.1–6); in Jamison, and Brereton. *The Rigveda – The Earliest Religious Poetry of India*. 1643–44.

30 *Vendīdād* – 1: 18–19; 16:1–12.

31 Hambly, Gavin R.G. (eds.) 1999. *Women in the Medieval Islamic World: Power, Patronage, and Piety*. New York: St. Martin's Press. 58.

32 Frederick Engels (1884), Claude Meillassoux (1972), Jack Goody (1976), Gerda Lerner (1986), Uma Chakravarti (1993, 2002) and others have drawn our attention to the close linkages between production and reproduction as a society transforms from one order to another.

33 Lerner, Gerda, 1986. *The Creation of Patriarchy*. Oxford: Oxford University Press. 149–50.

3

Prognostication as Goddess and Goddesses in Prognostication: A Contextual Study of Goddess Traditions in the Jaina *Aṅgavijjā*

Trisha

The anticipation of knowing what lies ahead fills most of us with a sense of wonder and excitement. Human beings of earlier millennia were no different. An ancient Jaina source that attests to such belief in prognostic or divinatory practices is the *Aṅgavijjā*.[1] The Prakrit term '*aṅgavijjā*' (Sanskrit '*aṅga-vidyā*') may be translated as 'knowledge from/of the body'. The text can broadly be dated to the Kuṣāṇa–Gupta time period (*c.* first –sixth century CE).[2] David Pingree and R.S. Sharma place the roots of prognostication in the *jyotiṣa* section of the *Vedāṅga* literature (*c.* 600–200 BCE).[3] Eventually, *jyotiṣa* or *joisa* became overarching terms used to accommodate and explore a wide range of inter-related themes such as divination, oneiromancy (dream interpretation), astral knowledge, fortune-telling by means of dice, omens and knowledge of birds and animals. Sharma posits that the gradual evolution of this knowledge system into a full-fledged discipline can be noted within the Brahmanical, Buddhist and Jaina traditions.[4] While the Sanskrit treatises on *jyotiṣa* comprise Brahmanical and non-religious sources, as well as certain Buddhist texts, the Prākṛta language treatises on the *joisa* tradition exclusively pertain to Jaina sources. There have been noteworthy studies on Sanskritic and Buddhist prognostic practices; for instance, Sujit Kumar Mukhopadhyaya has examined the *Śārdūlakarṇāvadāna* section of the *Divyāvadāna* (*c.* first century CE), and recently Virendra Singh Bithoo explored the socio-cultural context of Varāhamihira's *Jyotiṣaśāstra* literature (*c.* sixth century CE).[5] However, the implications of prognostication within the Jaina framework remain largely unexplored.[6] Since the *Aṅgavijjā* hinges upon a broad range of tangible and intangible facets like professions, ornaments, food-grains, conveyances, coinage and natural phenomena, aspects of everyday life in early India can be gleaned through the themes and activities classified in the text. Simultaneously, several religious and cultural facets permeate the source owing to its societal significance. Feminine divinity is one such aspect that occupies a considerable position within the *Aṅgavijjā* divinatory framework. This chapter analyses the conceptualization of goddess traditions in Jainism against the backdrop of prognostication reckoned in the *Aṅgavijjā*.

While the scholars of Jainism have focused on the over-arching religious, philosophical and ritualistic practices, as well as on the physical manifestation of worship in the form of Jaina art, architecture and iconography, we aim here to draw upon these themes in order to examine the hitherto unexplored realm of the Jaina school of prognostication and how it perceived and presented the aspects of feminine divinity. Jaina goddess traditions, especially their contexts and importance in the ancient period, are relatively under-researched. Scholars like B.C. Bhattacharya, Umakant P. Shah and Sonya Rhie Quintanilla have primarily focused on the iconographic analysis of female divinities like tutelary deities (*sāśanadevatā* or *sāśanadevīs*), who were the attendants (*yakṣīs*) of *tīrthaṅkaras*. Despite the sporadic iconographic presence of these goddesses since approximately the first century CE and their frequent representations from the post-Gupta period onwards, the dedicated appearance and classification of Jaina goddesses in literary sources occur much later in medieval period texts such as *Jvālāmālinīkalpa of Indranandi* (*c*. tenth century CE), *Bhāratīkalpa* and *Bhairavapadmāvatīkalpa* of Malliṣeṇa (*c*. eleventh century CE), *Ācāra Dinakara* of Vardhamānasūri (*c*. eleventh century CE), *Sarasvatīkalpa* of Arhaddāsa (thirteenth century CE) and *Vividhatīrthakalpa* of Jinaprabhasūri (*c*. fourteenth century CE).[7] Fortunately, *Aṅgavijjā* seems to represent early stages in the development of Jaina goddess traditions. Two interesting aspects about female divinities can be seen in the text – first, the practice of prognostication itself is deified as a goddess; and secondly, a rather small and obscure group of goddesses is enumerated in the text, who seemingly did not make it to the later age widespread goddess cults within Jainism. Therefore, the *Aṅgavijjā* provides an interesting premise for understanding the interaction between prognostic ideas and the goddess traditions in Jainism.

The Nature of the Jaina Religious Pantheon

In order to explore the above-stated facets of goddesses in the *Aṅgavijjā*, we first need to understand the conceptualization and the nature of the Jaina religious pantheon. Since salvation is the ideal goal in Jainism, a pivotal position is accorded only to those beings who have already achieved this aim and can inspire others in their soteriological journey. Thus, the *jinas* (victors) or *tīrthaṅkaras* (ford-makers who lead across the ocean of transmigration), who have successfully overcome worldly obstructions and attained liberation, are the ultimate revered figures. Thereafter, the next category of respected beings comprises the teachers and mendicants who propagate the principles envisaged by the *jinas*. Jaina devotionalism is, therefore, reserved for the omniscient beings, the knowledge instituted by them in the form of the canons, and the teachers who channel this ultimate knowledge into the lives of the Jaina followers (*Ratnakaraṇḍaka Śrāvakācāra* 1.7, 1.9, 1.10).[8] The veneration of these beings, who are considered 'greatly cherished' (*parameṣṭhi/parameṭṭhi*), is an essential component of both the Śvetāmbara and Digambara ascetic and lay orders.[9] Overall, there are five kinds of highly esteemed beings (*pañca-parameṣṭhi*): the worthy ones (*arhat*, who comprise the *tīrthaṅkaras*), the accomplished ones (*siddha*), the mendicant leaders (*ācārya*), the ascetic teachers (*upādhyāya*), and all other saints (*sādhu*).[10] Though this main assemblage of reverential figures serves as an exemplar for devoted Jainas, they cannot be supplicated for ordinary human needs. Lawrence Babb points out that such a premise makes the *pañca-parameṣṭhi* 'interactionally non-existent' for Jaina worshippers.[11]

The disengaged nature of the *pañca-parameṣṭhi* perhaps became the expedient cause for the worship of a different genre of 'gods' and 'goddesses' – those who were entrusted with the responsibility of catering to the mundane aspirations of certain Jainas. These sets of divinities were conferred an inferior position in comparison to the main devotional group. Fundamentally, Jainism does not accept the existence of universe-creating and wish-fulfilling deities.[12] The existence of such beings would imply that they could be propitiated for favourable results, thereby negating the role of human endeavour, which was considered to be the sole factor in achieving liberation. Besides, the involvement of deities in such matters was bound to be seen as an example of 'desire' on their part, thereby rendering them unsuitable for spiritual advancement. Also, as the Jainas viewed the universe as an ever-existing space, its creation and sustenance by gods and goddesses were implicitly negated. Thus, on the basis of these arguments put forward by F.W. Thomas, it can be ascertained that the 'deities' in Jainism were inferior in nature and position when compared to the *pañca-parameṣṭhi*.[13] As Padmanabh S. Jaini points out, this class of deities was perhaps necessary for 'weaker' Jains.[14] According to Jaini, Krishna Kant Handiqui and Vilas Adinath Sangave, this practice of deity-worship was most likely an imitation of the 'Hindu' deity traditions.[15] However, Paul Dundas posits that the occurrence of the deity tradition in Jainism cannot be wholly perceived as the process of 'Hinduization'; rather, these ideas were only 'passively' imbibed in Jainism.[16] Primary Jaina ideals of non-violence and continence were incumbent even upon Jaina female deities.[17] Thus, it can be concluded that the Jaina goddess pantheon retained a distinctive Jaina character and was essentially seen as being subservient to the *pañca-parameṣṭhi*.

This hierarchy of the Jaina pantheon is apparent even within the Jaina cosmographic framework.[18] According to the Jaina cosmography, the universe exists in the shape of a giant cosmic human (*loka puruṣa*) who stands akimbo with his hands resting on his waist and his feet set apart.[19] The top of the *loka puruṣa* is the place of perfection (*siddha loka*), where all liberated beings (*siddha*, including the *tīrthaṅkaras*) reside.[20] On the shoulders and in the chest-cavity (*ūrdhva loka*) resides a class of celestial divinities (*deva*) who have attained this place as a result of positive *karma* in their previous lives.[21] The waist of the *loka puruṣa* (*madhya loka*) is where humans, plants, animals, and a group of unliberated gods and goddesses reside.[22] These are the same divinities who assist devout Jainas in dealing with mundane problems.[23] The deities were not excluded from the cycle of rebirth and had to minimize their *karma* in order to become liberated. Principally, the deities of both the *ūrdhva loka* and the *madhya loka* were inferior to humans, as it was only through human birth that freedom from the cycle of rebirth was achievable.[24] Lastly, the pelvis, legs and feet (*adho loka*) are home to souls who have accumulated negative *karma*.[25] This broad framework of the Jaina pantheon and cosmological order is central to our discussion, as the obscure goddesses that find mention in the *Aṅgavijjā* belong to the realm of *madhya loka*. To contextualize this, we may note that by the early medieval period, several prominent goddesses were assimilated into the cosmological framework. The most prominent incorporation was that of sixteen *vidyādevīs* (female deities associated with tantric *sādhanā*), who were categorized as the deities residing in the *madhya loka*. Their position was firmly accepted by both Digambaras and Śvetāmbaras by the mid-eighth to ninth century CE. *Yakṣīs* or *śāsanadevatā* like Ambikā, Padmāvatī and Cakreśvarī, whose presence has been recorded in iconographic depictions as early as the first century CE and in textual traditions like the *Viśeṣāvaśyaka-bhāṣya* (*c.* sixth century CE), were viewed as tutelary goddesses who presided over the pilgrimage sites (*tīrtha*) of the *tīrthaṅkaras*. By the medieval period, they were accorded a position in the *adho loka*. Sarasvatī and Lakṣmī found a position in the *ūrdhva loka*, where the former was seen as the deity presiding over the teachings of *tīrthaṅkaras* (*śrutadevatā*), and the latter was revered by the merchant laity as the goddess of wealth.[26]

Before we move to these goddesses, let us see how prognostication itself is sanctified as a goddess in the text.

Prognostication as Goddess

Paying respect to the *pañca-parameṣṭhi* in the form of a salutation hymn (*namaskāra, nammokāra mantra/ maṅgala*) is a standard Jaina practice. It is generally offered at the beginning of Jaina sacred literature – this factor can be chronologically attested from the *Kalpa Sūtra* of Bhadrabāhu I (*c.* fourth–third centuries BCE); the *Hāthigumphā* inscription of Khāravela (c. 150 BCE); the *Paṇṇavaṇa Suttaṁ/ Prajñāpana Sūtra* (*c.* 79 BCE); and the *Bhagavatī* or the *Vyākhyāprajñapti Sūtra,* which can be dated to *c.* sixth century CE.[27] The *Aṅgavijjā* also begins with a homage to the *pañca-parameṣṭhi* (*Aṅgavijjā* 1.1).[28] Thereafter, reverence is offered to *Aṅgavijjā* as a goddess who is called *bhagavaīya/ bhagavatī* (*Aṅgavijjā* 1.2).[29] The divine position of prognostication is reiterated again in the ninth chapter titled 'Lesson on the Magical Formulae of the Body' (*aṅgamaṇi ajjhāo/ aṅgamaṇi adhyāyaḥ*). Here, the text attributes the genesis of goddess *Aṅgavijjā* to the twenty-fourth preceptor of Jainism, i.e., Mahāvīra himself. It states that the divine (*bhagavatīya/ bhagavate*) *Aṅgavijjā* has been inherited from (*mahābhāgāya/ mahābhāgāyai*) and granted by (*diṇṇāya/ dattāyai*) the mighty being (*mahāpurisa/ mahāpurūṣa*) Mahāvīra Vaddhamāṇa (Vardhamāna) (*Aṅgavijjā* 9.3).[30] The instant adulation of prognostication as a form of goddess right after the salutation hymn can be seen as an attempt to project *Aṅgavijjā* as an extension of the *namaskāra mantra* and the honourable figures. The introduction of the *Aṅgavijjā* in a manner similar to the introduction of the primary icons perhaps aimed to emphasize an explicit and acceptable position for the rather esoteric prognostic practice that depended upon the analyses of 'eight mighty omens' (*aṣṭamahāṇimittā*).[31] In fact, the Jaina position on prognostication prior to the *Aṅgavijjā* appears quite ambivalent. Canonical texts like the *Sūtrakṛtāṅga* (*c.* third–second century BCE), *Sthānaṅga* (*c.* second–third century CE) and the *Uttarādhyayana Sūtra* (early centuries CE) represent inconsistency in their opinion on *nimittās.*[32] Incidentally, the fifth Jaina *aṅga*, the *Bhagavatī Sūtra* (*c.* sixth century CE), mentions that the Ājīvika leader Maṅkhaliputta Gosāla plagiarized the idea of *ṇimitta* from the *pūrvas* and combined these with the two *maggas* of 'song' and 'dance' to form the Ājīvika canon.[33] B.M. Barua postulates that the term '*pūrva*' could mean 'older' traditions and did not necessarily refer to the Jaina *pūrvas.*[34] A.L. Basham adds that none of the titles of the fourteen Jaina *pūrvas* matched the names of the eight *nimittās*.[35] In fact, the Jaina *pūrvas* were a part of the twelfth *aṅga* named *Dṛṣṭivāda* ('discourse on the notions of the heretics'), which was believed to have been difficult to master and was eventually lost. Ludwig Alsdorf's summation on the nature of the *Dṛṣṭivāda* is important in this context. He believes that *Dṛṣṭivāda* actually served the purpose of ascribing hoary antiquity to later period texts.[36] Since its contents could never be known, it was easier to attribute esoteric traditions to the *Dṛṣṭivāda* in order to claim a sanctified position for them. Given the *odium theologicum* between the two religions, the Jaina texts tried to portray Gosāla as being subservient to Mahāvīra, discredit the Ājīvika doctrines, and show that their ideas emanated from Jaina thought.[37]

Thus, by taking into account the following three factors – (1) the inconsistent treatment of prognostication in Jaina canons, (2) the lucidity with which Jaina texts discredit the Ājīvikas, thereby implying that the sect had a well-institutionalized framework of theories and (3) Gosāla being the seventh Ājīvika preceptor, thereby indicating the doctrinal antiquity of Ājīvikan pre-determinism – it can be safely deduced that prognostication originated within the Ājīvika philosophy and that the Jainas developed and crystallized it in the form of a specialized text on prognostication, i.e. the *Aṅgavijjā*.[38] Given this context, the deification of *Aṅgavijjā* as a goddess becomes understandable. Probably, its proponents tried to project prognostication as a divine tradition and sought legitimacy for it by placing it after the main reverential beings. John Cort has also noted the tendency towards acceptance and deification of such forms of '*vijjā*' by *c.* 500–700 CE.[39]

In order to possibly highlight its vastness as being nearly equivalent to the grandiosity of the Jaina pantheon, the text indicates that the divine *Aṅgavijjā* has multiple branches, even though the names of these divisions are not mentioned. This hyperbole is repeatedly employed in the *Aṅgavijjā*, which is described as having a hundred-thousand branches (*sayasāhassa-sākhiṇo/ śata-sahasra-śākhinaḥ*), a thousand doors (*sahassa-dāra-juttassa/ sahasra-dvāra-yuktasya*) and a hundred thousand mouths (*saya-sāhassa-muhassa/ śata-sahasra-mukhasya*) (*Aṅgavijjā* 1.19).[40] The ninth chapter proclaims that prognostication is unmeasurable (*aparimita*), infinite (*aṇaṁtaṁ/ anantaḥ*) and boundless (*apāro/ apāraḥ*) (*Aṅgavijjā* 9.6).[41] Probably, the repeated mention of its vastness as well as its origin was designed to establish that the *Aṅgavijjā* was akin to the Jaina canon itself in terms of profundity. Since devotionalism was also reserved for the knowledge instituted by the omniscient beings in the form of the canons, as we have already seen, it is possible that such parallels were used to strengthen the claims of prowess of the *Aṅgavijjā*. Even though the text pertained to a very specialized type of knowledge system that found parallels with the larger *Jyotiṣaśāstra* framework, for example, the works of *Bṛhat Saṁhitā* of Varāhamihira, which can be broadly dated to the same time period, the *Aṅgavijjā* still catered to a Jaina audience specifically. As a result, the proponents of the *Aṅgavijjā* could have felt it necessary to place the text and the practice itself within the Jaina context of the supremacy of the venerable figures.

Goddesses in *Aṅgavijjā*

The *Aṅgavijjā* (9.269, 9.273) states that suitable feminine indications (*thī-ṇama-sama-lakkhaṇā/ strī-nāma-sama-lakṣaṇā*) should be fully mentioned (*saṅkittaṇā-saddā/ saṅkīrtanā-śabdā*) in the context of prevalent feminine-gender terms, some of which are Hirī (Hrī), Siri (Śrī), Lacchi (Lakṣmī), Kitti (Kīrti), Dhitī (Dhṛti), Buddhi, etc.[42] The editor of the *Aṅgavijjā*, Muni Punyavijaya, places these names in the category of divine beings (*deva-vibhāga*) in the index of the text.[43] Before we try to unravel the implications of these feminine divinities mentioned in the *Aṅgavijjā*, it is important that we understand the structure of the text and the context in which these names come up. The ninth chapter of the *Aṅgavijjā* follows a pattern where the human body is divided into the masculine (*puṇ-ṇāmāṇi/ puṁ-nāmāni*), feminine (*thī-ṇāmāṇi/ strī-nāmāni*) and neuter (*ṇapuṅsakā/ napuṁsakāḥ*) genders, and the prognosticators are guided that they should keenly observe the gendered body parts that the seeker touches while making interrogations about their future and provide them with prognostic counsel accordingly (*Aṅgavijjā* 9.8, 9.199, 9.379).[44]

Interestingly, when a seeker, who could either be a man or a woman, touches any of the listed masculine body parts – for example, the hair on the crown (*sikhaṅḍo/ śikhaṇḍaḥ*) or cheeks (*kavolā/ kapolau*) and enquires about topics like family welfare (*kuḍumba-vaddhiṁ/ kuṭumba-vṛddhiṁ*) or prospects of earnings in markets (*paṇiesu kaya-vikkaye/ paṇiṣu kraya-vikraye*) – the prognosticator is taught to generally give a positive reading (*pasatthaṁ/ praśastaṁ*) (*Aṅgavijjā* 9.1, 9.2, 9.11, 9.44).[45] On the other hand, if a seeker makes contact with any of the mentioned feminine body parts – for example, the neck (*givā/ grivā*) or vein (*dhamaṇī/ dhamanī*) – while asking about matters concerning the acquisition of wealth (*attho/ arthaṁ*) or prospects of pregnancy (*gabbhaṁ paripucchejja/ garbhaṁ paripṛcchet*), the prognosticator is guided to make unfavourable predictions like loss of wealth (*asiddha-attho/ asiddha-arthaḥ*) or infertility (*ṇatthi gabbho/ ṇa asti garbhaḥ*) (*Aṅgavijjā* 9.195, 9.197, 9.200, 9.206).[46] Similarly, the text advises that negative outcomes like disease and death (*rogaṁ maraṇaṁ atthi/ rogaṁ maraṇaṁ asti*) should be stated when the person seeking counsel touches neuter-gendered body parts like the space between the brows (*bhuṁantaraṁ/ bhū-antaraṁ*) or the interdigital folds (*aṁgulī aṁtarāṇiṁ/ aṁgulī antarāṇi*) (*Aṅgavijjā* 9.376, 9.392).[47]

Thus, it is evident that favourable outcomes were associated only with the body parts that were considered masculine. Adverse and often times disparaging results were tied to feminine and neuter-gendered organs. Once this basic order is established in the text, the composer of the *Aṅgavijjā* aims to enlighten practitioners and students about the various nomenclatures associated with the masculine, feminine and neuter genders, respectively. Thus, several adjectives, categories of human beings, celestial beings and spirits, plants and animals, relationship terminologies, professions, communities, planets and constellations, coins, foodgrains and colours are catalogued into the three genders. The names of feminine divinities like Hirī, Siri and Lacchi occur in this context. The author does not directly mention the prognostic implications of these divinities separately; rather, they are stated after a slew of negative results are expounded vis-à-vis the feminine body parts.

Efficacy of Invoking Goddesses in *Aṅgavijjā*

In order to understand the possible reasons for the inclusion of Hirī, Siri, Lacchi, Kitti, Dhitī and Buddhi in the *Aṅgavijjā*, let us now look at the *c.* fourth–fifth century CE text *Tattvārtha Sūtra* ('Manual on the Reality of Reason') composed by Ācārya Umāsvāti. Considered to be a seminal work by both the Śvetāmbaras and the Digambaras, possibly due to its composition before the split that took place in c. fifth century, the *Tattvārtha Sūtra* highlighted the Jaina cosmological, philosophical and ethical traditions. The *Tattvārtha Sūtra* can be placed in the same time bracket as the *Aṅgavijjā*, though the nature and utility of both texts were different. The Jaina cosmological scheme of the *Tattvārtha Sūtra* provides us with a description of the feminine divinities stated in the *Aṅgavijjā*. It is the middle plane, i.e., the *madhya loka*, that is of particular interest to us in the present context of Jaina goddesses. The *madhya loka* is the location of the central continent Jambūdvīpa, where human life is possible (*Tattvārtha Sūtra* 3.7).[48] Six mountain ranges run across Jambūdvīpa, dividing it into seven regions (*kṣetras*) (*Tattvārtha Sūtra* 3.10–11).[49] There are six lakes atop these mountains (*Tattvārtha Sūtra* 3.14).[50] Within each of these lakes lies one lotus (*Tattvārtha Sūtra* 3.17–18).[51] In these lotuses reside feminine divinities, namely Śrī, Hrī, Dhṛti, Kīrti, Buddhi and Lakṣmī, respectively (*Tattvārtha Sūtra* 3.19).[52] Neither the *Tattvārtha Sūtra* nor its *c.* sixth century CE commentary, the *Sarvārthasiddhi,* which was produced by the Digambara scholar Pūjyapāda Devanandi, elaborates on these six goddesses (*devīs*).[53]

Over the course of time, we see that most of these goddesses could not enter the popular deity pantheon of Jainism.[54] In certain cases, we find that one goddess was subsumed into another goddess cult; for example, John Cort points out that Śrī and Lakṣmī became one and denoted the abstract idea of wealth and prosperity in Jainism.[55] She is considered to be one of the fourteen dreams that the mother of the Jina sees upon his conception.[56] Interestingly, as pointed out by Cort, by the medieval period, Lakṣmī was promoted to the *ūrdhva loka*, where her qualities of non-violence and purity were extolled. Thus, it was only goddess Lacchi of the *Aṅgavijjā* who developed a remarkable position within the Jaina tradition. If we look at the names of the gods that are mentioned in the *Aṅgavijjā* in the context of positive prognostication based on masculine bodily features, these are Bhavaṇavāsī, Kiṁpurusa, Gaṅdhavva, Kinnara, etc. (*Aṅgavijjā* 9.68); i.e., those gods who existed in the *ūrdhva loka* as celestial beings according to the *Tattvārtha Sūtra* 4.1.[57] On the other hand, the goddesses are assigned negative prognostication in the *Aṅgavijjā* and belong to the *madhya loka* in the *Tattvārtha Sūtra*. However, their position in the intermediate zone could possibly signify that, at the time of the composition of the *Aṅgavijjā*, Śrī, Hrī, Dhṛti, Kīrti, Buddhi and Lakṣmī were considered available for mundane aspirations like fortune-telling. These goddesses were possibly replaced by the afore-mentioned *vidyādevīs,* who were propitiated for *sādhanā* by the medieval period. Overall, gendered prognostication as well as gradation is evident in both the *Aṅgavijjā* and the *Tattvārtha Sūtra*, even though the nature of both texts is immensely disparate. The conflation of the status of the feminine divinities and the outcomes of their divinatory association are important aspects that shed light on the perception of the goddess tradition in Jainism. It could be argued that their classification had been established in accordance with the theorized framework of the central pantheon of Jainism. Perhaps their subordinate position within the larger cosmographic framework of the primary and secondary pantheons also translated to their lesser position within a highly specialized esoteric discipline like prognostication.

From the above study, it is evident that while the esoteric idea of prognostication is held in supreme regard and is deified as the knowledge formulated by the Jaina preceptors, the goddesses mentioned within the prognostic fold are not considered significant enough to elicit a positive outcome. Thus, a two-pronged approach is essential for examining the representation of goddesses within the *Aṅgavijjā* – one from the lens of prognostic or larger *jyotiḥśāstric* traditions, and secondly, from a religion-specific perspective, as the *Aṅgavijjā* catered to a specific Jaina audience. The juxtaposition of the Jaina conceptualization of goddesses with respect to prognostic practices can be useful in understanding the trajectory of goddess worship within the religion. Overall, the *Aṅgavijjā* is an important Jaina treatise that not only contains ideas about obscure prognostic customs but also broadens our understanding of the religious, social and cultural aspects of ancient India.

Notes

1 The term 'prognostication' can be defined as the act of predicting or portending according to certain indications or signs. See, 'Prognostication', in *The American Heritage Dictionary of the English Language*. Available at: https://ahdictionary.com/ (accessed on 20 October 2019, 18:08). Also see, 'divination', in *The American Heritage Dictionary of the English Language*. Available at: https://ahdictionary.com/ (accessed on 2 May 2023). The *Aṅgavijjā* is considered to be one of the thirty miscellaneous texts (*prakīrṇakas/paiṇṇas*) of the Śvetāmbara canon. See, Jain, J.C. 2004. *History and Development of Prakrit Literature*. New Delhi: Manohar. 61.

2 On the basis of the numismatic data and the material culture incorporated within the *Aṅgavijjā*, Moti Chandra, V.S. Agrawala and Asim Kumar Chatterjee place it in early centuries CE. David Pingree states that the anonymous composer of the *Aṅgavijjā* was a near contemporary of Varāhamihira, the sixth century scholar from Avanti (western Malwa), who is credited with the composition of the Sanskrit text *Bṛhat Saṁhitā*, which also happened to contain forty-four verses that elaborated on prognostication related to marks on the body in the form of '*aṅgaviniścaya*'. However, J.C. Jain states that the *Aṅgavijjā* seems to have been composed before the *Bṛhat Saṁhitā*, though he believes that the roots of both the works were in an earlier tradition. See, Chandra, Moti. 1957. 'Introduction'. In *Aṅgavijjā*, edited by Muni Punyavijaya. Benaras: Prakrit Text Society, 36. Also see, Agrawala, V.S. 1957. 'Coin Names in the *Aṅgavijjā*', edited by Muni Punyavijaya, 88–9. Benaras: Prakrit Text Society. Also see, Chatterjee, Asim Kumar. 1978 (Reprint 2000). *A Comprehensive History of Jainism: Vol. I*. New Delhi: Munshiram Manoharlal. 225–6. Also see, Pingree, D. 1981. *Jyotiḥśāstra: Astral and Mathematical Literature*. Wiesbaden: Harrassowitz. 75. Also

see, Sastri, V. Subrahmanya, and M. Ramakrishna Bhat (eds.), 1997. *Bṛhat Saṁhitā*. New Delhi: Ranjana Publications. 406. Also see, Jain, *History and Development of Prakrit Literature*. 430.

3 Pingree, D. 1981. *Jyotiḥśāstra: Astral and Mathematical Literature*. Wiesbaden: Harrassowitz. 3. Also see, Sharma, R.S. 1983. *Perspectives in Social and Economic History of Early India*. New Delhi: Munshiram Manoharlal. 95.

4 Sharma, R.S. 1983. *Perspectives in Social and Economic History of Early India*. New Delhi: Munshiram Manoharlal. 95.

5 Mukhopadhyaya, Sujit Kumar (ed.), 1954. *The Śārdūlakarṇāvadāna*. Santiniketan: Viśvabharati Publishing Department. Also see, Bithoo, Virendra Singh. 2018. *Science and Society in Varāhamihira's Jyotiṣaśāstra*. Unpublished Doctoral Thesis: Centre for Historical Studies, Jawaharlal Nehru University, New Delhi. 174–8.

6 Apart from the *Aṅgavijjā, the Joṇipāhuḍa* (*Yoniprābhṛta*) *of Dharasena, the Karalakkhaṇa* (*Karalakṣaṇa*), the *Riṭṭhasamuccaya* (*Riṣṭasamuccaya*) of Durgadeva etc. are some important Jaina works that highlight the existence of prognostic traditions amongst the Jainas. See, Jain, *History and Development of Prakrit Literature*, 432–44.

7 See, Bhattacharya, B.C. 1939. *Jaina Iconography*. Lahore: Motilal Banarsidass. 16. Also see, Shah, Umakant P. 1987. *Jaina Rūpa Maṅḍana Vol I*. New Delhi: Abhinav Publications. 214. Also see, Quintanilla, Sonya. 2000. 'Āyāgapaṭas: Characteristics, Symbolism, and Chronology'. *Artibus Asiae*, 60: 79–137. Also see, Jaini, Padmanabh S. 2000. *Collected Papers on Jaina Studies*. Delhi: Motilal Banarsidass. 273. Also see, Dundas, Paul. 2002. *The Jains*. London: Routledge. 212–13.

8 The *Ratnakaraṇḍaka Śrāvakācāra* of Samantabhadra (*c*. fifth century CE) highlights the importance of the chief venerable figures of Jainism. See, Jain, Vijay K. (ed.), 2016. *Āchārya Samantabhadra's Ratnakaraṇḍaka Śrāvakācāra: The Jewel Casket of Householder's Conduct*. Dehradun: Vikalpa Printers. 22, 24, 26.

9 The Śvetāmbara ascetics and laity deified the *parameṣṭhi* in their 'necessary' (*āvaśyaka/āvassaya*) duties, through the 'eulogy of the twenty-four *jinas*' (*caturviṁśati-stava/cauvīsatthava*) and the 'adoration of the mendicant teachers' (*vandana/vandaṇaga*). The adulation of the central figures amongst the Digambaras can be ascertained from the *Ratnakaraṇḍaka Śrāvakācāra* of Samantabhadra. The text states that 'direction of right views' (*darśana-pratimā*) could be achieved by worshipping the 'superlative' pantheon (*Ratnakaraṇḍaka Śrāvakācāra* 7.136–137). See, Schubring, Walther. 2000 (Reprint). *The Doctrine of Jainas: Described after the Old Sources*. Delhi: Motilal Banarsidass. 268–9. Also see, Jaini, Padmanabh S. 1998 (Reprint). *The Jaina Path of Purification*. Delhi: Motilal Banarsidass. 189–90. Also see, Jain, Vijay K. (ed.), 2016. *Āchārya Samantabhadra's Ratnakaraṇḍaka*

Śrāvakācāra: The Jewel Casket of Householder's Conduct. Dehradun: Vikalpa Printers. 221–2.

10 Muni Punyavijaya, Dalsukh Malvania and Amritlal Mohan Bhojak point out that the stature of the *arhat* was higher than that of the *siddhas* as the former had not only institutionalized the Jaina faith but also devoted their efforts and teachings for the spiritual awakening and the advancement of the Jaina community. Meanwhile, the *siddhas* were those who had attained liberation. See, Punyavijaya, Muni, Dalsukh Malvania, and Amritlal Mohan Bhojak (eds.), 1971. *Paṇṇavaṇasuttaṁ*. Bombay: Shri Mahavira Jaina Vidyalaya. 236–7. The terms '*ācārya*' and '*upādhyāya*' were used even in the days of Mahāvīra to refer to different categories of teachers. Thus, the above-stated categories suggest different groups (and are not synonyms). See, Jain, K.C. 2001. *Mahāvīra and His Times*. Delhi: Motilal Banarsidass. 345. Also see, Cort, John. 2001. *Jains in the World: Religious Values and Ideology in India*. Oxford: Oxford University Press. 24.

11 Babb, Lawrence A. 1988. 'Giving and Giving Up: The Eightfold Worship among Śvetāmbara Mūrtipūjak Jains'. *Journal of Anthropological Research*, 44 (1): 68.

12 Thomas, F.W. 1968. *The Flower-Spray of the Quodammodo Doctrine: Śri Malliṣeṇasūri's Syādvādamañjari*. Delhi: Motilal Banarsidass. 29. Also see, Jaini, *The Jaina Path of Purification*. 89.

13 Ibid.

14 Ibid., 194.

15 Ibid., 163. Also see, Handiqui, Krishna Kant. 1949. Sholapur: Jaina Saṁsṛkti Saṁrakṣaka Saṅgha. 332–3. Also see, Sangave, Vilas Adinath. 1959. *Jaina Community: A Social Survey*. Bombay: Popular Book Depot. 237–8. 363–4.

16 Dundas, *The Jains*, 212–13.

17 Ibid. Also see, Cort, John. 1987. 'Medieval Jaina Goddess Traditions'. *Numen*, 34 (2): 236.

18 For Jaina cosmology, see, Upadhye, A.N. (ed.), 1943–51. *Tiloya Paṇṇattī of Yativṛṣabha*. Sholapur: Jaina Saṁsṛkti Saṁrakṣaka Saṅgha. Also see, Jain, Vijay K. (ed.), 2018. *Ācārya Umāsvāmi's Tattvārtha Sūtra: With Explanations in English from Ācārya Pūjyapāda's Sarvārthasiddhi*. Dehradun: Vikalpa Printers. Also see, Fischer, Eberhard, and Jyotindra Jain. 1978. *Jaina Iconography Vol. II*. Leiden: E.J. Brill.

19 Cort, *Jains in the World: Religious Values and Ideology in India*, 19.

20 Ibid., 20.

21 Ibid.

22 Ibid., 19.

23 Ibid.

24 Humphrey, Caroline. 1984. 'Some Aspects of the Jain Puja: The Idea of "God" and the Symbolism of Offerings'. *The Cambridge Journal of Anthropology Journal of Anthropology*, 9 (3): 5.

25 Cort, *Jains in the World: Religious Values and Ideology in India*. 19–20.

26 See, Cort, 'Medieval Jaina Goddess Traditions'. 236–7. 240–1. Also see, Shah, *Jaina Rūpa Maṁḍana Vol I*, 215. For Ambikā, see, Tiwari, M.N.P. 1989. *Ambikā in Jaina Art and Literature*. New Delhi: Bharatiya Jnanpith.

27 One of the first instances of the occurrence of the *namaskāra mantra* is in the *Kalpa Sūtra* of Bhadrabāhu (*c*. fourth–third centuries BCE). It begins with obeisance to the *arhats*, liberated souls, sacred guides, religious teachers and all saints in the world; and refers to the hymn as the key chant that can destroy sins. The next chronological mention of the hymn (though not in its entirety) is found in the *c*. 150 BCE *Hāthiguṁphā* inscription of Khāravela, which begins with the exaltation of only the *arhats* and the *siddhas*. Thereafter, the next mention is found in the fourth subsidiary *aṅga* (*upāṅga*), the *c*. 79 BCE *Paṇṇavaṇa Suttaṁ/ Prajñāpana Sūtra* of Ārya Śyāma. The subsequent textual tradition that begins with the benediction and also happens to be contemporaneous with the *Aṅgavijjā* is the fifth *aṅga*, the *Bhagavatī* or the *Vyākhyāprajñapti Sūtra* (*c*. sixth century CE). The introductory couplets offer salutations to the vanquishers, liberated beings, guides, teachers, all monks, and interestingly to the Brāhmī script and the scriptures additionally. See, Maharaj, Phulchandji. 1954. 'Kappasuttaṁ'. In *Suttāgame Vol. II*, edited by Phulchandji Maharaj. Gurgaon Cantt: Sūtrāgamaprakāśaka Samiti, 1. Also see, Sastri, Hirananda. 1983 (Reprint). 'The Hathigumpha Inscription of Kharavela, No. 7'. In *Epigraphica Indica*, Vol. XX, edited by Hirananda Sastri. Delhi: ASI, 79, 86. Also see, Punyavijaya, Muni, Dalsukh Malvania, and Amritlal Mohan Bhojak (eds.), 1971. *Paṇṇavaṇasuttaṁ*. Bombay: Shri Mahavira Jaina Vidyalaya. 231. Also see, Lalwani, K.C. (ed.), 1973. *Bhagavatī Sūtra Vol I*. Calcutta: Jain Bhawan. 1.

28 Punyavijaya, Muni (ed.), 1957. *Aṅgavijjā: Science of Divination through Physical Signs and Symbols*. Benaras: Prakrit Text Society. 1. Also see, Ratnesh, Rajendra (tr.). 2016. *Aṅgavijjā Prathama Khaṇḍa*. Jaipur: Prakrit Bharati Academy. 1.

29 Ibid.

30 Ibid., 57. Also see, ibid., 176.

31 The *Aṅgavijjā* (*Av.*1.2) advocates the use omens emanating from body (*aṅga*), speech (*saro/svara*), marks (*lakhaṇaṁ/lakṣaṇa*), moles on the body (*vaṅjaṇaṁ/vyaṅjana*), dreams (*suviṇo/svapna*), wear and tear (*chiṇṇa/chinna*), terrestrial phenomenon (*bhaummaṁ/bhauma*) and atmospheric omens (*antalikhāi/antarikṣa*). See, Punyavijaya, Muni (ed.), 1957. *Aṅgavijjā: Science of Divination through Physical Signs and Symbols*. Benaras: Prakrit Text Society. 1. Also see, Ratnesh, *Aṅgavijjā Prathama Khaṇḍa*, 2.

32 *Sūyagaḍo* 1.12.9 states that those who are proficient in the eight branches (*aṭṭhangameyaṁbahaveāhittālogaṁsi*) – astrology (*saṁvaccharaṁ*), oneiromancy (*suviṇaṁ*), divination from diagrams (*lakhaṇaṁ*), bodily

marks (*nimitta-dehaṁ*), and portents (*uppāyaṁ*), know the future *jānantianāgatāni*. See, Jacobi, Hermann, tr. 1895. *The Sacred Books of the East Jaina Sūtra: Sūtrakṛtāṅga-sūtra Part II*. Oxford: Clarendon Press. 317. The *Sthānaṅga* 8.23 is neutral in its judgement of prognostication and it mentions eight 'great signs' *mahānimittaaṭṭhavihemahāṇimitt epaṇṇase – bhome, uppāte, suviṇe, atalikkhe, age, sare, lakkhaṇe* and *vañjaṇe*. See, Shastri, Hiralal (ed.), 1992. *Thānānga*. Beawar: Shri Agam Prakashan Samiti. 634. On the other hand, the *Uttarādhyayana* states that a genuine monk does not subsist on prognostication (*jo vijjhāhiṇajīvaīsabhikkhī*) from perforation (*chiṇṇaṁ*), sounds (*saraṁ*), earthly omens (*bhaumaṁ*), atmospheric phenomenon (*antalikkhaṁ*), dreams (*suviṇaṁ*), marks (*lakhaṇaṁ*), sticks (*daṇḍa*), buildings (*vatthu-vijjaṁ*), changes in the body (*aṅgaviyāraṁ*) and from cries and screeches (*sarassa-vijayaṁ*) (*Uttarādhyayana Sūtra* 15.7). According to the preceptors, those who understand *lakkhaṇaṁ, suviṇaṁ* and *aṅga-vijjaṁ* should not be called monks (*Uttarādhyayana Sūtra* 8.13). See, Jacobi, *The Sacred Books of the East Jaina Sūtra*. 70–1.

33 Sikdar, Jogendra Chandra. 1964. *Studies in Bhagavatī Sūtra*. Muzaffarpur: Research Institute of Prakrit, Jainology and Ahimsa. 3. Also see, Basham, A.L. 1951. *History and Doctrines of the Ājīvikas*. London: Luzac and Company. 213.

34 Ibid., 214–15.

35 Ibid., 213.

36 Alsdorf, Ludwig. 1973. 'What Were the Contents of the *Dṛṣṭivāda*'. In *German Scholars on India Vol I*, edited by Cultural Department of the Embassy of the Federal Republic of Germany, New Delhi. Varanasi: Chowkhamba Sanskrit Series Office, 10.

37 Basham, *History and Doctrines of the Ājīvikas*, 47–8.

38 Sikdar, *Studies in Bhagavatī Sūtra*, 435–6. Also see, Mahalakshmi, R. 2023. *Symposium: Reason and Ideology in Ancient India*. Warangal: Indian History Congress 82nd Session. fn. 45. The idea that the future could be predicted suggested the inevitability of action or events, thereby indicating predeterminism.

39 Cort dates the *Aṅgavijjā* to *c*. fourth century CE and notes the process of deification in *Vasudevahiṇḍi*. However, the *Aṅgavijjā* exhibits prior-deification. Cort also notes that the origin of the medieval *vidyādevīs* can be seen in the context of the acceptance of occult practices. See, Cort, 'Medieval Jaina Goddess Traditions', 238–40.

40 Punyavijaya, Muni, ed. 1957. *Aṅgavijjā: Science of Divination through Physical Signs and Symbols*. Benaras: Prakrit Text Society. 2. Also see, Ratnesh, *Aṅgavijjā Prathama Khaṇḍa*, 4.

41 Ibid., 57. Also see, ibid., 176.

42 Ibid., 68–9. Also see, ibid., 212.

43 Ibid., 365.

44 Ibid., 60, 66, 72. Also see, ibid., 183, 204, 223.
45 Ibid., 59–61. Also see, ibid., 182, 184, 187.
46 Ibid., 66. Also see, ibid., 204–5.
47 Ibid., 72–3. Also see, ibid., 222, 224.
48 Jain, *Ācārya Umāsvāmi's Tattvārtha Sūtra*. 119–20.
49 Ibid., 121–3.
50 Ibid., 124–5.
51 Ibid., 126–7.
52 Ibid., 127–8.
53 Ibid., 111–27.
54 The afore-mentioned deities like *vidyādevīs*, *śāsanadevatā*, and goddesses like Sarasvatī and Lakṣmī became more prominent in the medieval period. See, Cort, 'Medieval Jaina Goddess Traditions', 235–55.
55 Cort, *Jains in the World: Religious Values and Ideology in India*, 188–9.
56 Ibid.
57 Punyavijaya, Muni (ed.), 1957. *Aṅgavijjā: Science of Divination through Physical Signs and Symbols*. Benaras: Prakrit Text Society. 62. Also see, Ratnesh, *Aṅgavijjā Prathama Khaṇḍa*, 190. Also see, Jain, *Ācārya Umāsvāmi's Tattvārtha Sūtra*, 146–7.

4

Devī and *Mahiṣa*: Puranic Narratives, Iconographic Representations

Sneha Ganguly

The worship of the divine feminine is common across religious traditions and appears to have had an early origin, resulting in extensive scholarship ranging from attempts to establish the presence of the feminine in the religious sphere as proof that 'historically women wielded power in ancient matriarchal, or at least pre-patriarchal, societies' to examining and appropriating the goddess tradition for generating feminist consciousness.[1] It was believed that such a system was later overthrown once male gods came into the picture simultaneously with male rule, primarily due to 'patriarchal (and) warlike developments'.[2] In the Indian context too, early scholars, while drawing attention to linkages between religion and material culture, foregrounded the fertility aspect of the goddess, albeit in a unilinear way.[3] The essentialist conceptualization of the goddess has been critiqued by scholars who show that she was conceptualized through complex processes and came to symbolize a variety of different elements at various historical junctures.[4]

Any discussion on the complex goddess tradition in the Indian context cannot be complete without examining the myth and imagery of Devī killing Mahiṣāsura, which is one of the most popular manifestations of the goddess in her *raudra rūpa*, more so textually than visually. In recent years, a debate over this imagery reflecting social contestations has emerged. A celebration of a goddess's slaying of the *asura* has assumed the form of a contest over the representation of communities through a putative association with the respective goddess and *asura*. The non-*savarṇa*[5] groups, as they have been referred to, protested in 2014 against the annual autumnal celebration of the slaying of Mahiṣāsura at the hands of what was seen as the Brahmanical goddess Durgā in some parts of the country. Members of another group complained that 'objectionable texts' on the goddess were being circulated, which could lead to social disharmony.[6] Others, also non-*savarṇa*, argued that some communities observed the eighth day of the autumn festival, the *Durgāṣṭamī*, as Mahiṣāsura's

‘Martyrdom Day’. Bahujan[7] scholars believed that the celebration of the slaying of Mahiṣāsura should be eschewed on two counts: first, it celebrated death; and second, it was based on a Brahmanical interpretation of an incident of contestation and conflict, with Mahiṣāsura, ostensibly an indigenous tribal king, being projected as a demon.[8]

While this is an important reference point in history that has shed light on the question of how and why associations with specific identities are forged and carried forward, and traditions are invoked to establish truth claims, the myths used to draw these identities need to be located within the time and historical context in which they appear and should not be used in a static and unilinear form. Even where they reveal certain inclusions and exclusions, these cannot be directly related to contemporary community identities.

The chapter will attempt to examine questions of contestation, conflict and negotiations in the *Purāṇas* through a reading of the *Mahiṣāsuramardinī* myth as found in two very important *Śākta* texts. The *Devī Māhātmya* (henceforth *DM*), part of the *Mārkaṇḍeya Purāṇa*, composed around the sixth century CE,[9] introduces Devī as an all-encompassing element for the first time, where her role is not only that of creation but also the preservation of the world – in a way, the myths in *DM* shape the nature of the goddess as she is to be known later. The other text that has been examined here is the *Kālikā Purāṇa* (henceforth *KP*), an *Upapurāṇa* dated to around the. eleventh century CE. The goddess was always embedded in the religious tradition of the subcontinent, but it is in the Puranic corpus that she becomes historically and significantly visible.

Religious Integration and the ‘Making’ of the Puranic Tradition

The historical juncture that scholars have discussed in connection with the ‘re-emergence’ of the goddess is linked to the creation of what is known as the Puranic religion, and therefore it becomes imperative to locate the myths in this context. The process of religious integration is to be seen against the backdrop of regional state formation and the incorporation of peripheral areas that characterized the early medieval period. The constant interaction between various groups situated in different locales had an impact on all spheres of society. These historical processes also led to certain innovations in the field of religion, which included the writing of new texts to incorporate the needs of the changing times. This led to the composition of the *Purāṇas*. With the rise of heterodox sects, the ideal Brahmanical social order was disrupted – women were becoming independent, people neglected caste rules and they did not observe the duties enjoined by the *Vedas*. The rise of heterodox religions also resulted in the *brāhmaṇas* losing power and patronage, which led them to feel the need to re-establish the *varṇāśramadharma* and the authority of the *Vedas*. R.C. Hazra argues that they were not only trying to improve their economic and social position but also attempting to preserve Brahmanical social culture in general.[10] This resulted in a new 'composite-syncretic' tradition embodied in the Puranic corpus, through which the Brahmanical ideologues not only addressed their anxieties by describing the *kaliyuga* – a depiction of society where chaos prevails – but also found a way to 'restore order', which could be achieved by following the rites and customs laid down in the *Purāṇas*.[11]

The processes of state formation fuelled by land grants in the post-Gupta period played a role in the integration of religious traditions. R.S. Sharma argues that the Gupta rulers, who had conquered new lands (and people), needed ideological and religious sanction to legitimize and consolidate their conquests, which were provided by the *Brāhmaṇas* who were offered land grants in regions that were on the periphery of the empire.[12] The land grants were also a means to expand agriculture. This led to the acculturation of 'the peripheral region' (from the point of the *madhyadeśa*). This further led to the 'Sanskritization' of the mother goddess cults and the compilation of the Tantric texts.[13] Günther-Dietz Sontheimer, in his work, *The Vana and the Kṣetra: The Tribal Background of Some Famous Cults*, argues that the integrative relationship between the forest society and state society (*vana* and *kṣetra*) led to a considerable and constant influence on religious attitudes, especially of those who lived beyond the forest, due to the attempts of the latter to penetrate it through the expansion of agriculture.[14] There was continuity from the *vana* to *kṣetra*, with the latter spreading into the former. This led to integration of tribal cults into the religious tradition of the *kṣetra*, although for Sontheimer this meant only a transformation and not abolition of the cults.[15] In the case of religion, 'the direct access to and experience of the divine in untamed nature became ritualized on a Sanskritic, "Hinduized" normative pattern'.[16] But the process was extremely slow and there existed the natural barrier of the forest. Thus, Sontheimer argues that there was assimilation of tribal cults into the Brahmanical tradition, which was majorly achieved through expansion of agriculture.[17] B.D. Chattopadhyaya attempts to show how *vana* and *kṣetra* are not separate entities but closely connected, as seen in the several instances of the 're-appearance of the goddess' during the third–fourth centuries CE. He argues that the 'reappearance of the goddess' must be linked to the 'process of amalgamation or convergence which wasn't a matter of accident' and be situated within the larger question of domination and subordination of elements in historical contexts. Chattopadhyaya also highlights through his readings of the copper plate inscriptions belonging to the eastern part of Madhya Pradesh how new political formations in the tribal region led to integration of the local goddess cult into the Brahmanical tradition and her expanding domain through the creation of new temples. The land grants also made sure that the goddess was worshipped from one generation to another, thus, cementing her longevity.[18] Further, there was an attempt to universalize the figure of the goddess like the attempt to associate Ghaṭṭavāsinī with Durgā.[19] There is also an attempt to juxtapose the goddess with the appropriate god and the names of 'tribal' people were getting more and more Sanskritized. He refers to this phenomenon as the 'brahmanical mode of cult appropriation' and links it to the conceptualization of the feminine theology (*Śāktism*) in Brahmanical tradition which allowed for the appropriation to take place in a bigger way. Finally, connecting the arguments of Sontheimer with his own study on religious process, he highlights (as has been stated before) that the *vana* cannot be imagined as a separate entity and must be situated within the larger religious process of appropriation, assimilation and contestation. Finally, the 'reappearance', or rather the entry, of the goddess into codified Hinduism, may also be taken to mark a disjunction between *vana* and *kṣetra* that was textually structured, where people appealed to the goddess to stop the *asuras* from killing them.[20]

In a more recent work, Bihani Sarkar examines the rise of the Durgā cult starting from around the third century CE and argues that the rise of the *āṭavika* kingdoms between around the third and seventh centuries CE saw the cult of Durgā gain prominence as she was intrinsically tied to their political processes. It is at this point of time that her cult was appropriated by the Vaiṣṇava and Śaiva traditions.[21] Interestingly, while in the *DM*, Devī is associated with Viṣṇu most clearly visible in the Madhu Kaitabha myth, in the case of *KP*, the situation is a bit more complex as there seems to be three-dimensional contestation between the Goddess, Śaiva and the Vaiṣṇava traditions, reflecting the milieu against which the text was composed, compiled and redacted. R.C. Hazra believes that the need for 'social discipline' (as understood by the followers of the *Vedas*) was one of the reasons for the composition of the *Purāṇas*. He highlights how the *brāhmaṇas* of Mithilā came to Kāmarūpa and tried to maintain the *varṇāśramadharma* but 'with the passing of the political power to the Mleccha', Kāpālikā Śaivism and Tantric Śāktism gained much popularity, and the 'Maithili Brahmins of Kāmarūpa experienced a great economic and social set back because of their Vedic inclination'. The *brāhmaṇas*, keeping in mind the local tradition would have wanted to appease the people for various purposes,[22] and this resulted in the composition of *Kālikā Purāṇa*, probably by the Maithili *brāhmaṇas* of Kāmarūpa, who wanted to popularize the 'brahmanical ideas of life and society' by associating the Vaiṣṇava faith with Śāktism and thus resurrecting it.[23]

Devī Kills Mahiṣa

In the *DM*, while explaining the majesty of the goddess, the sage Mārkaṇḍeya tells King Suratha the myth of Madhu-Kaiṭabha, Mahiṣa and Śumbha-Niśumbha. According to the myth, a battle took place between the *asuras* and the *devas*; Mahiṣa was the chief of the *asuras*, and Indra was the chief of the *devas*. The legend tells us that Mahiṣāsura had won the battle.[24] The *devas*, along with Prajāpatī (Brahmā), went to Viṣṇu and Śiva and told them about the extent of their defeat: "… He himself now wields sovereignty over Sūrya, Indra, Agni, Vāyu, Candra, Yama and over Varuṇa …'"[25] Viṣṇu and Śiva, upon hearing this, became angry, and from their anger emerged *tejas* which merged with the *tejas* of the other gods and finally took the form of a woman.[26] She was given *āyudha* and other *astra-śastra* not only by Brahmā, Viṣṇu and Śiva but also by the other gods who were present there. The goddess emitted a terrible laugh that shook the entire universe and the three worlds.[27]

Mahiṣa, along with the other *asuras*, heard the noise and, wondering about its source, rushed towards it, only to find the goddess. A great battle ensued between the *asuras* and the goddess.[28] The myth narrates how, along with Mahiṣāsura, other powerful *asuras* like Mahiṣāsura's general Cikṣura, Cāmara, Udagra, Asiloman, Bāṣkala, Parivārita and Viḍāla fought against the goddess.[29] However, Devī, wielding her various *āyudhas*, emerged victorious. Ambikā broke Mahiṣāsura's bow and chariot, killing the charioteer and the horse in the process. With no other option, Cikṣura, armed with a sword and shield, charged towards the goddess. He struck her *vāhana* – the lion – and then attacked her left arm, but his sword shattered upon impact. The *asura* then began hurling other weapons at Bhadrakālī, prompting her to release her lance, which slew the leader of the army. The battle continued, with the *asuras* desperately trying to defeat the goddess, all in vain.[30]

When the leader of Mahiṣa's army was slain, Cāmara came forward, but the goddess's lion *vāhana* fought with him, severing his head. Udgara too was slain in the battle, and Karāla was killed with her bare hands. The goddess, who was angry, killed Uddhata with her club, Bāṣkala with her javelin, and Tāmra, Andhaka, Durdhara and Durmukha with her arrows. She slew Ugrāsya and Ugravīrya and cut off Biḍāla's head.[31]

Seeing his army being defeated, Mahiṣa, in his buffalo form, made the goddess's troops tremble. While he killed some with the blow of his snout, he stamped over others with his hooves, lashed out at some with his tail and tore others with his horns.[32] He then ran towards Ambikā to kill her.

> In anger, he, of great valor, pounded the earth with his hooves, hurled up mountains with his horns, and bellowed. The earth, trampled by his rapid whirling, was crushed, and the ocean, flailed by his tail, flooded everywhere. Clouds were torn into pieces, rent by his swaying horns. Mountains by the hundred, thrown about by his breath, fell from the sky.[33]

Caṇḍikā, seeing all of this, ran towards him to slay him. She then threw a snare at him and bound the great *asura*.

> Thus, bound in the great battle, he abandoned his buffalo form, After which he became a lion. As soon as Ambikā cut off his head, he appeared as a man with a sword in hand. The Goddess cut the man to shred with her arrows, then he became a great Elephant. With his trunk, he dragged the lion, but the Goddess cut off the trunk.[34]

At this point, the *asura* assumed the buffalo form, causing the three worlds, along with everything movable and immovable, to tremble. The *asura*, drunk with might and power, hurled mountains at Caṇḍikā with his horns. The Goddess mocked him, after which she mounted the great *asura*. The next moment is what is majorly depicted in sculptural representations: 'Having struck him with her foot, she beat him with her spear. That great *asura*, who had come forth halfway fighting, was felled by the Goddess, who had cut off his head with a great sword.'[35]

In the *Kālikā Purāṇa*, the myth of Mahiṣa is mentioned thrice. According to Levi-Strauss, the structure of the myth is made apparent by continuous repetition.[36] Further, it also allows for the addition of new material. While discussing the ways in which an adept should celebrate Durgā Pūjā,[37] the myth of Mahiṣa is recounted. During the period of Manu Svāyambhuva, the great goddess Yoganidrā–Mahāmāyā was propitiated to destroy Mahiṣa and bring welfare to the world.[38] Bhadrakālī, placed her left foot on Mahiṣāsura and pierced him with her trident.[39] The story doesn't end here. She sends Brahmā, Viṣṇu and Śiva, along with other *devas*, to the hermitage of sage Kātyāyana and tells them that their desires will be fulfilled there. The gods, baffled by the order, started conversing amongst themselves about what desires were going to be fulfilled after reaching the hermitage, as the one desire they had was already fulfilled by the great goddess.[40] On reaching the hermitage, the hosts of Rudra came and informed them of *Asura* Mahiṣa and how he was controlling the heavens. The *devas* became infuriated, and from their bodies emerged Śakti, who came to be known as Kātyāyanī, as she was worshipped by Kātyāyana.[41] She then vanquished Mahiṣa in the same way as the goddess's ten-armed form did in a previous cycle.[42] Unlike the *DM* version, Mahiṣa is not really described here. The king Sāgara, getting confused, asked sage Aurva about the killing of Mahiṣa twice, upon which Aurva explained that the event took place in a different *kalpa* and started recounting the myth of Mahiṣa all over again.[43]

Once upon a time, Mahiṣa, who was asleep on a mountain, had a terrible dream. He saw that Mahāmāyā Bhadrakālī, looking extremely frightening, had chopped his head off and was drinking his blood.[44] Scared by the dream, Mahiṣa started worshipping the goddess for a long time, and she eventually appeared before him. Mahiṣa, who realized that the dream would come true and that it was his destiny to be killed by a woman – as he had been cursed by Kātyāyana – asked the goddess for a boon.[45] He requested a share in the sacrifice and also asked for a position under her feet, ensuring that he would never be moved from that position.[46] The goddess replied, saying that the share in the sacrifice had already been allotted and that there was nothing more to distribute. She accepted his request that he wouldn't leave her feet and assured him that in the battle and wherever else she was worshipped, he would be worshipped too.[47]

After propitiating the goddess, Mahiṣa asked her about her different forms and manifestations that he would be associated with, to which she replied, saying that the names he took [Ugracaṇḍā, Bhadrakālī, Durgā] would be the images through which he would be worshipped. It is revealed that during the period of the first creation, he was killed by her in the form of Ugracaṇḍā; while in the second creation, he was slain by her in the form of Bhadrakālī; and in the present *kalpa*, he would be killed by her in the form of Durgā.[48] Although in the previous battles he was not killed by her using her foot, because of the boon, he would be killed by her in a similar way so that he could get a share in the sacrifice. Then the goddess revealed her Ugracaṇḍā form, which was similar to the Bhadrakālī form but with two additional arms, bearing a club and a bowl with intoxicating liquor in the right and left hands, respectively. She was wearing a garland of skulls and a snake around her head and was the colour of collyrium.

Mahiṣa, after seeing the two forms, bowed to her and was trodden by her feet and killed by the two goddesses in the same way as Durgā had killed him in an earlier age.[49]

After seeing the buffalo's body pinned by the tridents, Mahiṣa lost his senses and started grieving. Later, he regained his senses and said to the goddess that if she was pleased with him, and if a share of the sacrifice had already been assigned to him, his destruction should occur at another time and in a different way. He requested her to take such measures that he would not be born again and engage in a fight with the *devas*.[50] The goddess replied, saying that his body would never decay because he would always be in touch with the soles of her feet, and he would always enjoy a share in the sacrifice. She also told him that his spirit would always remain with *jīvātma* due to the contact with the feet of Hara, and he would not be born for thirty crores and one hundred and eighty *kalpas*. Saying this, the goddess disappeared, and Mahiṣa, under the illusory power of the goddess, went back to his usual demonic self.[51]

The king asked the sage why, although many demons were killed by Mahāmāyā, they were 'not adopted' by her, yet in the case of Mahiṣa, such a peculiar event took place.[52] The sage explained by narrating the story of Rambhā, who had propitiated Śiva for the longest time and was granted a boon. Rambhā, bereft of a male child, asked Śiva to be born as his son, with a long and prosperous life, someone who 'famous and fortunate, and who will be victorious over all the gods and who cannot be killed by living beings'.[53] Śiva agreed to this and disappeared from there. Upon returning to his abode, Rambhā spotted a 'three-year-old she-buffalo' and copulated with her, resulting in Śiva being born in the form of the demon Mahiṣa. When Mahiṣa was cursed by Kātyāyana, Śiva told Caṇḍikā that she should incorporate the buffalo body of Mahiṣa, which was engaged in yoga, into herself and that she should kill him in the same way as she had done in the past. He further explained that since Viṣṇu, in the shape of the *siṁha*, was no longer able to carry her on his back, he, in his buffalo form, would become her mount.[54] This was the reason given for the incorporation of Mahiṣa by the goddess into her circle. This process was repeated in all three of Mahiṣa's births until he finally asked that he should not be born again.

Myth of Mahiṣa	***Devī Māhātmya***	***Kālikā Purāṇa***
Origin of the goddess	From the *tejas* of the gods: a detailed description of what each god has contributed.	1. Yoganidrā – Mahāmāyā, from whom Bhadrakālī manifests. 2. From the body of the gods.

Myth of Mahiṣa	*Devī Māhātmya*	*Kālikā Purāṇa*
Origin of Mahiṣa	No mention	Associated with Śiva; through him, the association of the goddess with the *asura* is mediated.
Changing forms of Mahiṣa	1) From buffalo to lion 2) Lion to man with a sword 3)Man to elephant 4)Elephant to buffalo	No change
Boon from the goddess	No mention	Second myth: he asks for a share of the sacrifice and to remain under the feet of the goddess.
Mount of the goddess	No mention	Context of the boon – Mahiṣa didn't want to take another birth and requested the goddess to find a way for his body to never decay.

The rise of the goddess

Thomas Coburn argues that the myths in the *DM* are of extreme importance, as never before does one see in the literary tradition the three myths woven together as a group, and where 'the Goddess has been portrayed as instrumental in effecting the divine triumph in all three encounters'.[55] He argues that the story of Mahiṣa formed the original kernel of the *DM* to which the myth of Śumbha–Niśumbha and Madhu-Kaiṭabha were added in that order.[56]

David Shulman states that the mythology of the slaying of Mahiṣāsura, the buffalo-demon, is the archetypal myth of the goddess in the Indic tradition.[57] D.C. Sircar has shown how this myth is not later than around the first century BCE, given the imagery found from different parts of the subcontinent, thereby attesting to its existence much before the *DM* was finally composed/ redacted. The telling of the myth of Mahiṣa is simple in the *DM* but in the *KP* it becomes extremely complex. One needs to keep in mind that both the texts are separated by a few centuries, which gave time for many local motifs and symbols to be added to the myth in *KP*. According to scholars like D.D. Kosambi and Gunther Sontheimer, this myth represents the appropriation of cults through the figure of the goddess; we will discuss this point later.[58]

There are many points of departure in the two retellings of the myth. In *DM*, the goddess appears from the *tejas* and *śakti* of the gods whereas in *KP* in the first episode, she seems to originate on her own (*svayambhu*) and is a manifestation of Yoganidrā – Mahāmāyā. It is only in the second telling that the goddess (this time Kātyāyani) emerges from the body of the gods. Heinrich von Stietencron argues that the two 'textual complexes' refers to two different theological standpoints. The *DM* refers to that point in the process when Śāktism was growing under the aegis of already-established

Figure 4.1 Devī slaying Mahiṣa, *c.* second century CE.
Mathura, LACMA

religious traditions like Vaiṣṇavism and Śaivism and, and which affected how the question of origin of the goddess was treated by the text. The treatment differs in the case of *Kālikā Purāṇa* because by then Śāktism had advanced to such a level where it could be assertive and articulate itself with greater independence.[59] What is interesting is the reference to 'Yoganidrā – Mahāmāyā'. Was there an attempt to associate the myth of Mahiṣa in particular, with that of the Vaiṣṇava pantheon by mentioning her?[60] This is particularly interesting if one talks about the myth primarily being a Śaiva myth.[61] In the Tamil myths of the Mahiṣa, the identification of Śiva with Mahiṣa is especially highlighted in the myth of Devī killing Mahiṣa, and the sprouting of the *liṅga* from the neck after the decapitation takes place.[62] Further, in his examination of the Mahiṣa myth, Stietencron argues that this particular myth opens up new vistas for understanding the *Śākta* tradition and also the '*śākta* reception of the myth'. One moment she is shown as blood thirsty and the other moment she is lauded as the source of ultimate knowledge, fount of salvation. This underlines the level at which the battle is fought in the *Śākta* theology. It represents a struggle waged within the individual: the *asuras* representing *avidyā* and *tamas* which is vanquished by the ultimate knowledge.[63] While Stietencron raises important issues, we will move beyond the theological reading, as the representation of the figure of *Asura* and his interaction with the Devī visible in the myths highlights a complex politico-religious process. To substantiate the arguments, three Mahiṣāsuramardinī images – because of their distinctive nature – are discussed.

Figure 4.1 depicts the *Devī* in her six-armed form slaying Mahiṣa. This sculpture, originating from Mathura, is crafted in its characteristic mottled red sandstone, dated to the Kuṣāṇa period, and is currently housed in LACMA. It represents one of the earlier depictions of the Devī killing Mahiṣa (the demon) and, as discussed earlier, attests to the myth circulating in oral traditions much earlier than it was written about. Here, the human form emerging from the body of Mahiṣa, or the anthropomorphic form of the *asura* characteristic of later periods, is not visible. An interesting aspect of this image is the way the Devī is intertwined with the buffalo. Is she killing him with her bare hands,[64] or is she embracing him? We know from earlier works by M.L.K. Murthy and later works by D.D. Kosambi that, in local tribal traditions and imagination, the assimilation of local cults into some traditions was achieved through the marriage ceremony between an agrarian goddess and a pastoral buffalo cult. This synthesis found expression in the Sanskritic Devī and Mahiṣa, respectively. Should or could this image not be read as a visual vestige of such a tradition?[65] If we adopt this interpretation, it would represent an important intervention, wherein the visual evidence does not align with the Sanskritic textual tradition. Instead, it presents an alternative narrative that appears rooted in local cultic beliefs.

The image (Figure 4.2) is one of the most famous, discussed extensively by R. Mahalakshmi. It bears close resemblance to the later depiction in Cave 16, Ellora (Figure 4.3).

Something that strikes the viewer immediately is the massive size of Mahiṣāsura where iconometrically; he is bigger than Devī, denoting his status as a ruler/ chief. The sculpture depicts a battle scene, the fight between Devī and Mahiṣāsura. The goddess is depicted in her eight-armed form, sitting on her *vāhana*, *siṁha*, holding her many *āyudhas*. The *gaṇas* surround her; one is even shown holding the *chhatri* cementing her identity as a divinity. The moving figure below the *Devī* has been identified by Mahalakshmi as Jayā, a *yoginī*.[66]

The left side of the panel depicts Mahiṣāsura. He, while shown retreating, is depicted as being larger in size iconometrically. He is represented in an anthropomorphic form with a human body and a buffalo head. The buffalo of the earlier Mahiṣamardinī has transformed into a human figure with a buffalo head. He is shown wearing a horned *mukuṭa,* holding a *mūsala* (club) and, like the goddess, he is depicted with the *chhatri*. He is also shown wearing a *yajñopavīta,* which is a marker of *Brāhmaṇa* identity.

Figure 4.2 Mahiṣāsura retreating, *c*. seventh century CE Mahiṣāsuramardinī Cave, Mamallapuram.

Figure 4.2(i) Details of Mahiṣāsura.

There are three figures behind him – they can be seen retreating. Two figures, the face of a man who has fallen down, and a dead body are visible between the goddess and Mahiṣāsura, confirming that it is a battle scene.

The image below (Figure 4.3) is from Cave 16, Kailashnatha, Ellora, and is dated to around the eighth century CE. Like in the Mamallapuram depiction, here too iconometrically Mahiṣa is shown almost towering over Devī who is seated on her *siṁha vāhana.*

Here too, a battle scene is depicted, but unlike the previous image, Mahiṣa is not seen retreating from the battle. Instead, he has raised his *mūsala* in a manner that seems as though he is about to fight with the Goddess. In the panel above Devī and Mahiṣāsura, one can see that the *devas* are watching the fight, with Indra among them, seated on his

Figure 4.3 Mahiṣāsura fighting with Devī, *c.* eighth century CE, Cave 16, Kailasanatha Temple, Ellora.

elephant. In this sculptural depiction, his crown, which has horns, is what identifies him with *Mahiṣa*, and the transformation from a buffalo to a human is almost complete. He is also dressed in fineries, reinforcing the association pointed out by R. Mahalakshmi with a chief or ruler.

The images clearly refer to the war in the *DM*. However, one of the most important takeaways is the transformation of the *asura* from a bull to a human, who is shown with markers of 'royalty/divinity' such as the *chhatri*, *mukuṭas* and other fineries. Mahalakshmi has argued that iconometric depiction/variation is a very important marker, as it redirects one's attention to what is significant and is also associated with notions of power – a case in point being the imagery of Umā-Maheśvara. In the depictions from Mamallapuram and Ellora, while in positions of flight and fight, Mahiṣāsura is iconometrically larger in size than the Goddess. One can, of course, interpret this to mean that even though he was larger, the Goddess succeeded in defeating him. But drawing from Mahalakshmi's work, it seems that such depictions are deliberate and encourage us to treat Mahiṣa, who is an *asura*, as significant. This particular imagery is too prolific to attribute to any specific symbolism, although the fact that it is found in the Pallava and Rāṣṭrakūṭa realms, which emerge from the early medieval context of regional formation, is noteworthy.

Further, juxtaposing the works of Kosambi and Sontheimer, such depictions allow us to discuss the appropriation of tribal cults through the figure of Mahiṣa, who is an *asura*, made to wear a *yajñopavīta* and identified with Śiva, as also highlighted in the myth from *KP*. Long ago, D.D. Kosambi, in his pioneering work *Goddesses at Crossroads*, brought to light the association of the local goddess Yogeśvarī with Durgā and the cult of Mhasobā/Mhātobā with that of Mahiṣāsura, who is further linked to Śiva through the myth.[67] It is in this context that the question of sacrifice becomes important.

With the rise of the heterodox sects and the spread of the doctrine of *ahiṁsā*, the Vedic sacrifices, which were the main source of income for *brāhmaṇas*, were becoming extremely unpopular, thereby affecting their livelihood.[68] Therefore, it is not surprising that in the *Purāṇas*, they would seek to re-establish the Vedic sacrifices. It is striking that in the myth in the *KP*, Mahiṣa asks for a share of the sacrifice, to which the goddess replies that she cannot grant it as it was already decided. This is reminiscent of the Dakṣa myth, where Śiva asks for a part of the sacrifice but is denied.[69] 'The exclusion from the sacrifice and the struggle to obtain a share are classic Śaiva themes, the underlying basis of the Dakṣa myth.'[70] Maybe the myth is suggesting a milieu where some groups, probably those who worshipped similar cults like that of Mhasobā (and identified Mahiṣa as their god), were asking for a part of the sacrifice – which would entail giving them space in the social order, and the *Brāhmaṇas* were denying this to them.

One of the most interesting points of difference that can be seen in the retelling of the two myths is that, in the *KP*, the association of Śiva with Mahiṣāsura is highlighted explicitly. This brings to light patterns of cult appropriation. Sontheimer argues that it is only through the figure of Śiva that one could bridge the gap between *vana* and *kṣetra*, as he was beyond the two realms but in contact with both. 'It was he who could hold the two different ecological, cultural, and religious areas together.'[71] Even Anncharlott Eschmann argues that one of the ways in which the tribal deities were incorporated into the pantheon was by associating the local cult, especially that of the goddess, with the *ugra* form of Śiva.[72] The attributes of *asura* associated with Mahiṣa points to his tribal origin, as was the case in Sanskrit textual traditions, which was written from the 'perception' of the people living in the *kṣetra*.[73] The initial fight between the two is attested in the contestation of the two cults, which was finally resolved through the marriage between Durgā and Śiva, or Yogeśvarī and Mhasobā.[74] Steitencron in his work discusses how in the later development of the myth of Mahiṣa, the asura's love is foregrounded. This, for him, is the case of genuine *bhakti* and the relationship between the two must be re-casted in tandem with the developments in the religious sphere.[75]

What is interesting is that Durgā herself isn't part of the Brahmanical pantheon, as discussed by Hazra, Mahalakshmi and more recently by Sarkar. Although there was the process of acculturation and integration, it was especially carried out through the figure of Durgā.[76] One doesn't find any mention of Durgā or similar deities in the Vedic *Saṁhitā* and *Brāhmaṇas*, which was probably due to the antagonism between the Vedic and the indigenous traditions. It was only later that a lot of non-Vedic deities came under the Brahmanical pantheon through processes of assimilation (and contestation). Gradually, non-Vedic deities came to be associated with the Brahmanical corpus, the first being Umā, who was seen (and known) as the wife of Rudra, a Vedic god who was later associated with the figure of Śiva.[77] This argument is being brought up at this point of the discussion to highlight that the reading of the myth isn't as simple as one might think it to be. There are complex webs and many ways through which various divinities are associated with each other, and there exists no one way (linear or otherwise) to read the myths.

The *Purāṇas* were composed in a context where socio-economic and political transformations were occurring across the subcontinent due to the shift in focus from the Gangetic core to other regions. This led to the emergence of state societies and the evolution of regional formations in many parts of the geographical expanse, marked by the spread of agriculture, the peasantization of the tribal population and the movement of the *Brāhmaṇas* as politico-religious ideologues, resulting in the process of religious integration. Furthermore, the context of Vedic sacrifice-centred worship was no longer relevant. Theistic cults, pilgrimage and devotion marked the religious traditions that were beginning to take shape at this time around the deities Viṣṇu and Śiva, and later the goddess as Devī. The rise of Śāktism required the composers to, if not re-write, add new material, myths and symbols to give space to the many goddess cults. It is in this context that one needs to read the myth of Mahiṣa. The myth highlights the religious process of acculturation and assimilation, although this process was neither easy nor one-way, and certainly not final, as there were contestations as well as negotiations.

Notes

1 The following works best exemplify this position: Erndl, Kathleen M. 2000. 'Is Shakti Empowering for Women? Reflections on Feminism and the Hindu Goddess'. In *Is the Goddess a Feminist? The Politics of South Asian Goddesses*, edited by Alf Hiltebeitel and Kathleen M. Erndl.

New York: New York University Press; Sunder Rajan, Rajeswari. 1998. 'Is the Hindu Goddess a Feminist?' *Economic and Political Weekly*, 33 (44): WS-34–WS-38. The latter problematizes the connections between Feminism and the Hindu goddess but herself uses the binaries of nature and culture in her discussion. See, *ibid.*, WS 36.

2 Rosemary Ruether in the essay 'Gender and the Problems of Prehistory' states that the association of fecundity in the Neolithic period in the Near East with these figurines are probably inherited from the Palaeolithic period. She is cautious in labelling the figurines as 'mother goddesses' and looks for alternate readings; see, Reuther, Rosemary Radford. 2005. *Goddesses and the Divine Feminine – A Western Religious History*. Berkeley: University of California Press. 13–40. 20.

3 Kosambi, D.D. 1962. 'At the Crossroads: A Study of Mother-Goddess Cult Sites'. In *Myth and Reality*. Mumbai: Popular Prakarshan; Agarwala, P.K. 1984. *Goddesses in Ancient India*. New Delhi: Abhinav Publications; Tiwari, J.N. 1985. *Goddess Cults in Ancient India (With Special Reference to the First Seven Centuries A.D.)*. Delhi: Sundeep Prakashan; Bhattacharyya, N.N. 1999. *The Indian Mother Goddesses*. Delhi: Manohar.

4 Coburn, Thomas B. 1988. *Devī-Māhātmya: The Crystallization of the Goddess Tradition*, Delhi: Motilal Banarsidass; Bernard, Elizabeth and Beverly Moon, eds. 2000. *Goddesses Who Rule*. New York: Oxford University Press; Chattopadhyaya, B. D. (2003) 2016. "Reappearance' of the Goddess or the Brahmaṇical Mode of Appropriation: Some Early Epigraphic Evidence Bearing on Goddess Cult'. *Studying Early India: Archaeology, Texts and Historical Issues*. Delhi: Permanent Black; Mahalakshmi, R. 2011. *The Making of the Goddess: Koṟṟavai -Durgā in the Tamil Traditions*, Delhi: Penguin Books; Sarkar, Bihani. 2017. *Heroic Shāktism: The Cult of Durga in Ancient Indian Kingship*. London: Oxford University Press.

5 *Savarṇa – sa + varṇa* means belonging to the same *varṇa*. According to Monier Williams it means having the same colour or appearance, to be similar, like or equal to. In the later *dharma* text, it is used to refer to the son of a *brāhmaṇa* and a *kṣatriya* woman. See, https://www.sanskrit-lexicon.uni-koeln.de/scans/MWScan/2020/web/webtc/indexcaller.php (accessed on 21 December 2023). The term is used to denote all those who fall within the *varṇa* category and therefore, non-savarṇa or avarṇa is used by the Dalit and Adivasi community to distinguish themselves. See, https://www.indiatoday.in/news-analysis/story/dalit-sawarn-caste-system-must-go-1989509-2022-08-18 (accessed on 21 December 2023).

6 S.N., Vijetha. 2014. 'Student Groups Come to Blows over Mahishasura Issue at JNU Once Again', *The Hindu*, New Delhi, 11 October. Available at https://www.thehindu.com/news/cities/Delhi/student-groups-come-to-blows-over-mahishasura-issue-at-jnu-once-again/article6491346.ece.

7 The term *Bahujan* literally means 'many people'. Gail Omvedt highlights the association of Buddhism with this term (*bahujan hitāya, bahujan sukhāya*) which is then used as a symbol of unity by the non-Brahmin, oppressed caste and class. It is often used along with the term 'Dalit' to talk of Dalit-Bahujan. See, Omvedt, Gail. 2003. *Buddhism in India – Challenging Brahmanism and Caste*. New Delhi: Sage. 65, 184.

8 Puniyani, Ram. 2016. 'Durga, Mahishasur and Caste Politics', *The Forward Press*, 3. Available at, https://www.forwardpress.in/2016/03/durga-mahishasur-and-caste-politics/.

9 Recent scholarship has tried to date the text to around the eighth century CE. See, Sarkar, *Heroic Shāktism.*

10 Hazra, R.C. 1987. *The Puranic Records on Hindu Rites and Customs.* Delhi: Motilal Banarsidass. 244.

11 It might seem like it is a very unilinear and simple process, but as scholars like R.C. Hazra, Kunal Chakrabarti and R. Mahalakshmi have shown, the process is extremely complex and continues to this day.

12 Sharma, R.S. 2014. 'Economic and Social Basis of Tantrism'. *Early Medieval Indian Society – A Study in Feudalism*. Delhi: Orient Blackswan.

13 Ibid., 237–64.

14 Sontheimer, Günther-Dietz. 2004. 'The *Vana* and the *Kṣetra*: The Tribal Background of Some Famous Cults'. In *Essays on Religion, Literature and Law*, edited by Brückner, Heidrun, Anne Feldhaus and Aditya Malik. New Delhi: Manohar, 353–60.

15 Ibid., 360.

16 Ibid., 373–4.

17 Romila Thapar drawing from Sontheimer's discussion argues that the duality between vana and *kṣetra* certainly existed, but over a period of time was ascribed meanings that went beyond the scope of ecology, and 'the perceptions accompanying it were neither static nor uniform'. See, Thapar, Romila. 2001. 'Perceiving the Forest: Early India'. *Studies in History*, 17(1): 1–16.

18 Chattopadhyaya, B.D., '"Reappearance" of the Goddess or the Brahmanical Mode of Appropriation; Some Early Epigraphic Evidence Bearing on Goddess Cult', 177–8.

19 Ibid., 179.

20 Ibid., 82.2.40–2.63, 43–4.

21 Sarkar, *Heroic Shāktism.*

22 The power and importance of the gift has been highlighted by Hazra in his discussion on the *Puranic Rites and Customs.*

23 Hazra, R.C. 1963. *Studies in the Upapurāṇas – Vol. II.* Calcutta: Sanskrit College. 24, 30–5.

24 Coburn, Thomas B. 1992. *Encountering the Goddess: A Translation of the Devī Māhātmya and a Study of Its Interpretation*. New York: SUNY. Chapter 82.2.1–2.2, 39.

25 Ibid., 82.2.3–2.5, 39.
26 Ibid., 82.2.6–2.12, 39–40. A description of the different body parts from different gods is given in the text, see. Ibid., 41–2.
27 Ibid., 82.2.13–2.32, 40–2.
28 Ibid., 82.2.35–2.38, 42.
29 Ibid., 82.2.39–2.45, 42–3.
30 Ibid., 82.2.51–3.18, 43–5.
31 Ibid., 82.3.13–3.19, 45–6.
32 Ibid., 82.3.20–3.22, 46.
33 Ibid., 82.3.23–3.26, 46.
34 Ibid., 82.3.28–3.31, 46–7.
35 Ibid., 82.3.32–3.39, 47.
36 Lévi-Strauss, Claude. 1955. 'The Structural Study of Myth'. *The Journal of American Folklore*, 68 (270): 428–44.
37 *Kālikā Purāṇa*, Shastri, B.N. 1994. *Kālikā Purāṇa*. Delhi: Nag Publishers. 60. 1–54, 431–5.
38 Ibid., 60.55–56, 435.
39 Ibid., 60.58b–63a, 435.
40 Ibid., 60.64b–71a, 436.
41 Ibid., 60.75–76, 436.
42 Ibid., 60.77, 437.
43 Ibid., 60.82–84, 437.
44 Ibid., 60.86, 437.
45 Ibid., 60.87.88, 90–1, 438.
46 Ibid., 60.104–105, 439.
47 Ibid., 60.106–107, 439.
48 Ibid., 60.112–117, 439.
49 Ibid., 60.118–121, 123, 440.
50 Ibid., 60.124–125, 127–8, 440–1.
51 Ibid., 60.131–133, 441.
52 Ibid., 60.136, 441.
53 Ibid., 60.137–138, 141a, 441–2.
54 Ibid., 60.151b–152, 442–3.
55 An interesting observation made by Coburn about the myths in the *Devī Māhātmya* is that the lesser known it is, the more it increases in length; see, Coburn, ibid., 211, 222.
56 Ibid., 102.
57 Shulman, David. 1976. 'The Murderous Bride: Tamil Versions of the Myth of Devī and the Buffalo-Demon'. *History of Religions*, 16 (2): 120–46.
58 See, Kosambi, 'At the Crossroads: A Study of Mother – Goddess Cult Sites'; Sontheimer, 'The *Vana* and the *Kṣetra*: The Tribal Background of Some Famous Cults'.
59 Stietencron, Heinrich von. 2005. *Hindu Myths, Hindu History: Religion, Art, and Politics*. Delhi: Permanent Black. 121–2.

60 It is entirely plausible that there was sectarian rivalry and the *brāhmaṇas* were trying to associate, like they seemed to have done before in the many myths found in *Kālikā Purāṇa*, the goddess tradition with that of the Vaiṣṇava pantheon, especially highlighted in B.D. Chattopadhyaya's discussion of the Naraka myth. This sectarianism as well as the supremacy of the goddess is visible in the reference where Śiva born as Mahiṣa tells Mahāmāyā that he will be her mount, since Viṣṇu can no longer be the one. The replacement of the lion by the bull as Devī's mount is an interesting phenomenon. K.R. van Kooij is of the opinion that bull as Devī's *vāhana* attests to the fierce nature of the goddess, for the buffalo is usually the vehicle of Yama, who rules the dead, and therefore, this myth has been interpreted as a *śākta* parallel to Śiva as Kālāntaka. It also highlights the superiority of the goddess tradition over the godheads. Further, the nature of worship is reflected in her conceptualization, as she is worshipped both by the Śāktas and the Vāmas, where the former marks her out as the supreme deity and the ultimate reality and the male gods are put in a subordinate position, which according to Kooij is pointed to by their association as her mount. The myth of Mahiṣa, especially, as it occurs in *Kālikā Purāṇa*, is important not just to understand sectarian conflict between the Vaiṣṇavas and Śaivas but also to understand the tensions between the goddess and the Śaiva tradition. See, Van Kooij, K. R. 1972. *Worship of the Goddess According to the Kālikā Purāṇa*. Leiden: E.J. Brill; Chattopadhyaya, B.D. 2017. 'Local and Beyond – The Story of Asura Naraka and Society, State and Religion in Early Assam'. *The Concept of Bharatavarsha and Other Essays*. Ranikhet: Permanent Black.

61 As Coburn seems to indirectly indicate in his discussion on the precedent of the myth and as has been highlighted by the discussions of Kosambi, Sontheimer and David Shulman.

62 Shulman, 'The Murderous Bride', 128.

63 Stietencron, *Hindu Myth, Hindu History*. 115–19.

64 It is interesting that she is seen with her *āyudhas* – one of which is the *cakra*. Does this establish her identity with the Vaiṣṇava tradition?

65 I would like to thank Prof. R. Mahalakshmi for drawing my attention to this visual peculiarity, and a possible alternate reading of this image.

66 Mahalakshmi, *The Making of the Goddess*, 256.

67 Kosambi, 'Goddesses at Crossroads', 91.

68 Hazra, *Studies in the Purāṇic Records on Hindu Rites and Customs*.

69 I would like to thank Prof. R. Mahalakshmi for bringing this to my notice.

70 Shulman, 'The Murderous Bride', 127.

71 Sontheimer, 'The Vana and the Kṣetra: The Tribal Background of Some Famous Cults', 367.

72 Eschmann, A. 2014. 'Hinduization of Tribal Deities in Orissa: The Śākta and Śaiva Typology'. In *The Cult of Jagannātha and the Regional Tradition of Orissa*, edited by A. Eschmann and G.C. Hermann Kulke. Tripathi. Delhi: Manohar, 135–56.

73 Sontheimer, 'The Vana and the Kṣetra: The Tribal Background of Some Famous Cults', 368.

74 Kosambi, *Myth and Reality*, 88.

75 According to Stietencron, 'In place of the bestial monster of the early versions, a noble, princely suitor for the goddess's hand now gradually takes shape. Her enemy is transformed into devotee and finally husband. Hate is transformed into love; and the formerly low-born adversary of the gods and impudent usurper of hegemony over the three worlds is transformed into an ascetic of Brahmin birth who finally turns out to be a partial incarnation of the god Śiva. What was initially depicted as repulsive has now become laudable and worthy of reverence: Mahiṣa is appearing as a symbol or prototype of the successful devotee (*bhakta*), who has attained to ultimate self-surrender *(prapatti)* and is rewarded by being released from the cycle of rebirth. From now on his place is in the immediate proximity of the supreme godhead,' *Hindu Myths, Hindu History*, 127.

76 R. Mahalakshmi makes an important observation while examining the importance of images from Mamallapuram. In one of the images, Durgā is standing erect and is given blood offerings. This image, she argues, captures the different elements that have gone into the making and understanding of the 'syncretic icon of Durgā in the Tamil region'. The stag and lion are associated with the Tamil warrior goddess Koṟṟavai and Durgā respectively, and the offerings of blood sacrifices to the warrior goddess are known both in the Sangam and the Puranic texts. 'The panel brings the practices and associations belonging to the two different milieus together and points to the process of acculturation that was transforming the Tamil landscape during the early medieval period.'

77 Hazra, *Studies in the upapurāṇa – Vol. II*, 24.

5

Of Power and Sexuality: Images of Śiva and Pārvatī from Kālañjara

Dolan Samanta

History is the intricate repository of human consciousness, a reservoir from which all existence has evolved. It is not just the illustration of political structures but the existence of bodies as a site that encompasses the structures predicated by normative prescriptions.[1] Throughout history, hierarchies have invariably materialized through the power of knowledge, imposing order upon societies.[2] Such an order of political and social hierarchies is visible in the images of Śiva and Pārvatī from Kālañjara. However, to understand why these images were sculpted, it is essential for us to understand the larger socio-political changes that were taking place in the subcontinent, which directly contributed to the religious development in central India.

The development of the new religious systems must be contextualized within broader political, intellectual and historical settings. There are two types of power apparatuses: ideological and coercive. The coercive power apparatuses are those directly controlled by the state and involve the direct coercion of the people. The ideological power apparatuses, either ideologically or through knowledge, justify or legitimize the state. Although these apparatuses work closely with the state, they may not appear to be part of state institutions. According to Foucault, political power exercises itself through the medium of these institutions, which may seem to have nothing in common with political power and appear independent of each other, but in reality, they are not. A prime example of the ideological power apparatuses is religious institutions. In early medieval central India, to understand the socio-political history of the region and Śaivism, *maṭhas* (monasteries) serve as one of the prime examples of such religious/ ideological state/power apparatuses. The kings patronized the *ācāryas* by donating land and building *maṭhas.* The *ācāryas,* in turn, legitimized their rule by consecrating them into Śaiva worship. Through this process, there was an institutionalization of power.

This institutionalization of power was not an isolated phenomenon but a process that changed the subcontinent's religious edifice. The heads of the *maṭhas* had become so influential that they acted as *rājagurūs* to the kings. The *ācāryas*, in their capacity as *rājagurūs*, were given the authority to officiate over royal decrees, administer land, collect taxes on goods in the marketplace and perform important rituals. This created an axis between the state and the religious institutions. The *rājagurūs* had also garnered enough wealth to patronize building activities themselves. The funding of temples and other religious institutions was not only an act of intellectual legitimation but also an active process of reconstituting monarchy around fresh forms of ritual knowledge and practice.

For understanding the discursive practices through which an ideological apparatus or religious institution operates, we need to take into account the production of extensive canonical literature, including Puranic and Tantric texts, which were produced in association with Śaiva *maṭhas.* Some of these textual traditions, pre-existing as early as the fifth century CE facilitated the institutional establishment and growth of the *maṭhas* themselves.

Scholars like R.C. Hazra, J.N. Banerjea and P.V. Kane, through their works, have shown the increasing Tantric influence in the *Purāṇas.* Devangana Desai and Alexis Sanderson have also demonstrated the growing blurring of distinctions between Smārta and Tantric traditions and rituals in the *Purāṇas.* The *Purāṇas,* as the epistemological and ideological discourse of religious traditions, succeeded in integrating the local and regional elements into a more comprehensive Brahmanical framework. The diverse regions underwent social and cultural changes during the time the *Purāṇas* were written, which necessitated a reformulation and negotiation of socio-religious rituals and observances. Myths were employed to emphasize the renegotiations with new groups.

Contextualizing Śaivite Monasticism

During this period, key theological developments influenced the organization of ascetic institutions. Both Śaiva Siddhānta dualism and Kashmiri Śaiva monism experienced revitalization, mainly in Tamil Nadu and Kashmir, through figures like Vasugupta, Somānanda, Utpaladeva and Abhinavagupta.[3] These systems were part of a broader Tantric Śaiva tradition rooted in the fifth century. Sanderson categorized Śaivism into three practices: Atimārga, Mantramārga and Kulamārga. Atimārga included Pāñcārthika Pāśupata, Lākula and Kāpālika traditions.

Kulamārga incorporated Śakta traditions with orgiastic worship, meat consumption and sexual contact. *Mantramārga* focused on Saiddhāntika Śaiva tradition and Śakta-oriented rituals. The right-hand Tantric system of *Śaiva Siddhānta*, combining Vedic and Tantric mantras, thrived in central India between the tenth and twelfth centuries, as evidenced by inscriptions in Gwalior, Malwa and Ḍahala regions. These inscriptions also reveal the spread of Śaiva Siddhānta branches (Mattamayūra, Mādhumateya, Āmardaka) in different areas.[4] The rise of Śaivite sects, their organizational activities and the expansion of temples paved the way for Śaivite monasticism.

With a decline in *Śrauta* sacrifice in religious ceremonies from about the fifth to the thirteenth century undertaken by the rulers of the subcontinent, their religious commitment generally took the form of Buddhism, Jainism or, more commonly, devotion to Śiva, Viṣṇu, Sūrya or the deities of the new initiatory religions. These allegiances were typically declared in the epigraphical sources by the inclusion amid their royal titles, of epithets to the deity/founder of whichever religion they favoured, illustrating sectarian affiliations.[5] Devotion to Śiva was common, and in this period, the epithet *paramamāheśvaraḥ* (entirely devoted to Śiva) is the most frequently encountered in declarations of the religious adherence of rulers.[6] Most of the Candella rulers referred to themselves as *paramamāheśvaraḥ.*[7] Their inscriptions also begin with the epithet *'om namaḥ śivāya'* paying homage to Śiva. Many inscriptions start with a eulogy of Śiva, which attests to the fact that they were Śaivaites.

Within this framework, Kālañjara emerges as a noteworthy site demanding exploration. The inscriptions discovered at the Nīlakaṇṭha temple highlight the interconnection of legitimacy between the royal authorities and the *rājagurus.*

Kālañjara, a hill fort in the Vindhya ranges at the border of modern-day Madhya Pradesh and Uttar Pradesh, has been a significant centre for Śaivism for centuries, hosting sculptures dating from the fifth to sixth century CE and rock-cut monuments from the eleventh to thirteenth century CE. Numerous sculptures at Kālañjara are associated with Śaivism. The site's religious importance is evident in textual sources, including the *Mahābhārata*, *Harivaṃśa*, *Purāṇas* and *Tantra*, which mention Kālañjara as an important *tīrtha* dedicated to Śiva. The name 'Kālañjara' symbolizes the destruction of time, associated with Mahākāla in Agamic texts.[8]

Yaśovarman, the seventh Candella ruler, conquered Kālañjara in 954 CE.[9] Kālañjara became the military capital of the Candellas due to its strategic location, with many Candella inscriptions from the time of Dhaṅgadēva referencing themselves as '*ādhipati*' (supreme lords) of Kālañjara'.[10] The Nīlakaṇṭha temple, with a striking Candella-style *maṇḍapa,* is one of the prime attractions. It was under the Candellas that this magnificent temple was constructed, possibly in the early part of the eleventh century CE. In the Khajuraho Stone Inscription of Yaśovarman, Kālañjara is mentioned as the dwelling of the lord Nīlakaṇṭha.[11] The temple is dedicated to Śiva, and the structure is replete with the representation of different anthropomorphic forms of Śiva, and the main shrine has a Śiva *liṅga.*

The Kālañjara stone inscription of Kīrttivarman from 1090 CE, affixed to the temple's sanctum wall, confirms the presence of the Śaiva Siddhānta in Candella territory. It mentions Kīrttivarman's guru Śrīmūrti, a Pāśupata sect follower, who patronized the temple's *maṇḍapa.* The inscription encourages the chiefs of Śrīkaraṇas and Vārikas (temples) to follow the Pāśupata path for merit.[12] This inscription helps us reiterate the point that the gurus had garnered not only prestige as royal preceptors but also enough wealth to patronize building activities.

Though the state seeks legitimacy through religious institutions and works in close association with them, the religious institution, even independent of the state, controls the social life of people in a wide range of aspects, including the regulation of their economic, social and cultural practices as well as their sexuality and sexual practices. A close reading of the mythology in the Puranic traditions shows that the relationship between religion and sexuality is central to the questions of power. Therefore, one of the most pertinent questions that arises is who controls and channelizes sexuality. The control of social and sexual life by *maṭhas,* in this context, was preconceived much earlier in the normative discourses on Śiva's sexuality in Puranic literature. Undoubtedly, all composed by men, these stories offer the advantage of providing a genuine representation of a masculine outlook.

This chapter focuses on analysing specific images of the *ūrdhvaliṅga* Śiva with Pārvatī from the Nīlakaṇṭha temple of Kālañjara. These images are significant as they depict erotic desire and simultaneously serve as a lens through which societal constructs of power and sexuality are conveyed. Analysing the representation of the body from a gender perspective is essential to uncover the underlying social dynamics that shape these depictions. These visual representations transcend mere biological aspects and serve as symbolic codes for societal constructs of gender identities. Moreover, they offer insights into the ways religious institutions and ideologies interpret gender identities within the framework of Brahmanical norms. The religious ideologies construct a societal gender framework that sets a paradigm within which gender identities are constructed, and these are manifest in the sculptures. A gendered theoretical perspective on the construction of these images and their underlying intentions will be undertaken here.

Śiva and Pārvatī: Discourses on Sexuality

Through a sculpture, the divine is represented as a body; therefore, how it was perceived is essential to what it is and why it was made.[13] The sculptures represent the understanding and articulation of sexuality by the belief systems. Puranic mythology serves as the epistemological foundation for numerous religious traditions in South Asia. Textual sources like the *Purāṇas* define and express 'religious' narratives of human sexuality and form moral norms around the subject. Therefore, to understand the discourses employed by the ideological apparatus, it is imperative to delve into Puranic mythology. Within this context, it becomes crucial to examine how religious and sacred knowledge, as well as perspectives on sexuality, originated and evolved within specific religious traditions. Additionally, it is equally important to explore how these understandings of sexuality are interpreted, articulated and perpetuated within the realm of religious traditions.

Simone de Beauvoir posited that women have historically been categorized as the 'Other', while men occupy the role of the 'prime subject'. This 'otherness' defines women in relation to men, positioning them as the weaker and less significant gender.[14] She further argued that religion, theology and philosophy played a role in reinforcing this representation of women as the 'Other'.[15] Women's objectification and subordination were institutionalized through religious ideology, with regulations and laws crafted predominantly by men to control women's sexuality and societal status through ideological and coercive power. Patriarchal ideology becomes deeply ingrained in cultural psyche when tied to religious doctrine, prescribing gender relations with divine sanction.

Patriarchy exerts its influence by conferring authority upon men, and this dynamic is evident in the mythology of Pārvatī, which predominantly revolves around her connection with Śiva. The codification of regulations and laws institutionalized the objectification and subjugation of women through these religious ideologies. The myths surrounding Śiva and Pārvatī and their sexual union strengthen the asymmetry between male and female.

The narrative of Pārvatī's birth and marriage, as depicted in the *Śiva Purāṇa*, unfolds as a predetermined event orchestrated by male deities for two key objectives. First, it is intended to produce a son capable of vanquishing the demon Tāraka, a feat prophesied to be achievable only by a son of Śiva.[16] Secondly, it aims to facilitate the process of creation, emphasizing the vital role of men in shaping these preordained events.[17] It is interesting to see how men, who have been conferred with divine status, wield authority to not only orchestrate the birth of the divine feminine but also control and channelize her sexuality in the name of the larger good, i.e., preserving the natural and cosmic order. Here, the control of a woman (Pārvatī) over her own body is taken over and justified by incorporating it into the narrative of the larger good, namely the maintenance of cosmic order, which, in turn, subordinates her own agency. Patriarchy utilizes religious ideology to objectify women's bodies, subjugating them within a masculinist system of representation that distorts their 'corporeality and sexuality'.[18] These representations are shaped and perpetuated by power systems, particularly religious institutions and ideologies.

Simultaneously, the myths are also making the reproductive roles of women anodyne, representing her as an aid for the greater purpose of creation and maintaining the cosmic balance. Beauvoir argues that the male gender assumed supremacy by controlling economic factors. The maintenance of life became an activity and project for men, whereas for women, the function of reproduction and motherhood made her akin to an animal. Therefore, men attached more value to their project of maintaining life rather than to women's creation of life, thus subjugating both nature and women.[19]

Within Puranic traditions, one of the creation myths surrounding Śiva and Pārvatī unfolds in the form of Ardhanārīśvara, an androgynous deity. According to this myth, for the purpose of facilitating creation, the female counterpart, Pārvatī had to be birthed from the male aspect, Śiva. The female entity is birthed only because of her reproductive powers, reinstating the idea that women are the 'Other', and their sexuality is directed and harnessed for the greater objective of creation. After the process of creation, the female principle returns to the male godhead, i.e., Śiva. Drawing upon Lerner's insights into the creation of patriarchy in Western civilization, we can find a parallel in the Judeo-Christian creation myths, particularly the narrative of Eve's creation from Adam's rib. Lerner argues that this specific event defines woman in a unique manner, as a 'natural' extension of man, flesh of his flesh, establishing a relationship akin to that of a mother to her child. This narrative frames man as 'the mother' of woman, with divine creativity mirroring the act of a human mother bringing forth life from her own body.[20]

Puranic writers utilize mythology as a tool to perpetuate specific discourses, beliefs and practices, primarily focused on creating ideal masculine embodiments for their deities. This serves to disseminate what they consider normative masculinity. These attributes are instilled and replicated extensively within the Brahmanical social order. R.W. Connell's framework identifies various forms of masculinity, hierarchically structured as hegemonic, subordinate, complicit and marginal masculinities. 'Hegemonic masculinity' is culturally esteemed, constructed through culture, institutions and persuasion, upholding men's dominant status and women's subordination.[21] In mythology, Śiva emerges as a prominent masculine archetype, embodying the symbolism of fertility. His portrayal is a nuanced blend of sensuality and asceticism, reflecting diverse facets of masculinity. Through the rich tapestry of mythological narratives that revolve around Śiva's various manifestations, he is characterized by features associated with hyper-masculinity – physical strength in the manifestations as Andhakāsuravadhamūrti and Tripurāntakamūrti; manliness, physique and desirability through the Bhikṣāṭana and the several myths around the *liṅga*.

Sexuality constitutes one of the most potent aspects of human existence, encompassing not only the physical act of intimate connection but also the potential for procreation. It serves as a means of conveying aspects of our identity to both ourselves and others. Due to the inherent embodiment of human beings, the world is experienced through a sexual and sensual lens, extending beyond the physical realm to encompass all the ways in which the corporeal realm is endowed with significance.[22] It is through sexuality that gendered identities take form, transmuting anatomical facts into multifaceted social constructs that transcend individual boundaries, shaping societal interpretations.

Within Śaiva mythology, the creation of the world and the emergence of humanity are rooted in the sexual union between Śiva and Pārvatī. This union plays a pivotal role in shaping the concept of what is deemed normative and socially acceptable, while also delineating those aspects perceived as transgressive, capable of unsettling the cosmological order. In one of Śiva's manifestations, he ventured naked into the Dāruvana forest. He is described as both deformed and attractive simultaneously. The women were not only drawn to him but engaged in making suggestive gestures as their garments slipped while they sang and danced, and in doing so, they breached societal expectations and norms.[23] Because of the transgression of normativity, the sages cursed Śiva's *liṅga* to fall, which caused chaos in all the three worlds and disrupted the cosmic order.[24] The myth categorically states that transgressing normative sexual boundaries can disrupt the cosmic balance; in other words, Śiva's sexuality, unchannelled within norms, causes a catastrophe. However, the myth also highlights that restoring balance requires not chastity but the fulfillment of desire. Cosmic harmony is re-established when Śiva's sexuality conforms to the normative, as symbolized by the *liṅga* fitting into Pārvatī's *yoni*.[25] It represents the erotic, which is simultaneously channelized within the normative and, therefore, becomes acceptable. It is a symbolic representation of creation.

While the canonical texts might not have been accessible to people of all genders and castes, the sculptural representations were available for everyone to engage with. The sculptures of the divinity, therefore, became very important and significant in the social production of normativity, setting boundaries between what was acceptable and what was not.

Images of Power, Power of Images

Erotic desire holds a pervasive presence in both our private and public spheres, permeating popular culture through cinema, television, literature, advertising and music. Regardless of how we choose to engage with or suppress these desires, and despite differing views on permissible forms of eroticism, representations of the erotic inherently resonate with us all. However, the challenge of eroticism is most pronounced when it takes visual form in art. Erotic art presents us with the opportunity to simultaneously indulge in and confront our fantasies. It directly addresses themes of love, sexual desire, titillation and sensual attraction, thereby testing our individual and collective notions of what is deemed 'pleasing' and what is considered 'decent' or 'appropriate'.

The widespread prevalence of erotic sculptures in the art of the subcontinent has posed an intriguing set of questions for historians. However, one needs to take into account that the representation of erotic sculptures is neither limited to a specific region nor an isolated phenomenon. The development of the *Tantric* religion and its influence on societal interactions directly contributed to such representations in temples across the subcontinent. The *Śilpaśāstras, Vāstuśāstras* and other authoritative texts embodying rules and procedures for sculpture and architecture refer to the portrayal of erotic figures on different parts of temples. Erotic imagery can be found in Brahmanical, Buddhist and Jaina temples.

In this context, studying the representation of Śiva in his *ūrdhvaliṅga* form with Pārvatī presents us with an intriguing issue because although it represents the erotic form of Śiva, it also represents the social paradigm wherein the notions of power and sexuality are being represented through these sculptures. They are divine bodies, the role they are playing is divinely ordained and therefore they go a long way in establishing normativity of gender roles and sexuality. I will be discussing two images of Śiva and Pārvatī from Kālañjara, both of which were sculpted between the ninth and eleventh centuries CE as part of the Nīlakaṇṭha temple during the Candella reign.

In this image, Śiva assumes his Bhairava form, adopting a *tribhaṅga* posture with eighteen hands, deviating from the typical sixteen hands associated with Bhairava. He adorns a *mundamālā* (garland of skulls) and a *mekhala* (girdle of bells). Conforming to tradition, snakes are integrated into Bhairava's ornamentation, evident in the serpents adorning his ears. He is holding an *asi, ḍamaru*, a bunch of arrows, *triśūla, akṣamālā* and a dagger, while one hand assumes the *varada mudrā on* his right side. One of his hands on this side is damaged. On the left, he grasps a *kheṭaka*, a snake, *pāśa*, a bow and a *muṇḍa*. Another hand clutches a skull, potentially

Figure 5.1 Śiva in Bhairava form, Kālañjara

a component of the *khaṭāvaṅga* staff, albeit it remains somewhat unclear. Additionally, two of his hands support an elephant hide, possibly symbolizing the epithet *kṛttivāsa*, i.e., a god who has the hide of an animal for his garment.[26] Śiva wears a *jaṭāmukuṭa*, and his formidable demeanour is apparent through raised brows, large round eyes, flared nostrils, moustache, open mouth and beard.

The *pratimālakṣaṇa* highlights the presence of Śiva in his Bhairava-Mahākāla form, particularly when engaged in the act of frightening the goddess Pārvatī with a snake. This description indicates the coexistence of two manifestations of Śiva – Bhairava and Mahākāla – with the distinction lying in their representation. A side profile typically represents Bhairava, while a frontal view depicts Mahākāla. The implied sense is the dual presence of both figures engaged in the *līlā* of scaring Pārvatī with a snake.[27]

In this image, Pārvatī is seated on an elevated platform, distinguishable from other female devotees due to the image's size and placement alongside the other images. She adorns an elaborate headdress and an array of ornate jewellery. Her gaze appears to alternate between apprehension towards the *ugra/saṁhāra mūrti* of Śiva and an underlying, albeit subtle, hint of eroticism, as her left hand delicately grazes her right breast.

In this image, Śiva is depicted in the Gajāsurasaṃhāramūrti form. He is adorned with a *sarpahāra* (snake ornament) and a *muṇḍamālā* (garland of skulls). Śiva is shown with ten hands, two of which support the elephant hide, adorned with snakes as bangles. On his right side, he wields a *vajra, asi* and a *muṇḍa*, with one hand positioned between his waist and

Figure 5.2 Śiva as Gajāsurasaṃhāramūrti, Kālañjara

thigh, symbolizing masculine power. To his left, he holds a *paraśu* (axe), *triśūla* (trident) and a basket, and he appears to be holding an animal. The vanquished *gajāsura* beneath his left foot signifies Śiva's victory over the asura. His appearance exudes awe, featuring prominent round eyes, flared nostrils, a moustache and an open mouth. The narrative behind this depiction involves Śiva emerging from his *liṅga* to thwart an asura who had taken the form of an elephant to disturb the meditation of numerous *Brāhmaṇas* assembled around the *liṅga*. Śiva subdues the elephant and employs its skin as his upper garment. While variations exist in the recounting of this story, the commonality is that Śiva killed the elephant asura and made the elephant's skin his upper garment.

Pārvatī is seated atop a *pīṭha* (pedestal) veiled with a sheet, accompanied by an attendant at her feet. Elegantly adorned with an intricate headdress, she gazes towards Śiva while gently touching her breast. Pārvatī is notably distinct from the other female devotee images dispersed in small niches throughout the space. Positioned on the left wall in direct alignment with Śiva's image, she maintains a central role in the overall composition.

Both these images hold significance within the temple context, serving as focal points within the public space of the temple. Their placement and iconography indicate their purpose for public viewing by temple visitors. While looking at these images, a notable aspect that immediately captures one's attention is the proportion of the *liṅga*, specifically in the case of the Gajāsurasaṃhāramūrti, in comparison to the visual image of Śiva. The *liṅga* is markedly larger than the relative body proportions. There is a clear accentuation of masculine power. It is within this context that the symbolism of the goddess touching herself presents a particularly intriguing significance.

Judith Butler's perspective sheds light on the performative nature of masculinity and femininity, emphasizing that these gendered identities are not intrinsic or biologically determined but rather acquired through learned bodily behaviours and actions. These performances often mask themselves as natural and innate, employing physical cues as their distinctive markers. Gender, according to Butler, is a social construct, constituted by a repertoire of bodily enactments that are frequently adopted unconsciously, yet they present themselves as natural expressions. These performances not only serve the individual but also contribute to the societal framework. The male and female bodies, in this context, function as symbols of society, embodying and reflecting the powers and restrictions imposed by a particular culture. The boundaries of desire, too, are circumscribed by the broader social context and the established norms that delineate what is considered acceptable and what is not. Consequently, even desire operates within these pre-defined normative boundaries, reinforcing the idea that it must conform to established societal norms.

In this context, examining the images of Śiva and Pārvatī is extremely interesting. There is a performance of the 'masculine' and the 'feminine' in tandem with the religious and social constructs of gender. The concept of power is evident not only in the *ūrdhvaliṅga* but also in Śiva's gestures and expressions. He is overpowering through his angry form, and the images convey the idea that there is a direct correlation between his masculinity and sexuality. While he is sexualized through the iconography of his phallus, other gestures depict his dominance and might. While Śiva displays various overpowering signs of masculinity and power, in contrast, Pārvatī is shown as the object of Śiva's desire and bereft of any sign of power. In this context, it seems extremely intriguing that Pārvatī is touching herself while Śiva is represented through angry images. It is only through Pārvatī that Śiva's sexuality can be channelled or actualized based on preconceived norms because Pārvatī is the only one who can make Śiva's semen flow. Therefore, while she is the 'Other', she is essential for creation.

She is represented in a state of undress, and her breast is clearly outlined and exposed. Her breasts are modelled in the erotic ideal of 'firm', slightly muscular bosoms. In the image, Śiva is presented entirely nude and upright, effectively conveying not only power but also his embodiment of masculinity. In stark contrast, the goddess assumes a slightly forward bend in her posture, reflecting a sense of modesty and shyness, which aligns with the societal expectations for women. She is touching her breast as a sign of submission. One of the most critical questions that one might ask is whom does the breast belong to? The very eroticization of the woman's body through the sexualizing of the breast is a power that the patriarchal ideology is exercising. Although a divine goddess in her own right, she is reduced to the object of the man's desire personifying the performance of the woman's role. It is in this context, Pārvatī appears as a sexualized body in tandem with the images where Śiva is in his angry form. Pārvatī represents the divine woman who is the object of the Śiva's sexual desire. Like Pārvatī, women are expected to become the object of desire for men.

The hegemonic masculinities depicted in religious discourses create a social narrative about what ideal, normative masculinity should be and how it should function, which, in turn, empowers and valorizes these religious discourses.[28] This perspective could be used to explore gender in terms of the female body and femininity, as well as how female figures are portrayed in sculptures embodying the ideal and normative female according to textual sources. Women are frequently reduced to their physical forms, leading to their objectification, particularly in the context of their sexuality, where their bodies are commodified as sexual objects. Artistic traditions in the Indian subcontinent have persistently depicted sensuous female figures provocatively posed, commonly associating women with nature. This connection primarily emphasizes women's association with fertility and motherhood, seen as their naturally ordained roles.

It is essential to understand that these images were a creation of the male imagination; hence, the concept of the male gaze cannot be overlooked. Therefore, in that context, it is important to understand that the breast is not only erotic but also a source of masculine pride, as it is his seed that impregnates the female and transforms her into a milk-bearing mother.[29] There was a projection of men's desires and erotic longings onto women's bodies. The erotization of women's breasts has been a predominantly male affair, obviously influenced by the male gaze of desire.[30] The erotization of the breasts, as understood from these images, was a result of the overshadowing of the maternal symbolism through the sexualization of the breast.

Stephen Ellingson highlights that the appeals religions make to various dimensions of extra-human reality function as a source of legitimation, wherein religious constructions of sexuality, family or gender are posited as natural, sacred and transcendent.[31] These constructions of female and male sexuality in Śaiva mythology extend beyond the reach of human understanding because they are situated in a metaphysical reality where the beings are sacred and transcendental – they are the reason for creation and destruction. Śiva's sexuality is destructive, yet it aids in the process of creation. When Śiva's sexuality is not satiated, it threatens the cosmic balance, and when his sexual desire is fulfilled, it leads to the process of creation.

The ideological discourse directed through religious institutions was asserting the gendered identities accepted in society as norms. The dominant social ideologies, norms and expectations are given symbolism within the domain of religion. Gender hierarchies and roles are legitimized through the continuous reiteration of myths. Through the stylized retelling of myths asserting gendered identities, a woman's sexuality is controlled. Moreover, by limiting women's social roles solely to their reproductive functions, men have consistently tried to prove that women's subordinate condition was divinely, and therefore naturally preordained. These images of Śiva and Pārvatī, therefore, need to be seen within this context.

Erotic is not merely about sexual procreation but also the production of pleasure. When incorporated into art, it encompasses a range of expressions. However, eroticism is not equivalent to pornography. Though pornography and erotica refer to verbal or pictorial representations of sexual behaviour, there is a difference between the two. Erotic art may draw on aspects of pornography, notably the depiction of sexual organs and sexual practices, but it does not do so for sexual arousal alone. It also plays on the aesthetic imagination, usually employing sexual imagery to express social and political relations. Eroticism in art, therefore, has a deeper philosophical context. The philosophical ideas of a given culture are an essential medium through which sexual behaviour is represented.

The sculptures of Śiva and Pārvatī are also a reflection of the idea of the male gaze, where the sexual politics of a particular gaze empowers men while objectifying women. Through the male gaze, the woman is constructed as the objectified 'other', whose function is to satiate male desire. In doing so, the woman, as a body of feelings, thoughts and sexual desires, is rendered less significant. Thus, one can interpret the gaze as a narcissistic ego, where one reflects his incomplete desires. These images should not just be seen as a temporal phenomenon of the past; rather, they should be scrutinized as a perpetual historical narrative of female bodies. History can be perceived from the experiences of those who are subjected to power and domination and who did not have tangible forms of expression.

Today, the perverse male gaze dominates the iconography of female bodies. From cinema to comics, most women are portrayed as tools of male sexual desires. The female body is constructed as the 'other' that constantly needs to be worked upon to achieve a 'flawless' form that is desirable and aligns with the male fantasy. This is particularly evident in how a woman's body is represented in the visual forms of popular culture. The image and representation of women have been marginalized to serve the functionality of male sexual desires. Although we claim to be 'modern', our times seem to be flowing in continuity since historical times, specifically in constructing gendered identities.

Notes

1 Foucault, Michel. 1989. *The Order of Things: An Archaeology of the Human Sciences*. New York: Routledge. 237–8.
2 Ibid., 236–7.
3 Pandey, K.C. 1954. *An Outline of the History of Śaiva Philosophy*. Delhi: Motilal Banarasidass. 56–7.
4 Desai, Devangana. 1996. *Religious Imagery of Khajuraho*. Mumbai: Project for Indian Cultural Studies Publication. 58.
5 Sanderson, Alexis. 2009. 'The Saiva Age'. In *Genesis and Development of Tantricism*, edited by S. Einoo. Tokyo: Institute of Oriental Culture, University of Tokyo. 43–4.

6 However, the dominance of Śaivism did not mean that only one sect existed but multiple sects were coexisting. The worship of the goddess was progressively subsumed within Śaivism and was promoted by its adherents as a higher form of that religion. This can particularly be seen in the earliest forms of the religion which later Śaivas would call the Atimārga, practised by the ascetics – Pāñcārthikas, Lākulas and the Somasiddhāntins and it continued to be so in the Siddhānta, the core tradition of the Mantramārga that emerged out of the Atimārga from about the fifth century onwards. Ibid., 44–5.

7 With the exception of Harṣha, Yaśovarman and Jayāvarman who were believers of Vaiṣnavism.

8 Bakker, H.T. 2016. *The World of Skandapurāṇa: Northern India in Sixth and Seventh Centuries*. Leiden and Boston: Brill. 211, 213.

9 Trivedi, H.V. 1989. 'Stone Inscription of Yaśovarman'. In *Corpus Inscriptionum Indicarum: Inscriptions of the Paramāras, Candellas, Kachchhapaghātas and Two Minor Dynasties*. Vol. 7. New Delhi: ASI. 337–46.

10 Trivedi, H.V. 1989. 'Nanyaurā Copper Plate Inscription of Dhaṅgadēva'; 'Nanyaurā Copper plate inscription of Dēvavarman'; 'Kālañjara Rock Inscription of Mandānavarman'. In *Corpus Inscriptionum Indicarum: Inscriptions of the Paramāras, Candellas, Kachchhapaghātas and two Minor Dynasties*. Vol. 7. New Delhi: ASI.

11 Trivedi, 'Stone Inscription of Yaśovarman', 337–46.

12 Trivedi, H.V. 1989. 'Kālañjara Stone Inscription of Kīrtivarman'. In *Corpus Inscriptionum Indicarum*. 7: Part 3, edited by H.V. Trivedi. New Delhi: ASI. 367–71.

13 Meister, M.W. 2007. 'Image Iconopraxis and Iconoplasty in South Asia'. In *RES: Anthropology and Aesthetics*. Harvard University: Peabody Museum of Archaeology and Ethnology. 13.

14 De Beauvoir, Simon. 2011. *The Second Sex*. Translated by C. Borde and S. M. Chevallier. New York: Vintage Books. 105.

15 Ibid., 31.

16 P, *Rudrasaṁhitā,* 3.24.13, 566.

17 P, *Rudrasaṁhitā,* 2.16.23, 344.

18 Mahmood, S. 2006. 'Agency, Performativity, and the Feminist Subject'. In *Bodily Citations: Religion and Judith Butler*. Edited by E. T. Armour and Susan M. ST. Ville. New York: Columbia University Press. 197–8.

19 De Beauvoir, S. 2011. Ibid., 100.

20 Lerner, Gerda. 1968. *Creation of Patriarchy*. New York: Oxford University Press. 181.

21 Connell, R.W., and J.W. Messerschmidt. 2005. 'Hegemonic Masculinities: Rethinking the Concept'. *Gender and Society*, 19 (6): 832.

22 Ellingson, S. 2002. 'Introduction'. In *Religion and Sexuality in Cross-cultural Perspective*, edited by S. Ellingson and M. Christian Green. London: Routledge, 2.

23 P, *Koṭirudrasaṃhita*, 12.11–13, 1297–98; *Liṅgapurāṇa*, part I, 29.12–21, 116–17.

24 *Liṅgapurāṇa*, part I, 29.18–21, 116–17; ŚP, *Koṭirudrasaṃhita,* 12.14–17, 1297–98.
25 P, *Videśvarasaṁhitā,* 16.87–95, 103–4.
26 Banerjea, J.N. 1956. *Development of Hindu Iconography*. New Delhi: Munshiram Manoharlal Publishers. 487.
27 Bhattacharya, D.C. 1991. *Pratimālakṣāṇa of the Viṣṇudharmottara*. New Delhi: Harman Publishing House. 90.
28 Taylor, M.C. 2013. 'Purāṇic Masculinities and Transgender Adventures in the Garden of the Goddess'. *International Journal of Hindu Studies*, 17 (2): 155.
29 Ibid., 62.
30 Ibid., 90.
31 Ellingson, S. 2002. Ibid., 3.

6

Iconographic Prescriptions for Goddesses in *Śilpa Śāstras*: A Contextual Study

Ashima Ahuja

In the early medieval period, temples emerged as wielders of substantial authority in the social, economic, and political realms, and they increasingly began to be employed as powerful instruments to propagate and vindicate the ideologies relevant to the ruling elite or Brahmanical institutions. Temple iconography, besides being a display of religious beliefs and outlook, became an important avenue to propagate specific social and political ideologies. The architectural texts that guided the delineation of such icons and imagery undoubtedly did not remain uncharged with these conceptions. For example, the architectural rules could be used to illustrate the social ethics crucial to the regime and to broadcast the power and fame of the sovereign; the prescriptions for the making of images could be used as vindicators of social hierarchy, gender conventions, and as hallmarks of the sacred and profane, propitious and unfortunate. All the earlier studies have focused on the study of the divine feminine through visual and mythological sources, employing the *śilpa* texts merely for the architectural details and terminology. Deviating from the earlier approaches, this chapter aims to draw chiefly upon the *śilpa* texts not only for the specific details but also to extract the embedded ideologies in order to contextualize the making of the images during the early medieval period.

Out of the larger corpus of texts dealing with the *śilpa* tradition, those selected for the study are the *Mānasāra*[1] and the *Mayamatam*.[2] There is no direct reference to the date or the time bracket that these texts can be ascribed to, albeit there being a few indirect references, internal and external to the text, on the basis of which the scholars have attempted to determine the date and provenance. A larger consensus places these texts broadly between the time period of ninth to thirteenth century CE, and both of them have been recognized as having a south Indian provenance.

For a systematic analysis of the *śilpa śāstras*, the chapter is divided into three sections: the first section examines the distribution of goddess temples in different types of settlements and aims to uncover the rationale behind their placement at definite locations within a settlement. The second section concerns the representation of goddesses in the *śilpa* texts; an endeavour is made to corroborate the prescriptive representations of goddesses with the epigraphical representations of the same temporal frame, across different regions, in order to identify interconnections and deviations. The third section investigates how certain social ideas and cosmological concepts are infused into the prescriptions for the making of images. Before we proceed with an investigation into the making of goddess images, let us examine the criteria for the distribution of goddess temples within settlements.

Distribution of Goddess Temples: Concepts and Contexts

Diagram 6.1 represents *Vāstupuruṣamaṇḍala.* Following the selection of a site for the construction of a village, a town or a temple, the texts deem it imperative to draw the *Vāstupuruṣamaṇḍala* on the selected ground before the beginning of construction. The plots of the *Vāstupuruṣamaṇḍala,* together with their aligned deities, can be seen as the bedrock to which most of the architectural distribution and location are affixed, as the texts occasionally refer to these plots while prescribing the allocation of various buildings or functional spaces. Thus, it is crucial to understand the scheme of *Vāstupuruṣamaṇḍala* for the purpose of understanding the distribution of structures within a settlement.

The concept of *Vāstupuruṣamaṇḍala* can be understood with reference to the myth of *Vāstupuruṣa.* As per the narration of the *Bṛhat Saṃhitā,*[3] the body of a Being (*sattva*) overran the earth and the sky. It was then captured by the various gods and was put upside down in a manner that the gods pinning down the various limbs of the creature became the presiding deities of those limbs. This Being is described as the house-god (*Vāstupuruṣa);* he is set inside the *maṇḍala* of either 64 or 81 squares, and has his head towards the north-east and face hung down.[4] The central part of the site/*maṇḍala* is occupied by the *Brahmā*; the first round encompassing the *Brahmā* part is called *Daivaka* part (region of gods); surrounding this, the second last round of the settlement is called *Mānuṣa* part (region of men); and the outermost round is *Paiśāca* part (region of demons)[5] (Diagram 6.1). The treatises refer to the plots of *Vāstupuruṣamaṇḍala* while determining the placement of various temples. Thus, the placement of the goddess temples interwoven with this scheme will be contextually analysed in different types of settlements.

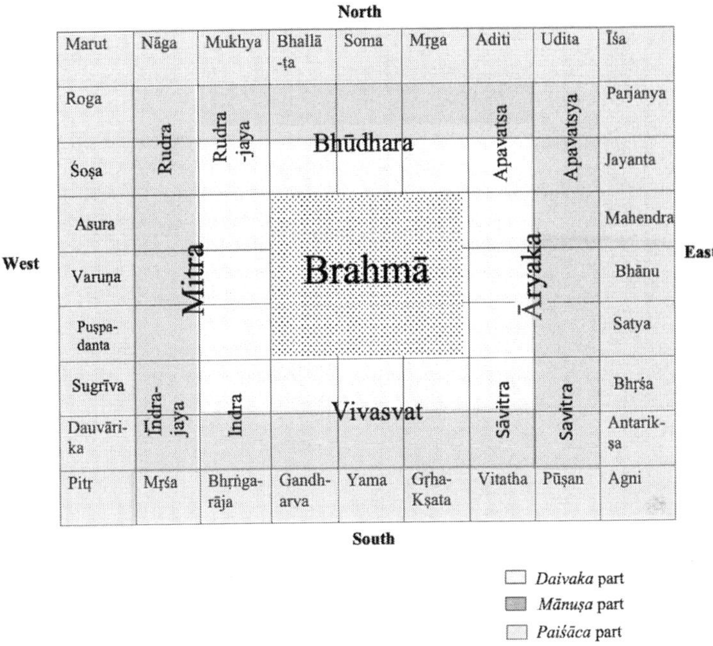

Diagram 6.1 Scheme of *Vāstupuruṣamaṇḍala* of 81 squares, as per *Mānasāra*.[6]

In the *Mānasāra*, the distribution pattern of temples varies according to the type of settlement.[7] From Table 6.1, we gather that the temples of female deities are assigned spaces in the *Sarvatobhadra* (for *Brāhmaṇas* and gods), *Nandyāvarta* (for *Brāhmaṇas* and gods), and *Svastika* villages (for *Kṣatriyas*), in contrast to the other types of settlements, which only have temples of male deities.

Durgā Temple: The prominence given to the goddess Durgā in *Svastika* village,[8] meant for the kings, is explicable in terms of her combative skills and valour. Here, the temple of Durgā is placed at the four cardinal and intermediate points[9] (Diagram 6.4). In the *Nandyāvarta* village, it is placed in the *Rākṣasa* or *Puṣpadanta* plots, which are located on the inner margins of the village, in the western direction[10] (Diagram 6.3).

Kālī Temple: In the *Nandyāvarta* village, the temple of Kālī is located on the village outskirts, two miles away from the village, towards the north[11] (Diagram 6.3). According to the myth in the *Vāmana Purāṇa*,[12] Kālī emerged from the forehead of the great goddess (Kauśikī), as her ferocious form, to assist her in a battle with the demons. The presence of

Table 6.1 Distribution of Temples in Different Types of Settlements, as per *Mānasāra*.[13]

Kind of village	Occupancy	Temples
Caturmukha village	*Śūdras*	Temples of Śiva, Viṣṇu and other gods
Daṇḍaka village	*Brāhmaṇas* retired life.	**Male Deities:** Temples of Śiva and Viṣṇu
Sarvatobhadra village	*Brāhmaṇas* and gods	**Female Deities:** Temples of Vaiṣṇavī and Cāmuṇḍā **Male Deities:** Temples of Brahmā, Śiva, or Viṣṇu
Nandyāvarta village	*Brāhmaṇas* and gods	**Female Deities:** Temple of Sarasvatī, Lakṣmī, Bhuvanā (Earth Goddess), Durgā, Kālī **Male Deities:** Temples of Śiva, Viṣṇu, Śrīdhara, Vāmana, Vāsudeva, Ādiviṣṇu or Janārdana, Keśava or Nārāyaṇa, Narasiṁha, Rāma or Gopāla, Vaināyaka, Subrahmaṇya or temples of Jainas or of Sugatas, Bhairava.
Kārmuka village	*Vaiśyas, Śūdras*, or *Pṛthuloman*	**Male Deities:** Śiva (Īśvara) and Viṣṇu Temple
Padmaka village	*Brāhmaṇas*	Temple pavilion
Prastara village	*Kṣatriyas* and *Vaiśyas*	Unspecified temples in the second round of the settlement.
Svastika village	*Kṣatriyas*	**Female Deities:** Temples of Durgā and Cāmuṇḍā **Male Deities:** Temples of Viṣṇu, Śiva, Bhairava, Gaṇeśa, six- headed Kārttikeya, Jvara-deva (god of fever), Bhāskara (Sun)

her temple on the village outskirts can be interpreted as a requisite for the village's defence.

Sarasvatī Temple: The Sarasvatī temple is to be located in the *Mukhya* or *Bhallāṭa* part of the *Nandyāvarta* settlement,[14] which is designated for the *Brāhmaṇas* and gods. These parts lie on the inner edge of the village, in the northern direction (Diagram 6.3).

Lakṣmī Temple: The Lakṣmī Temple is also located in the *Nandyāvarta* settlement, in the *Aditi* or *Mṛga* parts, which lie on the northern edges (Diagram 6.3).

Bhuvanā Temple: The Temple of Bhuvanā (Earth Goddess) is situated alongside the Lakṣmī Temple in the *Aditi* or *Mṛga* sections (Diagram 6.3).

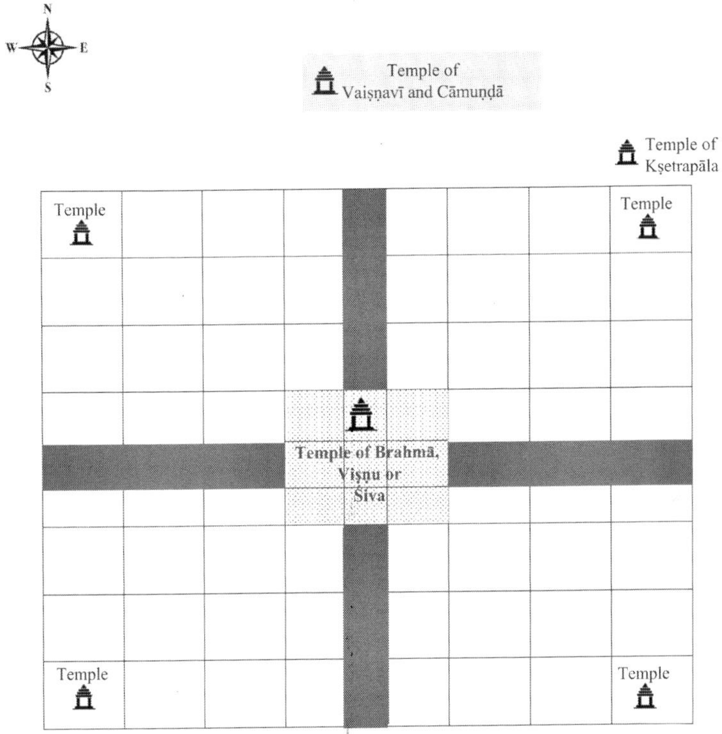

Diagram 6.2 Distribution of Temples in *Sarvatobhadra* Village.

Both goddesses are consorts of Viṣṇu, and their prominence is evident in the inscriptional records from the same time period.

Cāmuṇḍā Temple: The Cāmuṇḍā Temple is located on the outskirts of villages in *Svastika*[15] as well as *Sarvatobhadra*[16] settlements (Diagrams 6.2 and 6.4). Cāmuṇḍā is an epithet given to Kālī by the great goddess Kauśikī, as she adorned her head with a crest made from the skulls of the demons Caṇḍa and Muṇḍa.[17] Cāmuṇḍā appears in early medieval temples either as an independent goddess or collectively as one of the Saptamātṛkās, most often depicted on the outer walls (*jaṅghā*). Devangana Desai states that the Mātṛkās are positioned as *avarṇa* deities, forming a protective fence around the temple.[18] The presence of the Cāmuṇḍā temple on the village outskirts can be understood within this same context.

Vaiṣṇavī Temple: Vaiṣṇavī is also represented both as an independent goddess and as one of the Saptamātṛkās in the *Purāṇas*, born to fight the

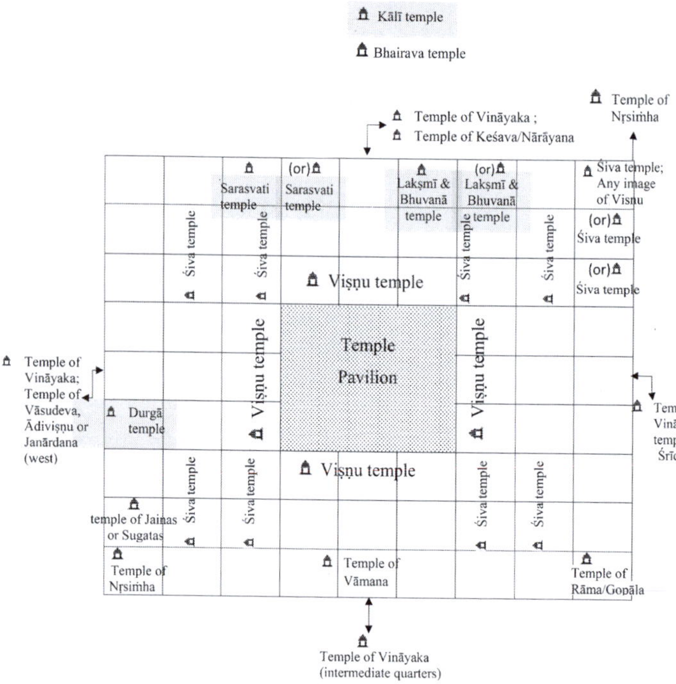

Diagram 6.3 Distribution of Temples in *Nandyāvarta* Village.

army of demons. According to the account in the *Vāmana Purāṇa*,[19] she was born from the arms of Kālī and is described as seated on *Garuḍa*, holding weapons. The *Varāha Purāṇa*,[20] on the other hand, portrays her independently as the slayer of Mahiṣa (*asura*) and states that devotion to her protects one from ferocious animals and thieves, while also preventing one from causing displeasure to kings.[21] The temple of Vaiṣṇavī is assigned a space on the village outskirts, in the *Sarvatobhadra* settlement,[22] towards the north, along with the Cāmuṇḍā temple. Thus, her placement can also be interpreted in terms of a defensive function for the village inhabitants.

From the placement scheme in *Mānasāra* (Diagrams 6.2, 6.3 and 6.4), it is apparent that while the temples of Viṣṇu and Śiva are distributed all across the plots, the temples of female deities are assigned a direction either on the periphery of the village (*Paiśāca* part) or further away on the outskirts. A similar scheme of placement is apparent in *Mayamatam* (Diagram 6.5), which places the temples of female deities in the periphery of the village, in contrast to the temples of Viṣṇu and Śiva, which could be

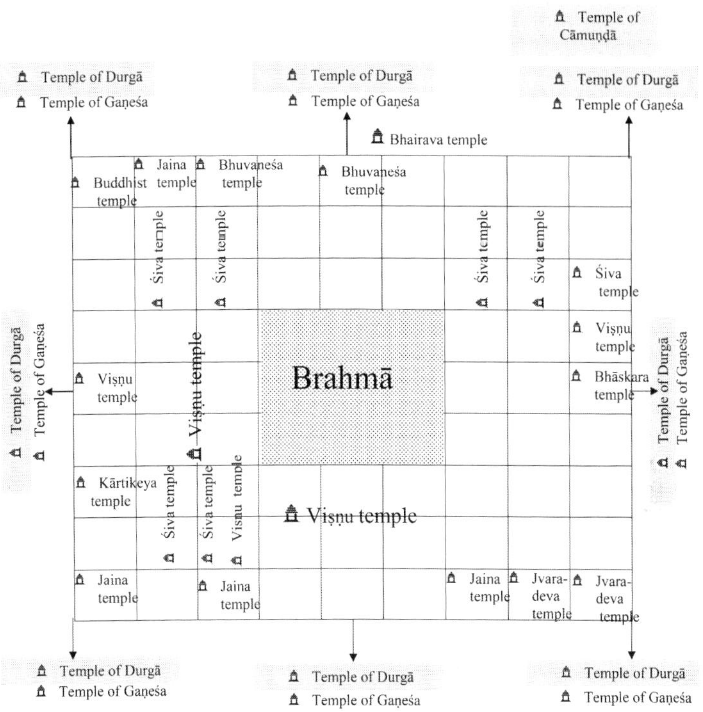

Diagram 6.4 Distribution of Temples in *Svastika* Village.

placed in any part of the settlement, including the Brahmā part, and even outside the village.[23]

Visual Representations of the Goddess

The imagery in the *śilpa* texts is broadly divided into three categories: Brahmanical, Jaina and Buddhist, but the discussion of the deities in the texts is held within the Brahmanical framework. In our discussion, the divine feminine is organized into three broad groups, indicating the range of forms she appears in the *śilpa* texts. These are: (1) goddesses represented independently, (2) goddesses represented with their divine consorts, and (3) goddesses represented collectively. Many variants of the divine consorts are depicted across temples, each narrating the story of conjugal and householder life. However, the dominant representation

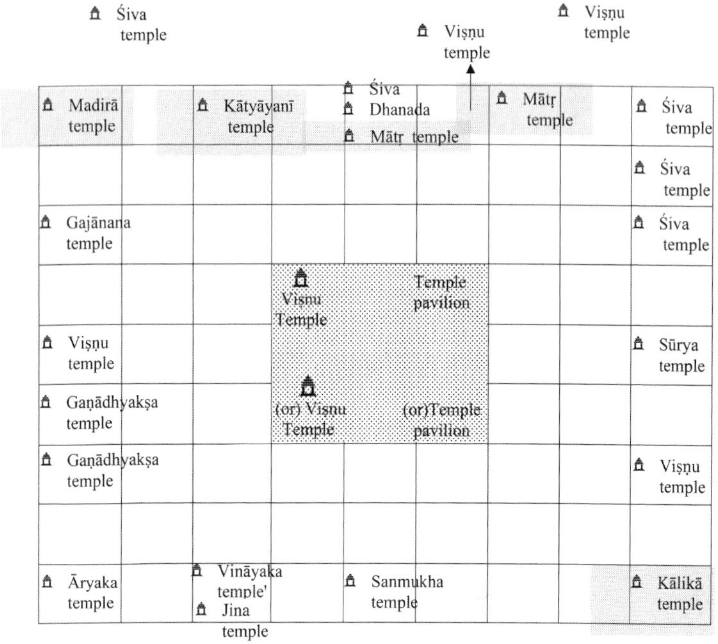

Diagram 6.5 Distribution of Temples in a Settlement, as per *Mayamatam*.[24]

found in treatises is the consorts seated or standing beside each other, with two or four arms, and the attributes are intricately detailed. For instance, according to *Mānasāra*, Sarasvatī is portrayed in an erect or seated posture on Brahmā's right side, whereas his left side is taken by Sāvitrī, the other consort. With a pleased face, Sarasvatī is to be shown seated in *padmāsana* (lotus position/cross-legged), on a *padma-pīṭha* (lotus pedestal).[25] When four-armed (*caturbāhu*), she holds a *saṃdarśa* (mirror), *pustaka* (book), *akṣamāla* (string of rosary) and a *kuṇḍikā* (pot).[26] However, when two-armed (*dvi-bhuja*), her right hand is shown in a boon-giving posture and her left hand holds a *padmaka* (lotus).[27] Wearing yellow clothes (*pīta-ambara*)[28] and fine silk garments (*dukūla*[29]*-ambara*), she appears shining/white like pure crystal (*śudha-sphaṭika-sama-kāśa*).[30] Alternatively, she may have a gold complexion (*hema-varṇa*), or a white (*śveta*), red (*rakta*), or dark blue (*śyāma*) complexion. The details of the ornamentation of each deity are intricately laid out.

Goddess Pārvatī,[31] two-armed, is represented in standing or seated posture, on the left side of *liṅga* or Śiva. She is dark-complexioned (*śyāma-*

varṇa), having large and broad (*viśāla*) two eyes (*dvi-netra*); broad smiling face, high neck, large belly (*mahodara*), plump breasts; wide buttocks (*vistīrṇa-śroṇi*)[32] and thighs. She wears yellow clothes (*pīta-ambara*) and fine silk garment (*dukūla-vasana*). On the other hand, Śiva is four-armed (*caturbāhu*) with three eyes.

Further, as prescribed by the text, Lakṣmī is represented in an erect or seated posture on the right side of Viṣṇu, embellished with all the ornaments.[33] She is two-armed, having a gold-complexion (*hema-varṇa*). Mahi-Śakti, the other consort of Viṣṇu, is shown on his left side; she is portrayed as dark-complexioned and with two arms.[34]

When independent of Viṣṇu, the goddess Lakṣmī is represented as two-armed, holding a *rakta-padma* (red lotus), with *Airāvata* (Indra's elephants) on her both sides. She is called *sāmānya* (ordinary) Lakṣmī.[35] The Mahā-Lakṣmī, on the other hand, with a pure gold complexion, is represented with two or four arms, seated on a lotus throne.[36] She has three broad eyes (*tri-netra*), plump breasts, a pleased face (*prasanna-vadana*), smiling from the corners of her eyes. Her forehead bears a *bhrama-raka* (bee-crystal), or *ratna-paṭṭa* (jeweled band).[37]

Manonmā, or Nā-unmādinī, another independent goddess, is described as having a reddish-white (*śveta-rakta*) or dark blue (*śyāma*) complexion and three eyes (*tri-netra*).[38] She is depicted as four-armed, seated on her *vāhana*, the bull (*vṛṣabha*), occupying three-fourths of its back with her right leg in a cross-like *svastika* position and her left leg bent.[39] Additionally, the iconographic prescriptions for the Saptamātṛkā (Vārāhī, Kaumārī, Cāmuṇḍī, Bhairavī, Māhendrī, Vaiṣṇavī and Brahmāṇī) are also detailed, all of them shown as four-armed and adorned with all the ornaments.

Attributes similar to these are prescribed in the *Mayamatam*; however, the text has a longer list of deities (Table 6.2). We have seen prominence given to these goddesses in the distribution scheme of the temples. We also notice the wide popularity of these goddesses (Lakṣmī, Bhūmi, Pārvatī and Durgā) in the inscriptional records of the same time period (Table 6.3). Let us look at the context in which the goddesses appear in the inscriptions.

From the epigraphic records spanning across central and southern India, which belong to the early medieval period, it can be deduced that the kings principally displayed devotion and allegiance to the male deities. In the accounts of the kings' eulogies, goddesses are referred to, but mostly in relation to their consorts, kingship, and power. In the Tanjavur temple inscriptions of Rājarāja, there is a repeated comparison of the king with Viṣṇu, and the representation of goddess Lakṣmī and goddess Earth as the king's wives in the context of his growing fortune, fame, and extended

Table 6.2 List of Goddesses in *Mānasāra* and *Mayamatam*

Mānasāra	*Mayamatam*
I. Goddesses Represented Independently	**I. Goddesses Represented Independently**
Mahālakṣmī	Lakṣmī
Sāmānya (ordinary) Lakṣmī	Yakṣinī/ Hemamālā
Manonmā, or Nā-unmādinī	Kātyāyanī
	Durgā
	Sarasvatī
	Bhūmi
	Jyeṣṭhā
	Pārvatī
II. Goddesses Represented with Divine Consorts	**II. Goddesses Represented with Divine Consorts**
Brahmā- Sarasvatī – Sāvitrī	Brahmā-Sāvitrī-Bhāratī
Viṣṇu – Lakṣmī – Bhūmi	Viṣṇu-Śrīlakṣmī-Bhūmi
Gaurī/Pārvatī – Śiva/*liṅga*	Sūrya-Prabhā-Sandhyā
	Agni-Svāhā
	Kubera-spouse
	Candra-Revatī-Rohiṇī
	Kāma-Rati
	Śāstā-Pūrṇā-Puṣkalā
III. Goddesses Represented Collectively	**III. Goddesses Represented Collectively**
Saptamātṛkā:	**Saptamātṛkā:**
Vārāhī	Brahmāṇī
Kaumārī	Māheśvarī
Cāmuṇḍī	Kaumārī
Bhairavī	Vaiṣṇavī
Māhendrī	Vārāhī
Vaiṣṇavī	Indrāṇī
Brahmāṇī	Kālī/ Cāmuṇḍī
	Seven Rohiṇīs

control over the eight directions through the conquering of kingdoms. For example, inscription number 3 of Rājarāja states:

> *Rājarājadeva ... his heart rejoiced, that, like the goddess of fortune, the goddess of great earth has become his wife,– in his life of growing strength ... the conquest made him famous in the eight directions.*[40]

Inscription number 9 of Rājendra-Choladeva mentions that while the goddess of fortune became his constant companion, the goddess of the great earth, the goddess of victory in battles, and the goddess of fame became his wives.[41] In another inscription of Devarāya II of the Vijayanagara empire, it is mentioned in reference to King Devarāya II:

Table 6.3 Inscriptional References to Goddess in Early Medieval India.

S.No.	Inscription	Date	Ruler	Provenance	Donor	Donee	Donation	Reference
	Inscription No. 3 of Rājarāja Chola	10–11th century CE	Rājarāja	Thanjavur temple: on the north wall, lower tier	Rājarāja	Rājarājeśvara temple	Gold ornaments and other precious objects.	E. Hultzsch, ed. and tr. 1891. *South-Indian Inscriptions: Tamil Inscriptions of Rajaraja, Rajendra-Chola, and Others in the Rajarajesvara Temple of Tanjavur*, Vol. II-Part I. Calcutta and Bombay: Thacker, Spink & Co., pp. 21, 35.
	Inscription No. 9 of Rājendra Chola	1021 CE (6th regnal year)	Rājendra Chola	Tanjavur temple: south wall, first tier	Guru Īśānaśiva-paṇḍita, minister Udayadivākaran Tillaiyāliyār, Valaṅgai-paṛambaḍaigalilār, and the temple treasury	Rājarājeśvara temple: temple's lord and two more images	Money deposit (to be given out for interest to the villagers for the requirements of the chief idol and other images).	E. Hultzsch, ed. and tr., 1891. *South-Indian Inscriptions*, Vol. II, Part I, pp. 90–93.

S.No.	Inscription	Date	Ruler	Provenance	Donor	Donee	Donation	Reference
	Satyamaṅgalam Plates of Devarāya II of Vijayanagara	Śaka-Saṁvat 1346	Devarāya II	Satyamaṅgalam village, Vellore, Tamil Nadu	Devarāya II	Eight *Brāhmaṇas*	*Agrahāra* named Ciṭeyāṭyūru	E. Hultzsch, ed. 1979. *Epigraphia Indica*, Vol. III (1894–95). New Delhi: Archaeological Survey of India, pp. 35, 40.
	Torkhede Plates of Govindarāja of Rashtrakutas	Śaka-Saṁvat 735	Govindarāja	Torkhede village, Khandesh, Maharashtra	Mahāsāmanta, named Buddhavarasa of Śalukika race	*Brāhmaṇas*	*Agrahāra*, named Govaṭṭana	E. Hultzsch, ed., 1979. *Epigraphia Indica*, Vol. III, pp. 53, 57, 58.
	Chiplun Copper-Plate Grant of Pulikeśin II of Chalukya dynasty	609–642 CE	Satyāśraya-Pulikeśin II	Chiplun, Ratnagiri District, Maharashtra	King's maternal uncle, named, Sendraka Raja Śrivallabha-Senānandarāja	Brāhmaṇa, named Maheśvara	Avañcapali village, in the Avaretikā Viśaya	E. Hultzsch, ed. 1979. *Epigraphia Indica*, Vol. III, pp. 50, 52.

> *He made the whole world the dwelling of his wife – (the goddess of) fame.*[42]

The inscriptions across the regions refer to the earth as the goddess of fame, and to the king as the enjoyer of this fame as well as its protector. The Torkhede Plates of Govindarāja of the Rashtrakutas state:

> *The king of favourites of fortune, by name Govindarāja III- an enjoyer of the young woman the Earth. which is his fame.*[43]

Besides the symbolic association of goddesses with the king's fortune and fame, the devotion towards the husband/king by these goddesses is also emphasized in the inscriptional records. For instance, in the inscription of Pulikeśin II of the Chalukya dynasty, it is stated:

> *The glorious (Pulikeśin II)..whose besmearing with sandal-wood oil is rubbed off by (the clinging of) the bulky breasts of the goddess of fortune who practices (towards him) the vow of treating a husband like a god.*[44]

It is discernible from the epigraphical sources that the goddess Lakṣmī and the goddess Earth were the most popular goddesses among the kings during the early medieval period, especially in the southern part of the subcontinent, as they consistently appear in the records during this time. The goddesses frequently appear in relation to the king as his queens/wives and as the sources of his fortune and fame. The goddess Earth is portrayed in the context of the king's rising influence over the eight directions. Most importantly, in one of the inscriptions (inscription number 9 of Rājendra-Choladeva), we also notice the appearance of the 'goddess of victory in battles', who is apparently the goddess Durgā, as the king's wife. This may be deciphered as an attempt to undermine the stature of the goddess in order to fit her within the patriarchal frame. The goddess Pārvatī always appears in relation to her consort Śiva, and even in relation to the king in the Chola inscriptions. In some instances, the union of Hara and Gaurī is celebrated, as it is stated:

> *Victorious, victorious, be that union of (the god) Hara and (the goddess) Gaurī, in which the face and breasts (of the goddess) are passionately kissed by the left arm (of the god); in which the fingers (of the god) separate themselves among the curled tresses (of the goddess).*

Thus, a correspondence can be drawn with respect to the occurrence of the goddesses in the textual and epigraphic records, and their perceived social status, which also reflects the attitude of the ruling and authoritative classes towards the feminine at the social plane. The perpetual emphasis on the role of goddesses as the king's devoted wives, as sources of fortune, fame and victory, appears to be their mode of promoting such qualities and ethics for the feminine at the social level, using goddesses as exemplars to achieve this aim, portraying them as the upholders of dharmic values. We notice that the visual representations of the couples are dominantly exhibited at all prime locations of the temple, and the majority of the time, the feminine is portrayed in smaller proportion than her spouse. Figures 6.1–6.9 below show the sculptural representation of some of the goddesses from the early medieval temples in Tamil Nadu. These, are also the goddesses who are uniformly mentioned in the epigraphic and prescriptive sources.

We cannot omit to note here that the texts intricately specify the details of the ornaments with which the deities are embellished. In the epigraphy,

Figure 6.1 Sculpture of Gajalakṣmī in Varāha Cave, Mamallapuram, Tamil Nadu.

Figure 6.2 Sculpture of Gajalakṣmī in Kailāsanāthar Temple, Kanchipuram, Tamil Nadu.

Figure 6.3 Sculpture of Durgā in Kailāsanāthar Temple, Kanchipuram, Tamil Nadu.

Figure 6.4 Sculpture of Mahiṣāsuramardinī in Bṛhadīśvara Temple, Thanjavur, Tamil Nadu.

Figure 6.5 Sculpture of Ko<u>r</u><u>r</u>avai Durgā in Varāha Cave, Mamallapuram, Tamil Nadu.

Figure 6.6 Representation of Varāha saving the earth goddess, in Varāha Cave, Mamallapuram, Tamil Nadu.

Figure 6.7 Umasahitamūrti in *sukhāsana*, Bṛhadīśvara Temple, Gaṅgaikoṇḍa Cho̱lapuram.

Figure 6.8 Umasahitamūrti, standing figures, Bṛhadīśvara Temple, Gaṅgaikoṇḍa Cho<u>l</u>apuram.

Figure 6.9 Representation of Śiva and Pārvatī in Bṛhadīśvara Temple, Gaṅgaikoṇḍa Cho<u>l</u>apuram, Tamil Nadu.

we find references to the gift of ornaments by the queens to the temple goddesses; for instance, the elder sister of Rājendra Chola, Āḻvār Parāntaka Kundavaiyār, gifted to the goddess Umāparameśvari (the consort of Dakṣiṇa-Meru-Viṭaṅkar) the following ornaments of gold: girdle, foot-ring, pendant, earrings, necklace, bracelets, arm-rings and other ornaments of jewels, such as a crown and garland.[45] There are many more instances of the gift of ornamentations to the deities, and hence, the striking importance given to the ornamentation in the treatises can partly be understood in this context.

Unravelling the Social Landscape from Prescriptions

It can be deduced from the prescriptions that the authors orchestrated the rules concerning the making of images within the framework of socially constructed notions related to caste, gender, auspiciousness and inauspiciousness. Hence, a careful analysis of these prescriptions reflects the authors' mindset and, through it, allows an insight into society's perception of the surroundings.

Gender Conventions: The stones used for making idols are classified into three gender categories (male, female and neuter), and the physical contours stereotypical to each gender category are accorded to the different stones (Tables 6.4 and 6.5). The stones having a uniform shape from top to bottom are viewed as male stones; the stones with a wide bottom and thin top are treated as female stones; whereas the stones with an irregular shape (as per *Mānasāra*, wide bottom and top, and thin middle part; as per *Mayamatam*, thin bottom and top, and wide middle part) are treated as neuter stones.[46] *Mānasāra* also construes the shape of a neuter tree as similar to the shape of a eunuch.[47] It cannot be said with certainty if a neuter stone is understood within the same context, or if it is conceptualized as a non-living object with an irregular shape, or as a neuter stone with the features of both male and female.

In addition to the shape, the sound conventional to each gender is set comparable to the sound of the stone belonging to that gender. In both texts, the sound of the male stone is construed as synonymous with harsher and louder sounds, such as those of a jewel box and an elephant bell, while the female sound is associated with the low clinking sound like that of a bell metal and a cymbal. A neuter stone is perceived to have no sound,[48] the reason for which can probably be attributed to its lifelessness, particularly in case if it is regarded as non-living.

Mayamatam takes a step further, sub-categorizing the male, female and neuter stones into young, mature and old stones, and also adding pregnant stones to the list[49] (Table 6.5). The age of a stone is ascertained on the basis of its texture, temperament and sound, just as the age of a person is determined from their skin, and sound to some extent.

Male stones are deemed appropriate for making male idols as well as *liṅga* (as per *Mānasāra*), or for iconic, symbolic and mixed representations (as per *Mayamatam*); female stones are considered appropriate for the representation of female deities and *pīṭha*; neuter stones are considered appropriate for all kinds of buildings (as per *Mānasāra),* or for *Brahmā* stone, *Kūrma* stone and *nandyāvarta* stone (as per *Mayamatam*). Similarly, a young stone is considered suitable for making anything; a mature stone, being young and in the 'prime of life', is considered suitable for making everything, with the implication of definite success in the process.[50]

Table 6.4 Gender Labelling of Stones, as per *Mānasāra.*[51]

Stone	Shape/texture	Sound like	Suitability
Male	Uniform bottom, middle and top; quadrangular	Jewel box	For male idols & *liṅga*
Female	Wide bottom, thin top; circular	Bell metal; Low sound	For the altar of the phallus (*pīṭha*) and female deities (*śakti*).
Neuter	Wide bottom and top, Thin at middle; with many horns	No sound	For buildings of all kinds
Tree-stone (*vṛkṣa*)	-	Buffalo	-
Barley-stone (*yava*)	-	'Half of aforesaid'	-

Table 6.5 Gender Labelling of Stones, as per *Mayamatam.*[52]

Stone	Shape/texture	Sound like	Suitability
Male	Cylindrical; smooth	Elephant bell	For iconic, symbolic and mixed representations.
Female	Wide bottom, thin top	Cymbal	For female deities or a pedestal (*piṇḍikå*).

Stone	Shape/texture	Sound like	Suitability
Neuter	Thin bottom and top, wide at middle;	No sound	For Brahmā stone, Kūrma stone, and *nandyāvarta* stone.
Young	Soft	Partly baked brick	For anything
Mature	Round; Smooth, glowing; cold and sweet – 'in the prime of life.'	Deep sound	For everything (leads to the accomplishment of the work it is used for)
Aged	Rough like the skin of a toad or a fish, with lines and spots; it requires delicate handling. inauspicious	-	-
Pregnant	Carries convolutions, which are visible when cutting the stone. (weathered or volcanic stones); Careful disposal	-	-

Act of Chiselling: Conformity to the Cosmic Scheme

We find that the *śilpa* texts introduce various cosmic metaphors in the making of images as well as in the planning of architectural spaces. While the chief architect (*sthapati*) is called the creator (*prakṛti*), the sculptor (*sthāpaka*) is the one who brings life into the images.[53] The process of chiselling of the eye is equated with withdrawing darkness from the eyes and bringing the sight.[54] In *Mānasāra*, the opening and closing of the eyes is conceptualized as the rising and setting of the sun, with the eyes sending across rays like the sun when they are opened:

> *When the sun rises the rays spread all over, so also the case with the eye of an individual as regards its rising and setting.*[55]

Chiselling of the eyes is treated as a significant act, for a special setting is designed for this occasion: the entire process is staged on a pavilion built in front of the main temple or to its left or right side.[56] The pavilion is square (nine, seven or five cubits), provided with sixteen or twelve pillars (*stambha*), an altar/platform (*vedi*) in the centre, and is optionally furnished with a pinnacle (*kūṭa*).[57] It has four doors (*dvāra*) in the four directions and is also provided with four arches (*toraṇa*). The decoration of the pavilion is done with ceremonial flags, ornamental clothes, garlands of plantains, garlands of flowers, jewels etc.[58] Upon the pavilion, the chiselling of the eyes is performed, a process that is crucial to bringing life into the images by way of instilling the light. The idol is particularly placed on the western, southern or south-western direction of the *vedi*, upon the *vāstupuruṣamaṇḍala* of forty-nine squares or nine squares, which is marked on one of these sides.[59] The reason for such a placement can be explained on two grounds: first, higher radiance of the sun in these directions throughout the day, which is necessary for the convenience and intricacy of carving; secondly, again with relativity to the sun, for fiercer the lustre, larger the light drawn to illuminate the eyes. This conjecture can be supported with reference to the text, according to which, having marked the eyes, the iris and the pupil, the *Sūrya mantra* (sun hymn) is recited for introducing the light into the eyes; the *Śaśi mantra* (moon hymn) is recited for the left eye; the *Agni-bīja* (fire hymn) is recited to kindle the third eye, which is present on the forehead.[60] It is stated:

> *Like a lamp it (the eye) should be the chief (shining) thing in the lotus like heart (of the artists).*[61]

The sun and the moon, in harmony with the right and left eyes of the sculpture, seem to be in conformity with the *Atharvaveda*'s[62] description of *vratya*[63] based on the principle of duality: the right eye of the *vratya* is described as the sun, and the left eye as the moon:

> *Of that Vratya*
> *The right eye is the Sun; the left eye is the Moon.*
> *His right ear is Agni, and his left ear is Wind.*
> *Day & Night are his nostrils*
> *Diti & Aditi are his head and skull*
> *By day, the Vratya is turned westward; by night, he is turned eastward.*
> – *Atharvaveda* (*Kāṇḍa* 15, *Sūkta* 18, Verses *1–5*)[64]

The principle of duality with respect to the sun and the moon is also indicated in the *Viṣṇudharmottara Purāṇa*.[65] The sun and the moon are respectively described as the *Puruṣa* and the *Prakṛti*, which are held as attributes in the hands of Vāsudeva, the creator of the world, in the form of a wheel and a mace.[66] The comparison is also drawn in the context of Śiva, as his three eyes are equated with the sun, the moon and the fire.[67]

This allegorical scheme indicates the importance of cosmic intervention and the relevance of the principle of duality (or the existence of complementary forces) for the making of images, in a similar fashion to how these forces are believed to have played a significant role in the creation of the universe. It is also to be noted that the placing of the idol upon the plot is preceded by other ceremonial acts.[68] The plot of *Vāstupuruṣamaṇḍala,* upon which the idol is carved, can be seen as an imitation of the micro-world or the universe,[69] further making it apparent that the process of inducing life into the idols is performed in conformity with the cosmic order.

It is discernible from the study that *śilpa śāstras* not only served as the reference ground for extracting the prescriptive details for the creation of architectural spaces or pieces. A careful analysis reveals that the ideas of cosmic replication, as well as social ideas related to caste, gender, notions of auspiciousness and inauspiciousness, sacred and profane are repeatedly employed within the prescriptions with the objective of imbuing cosmic principles and social ethics even within the built spaces. For the study of sculptures, the textual and epigraphical juxtaposition revealed the uniform occurrence of certain deities in both records, who occupied a prominent place in worship; these include Śiva, Viṣṇu, Lakṣmī, Bhūmi, Pārvatī and Durgā. The study of the epigraphical sources, from the same time frame, reflects the appearance of goddesses prominently in relation to their consorts or kingship, and their representation as symbolic, subdued wives. The study identified efforts at promoting gender and patriarchal norms through the illustration of goddesses as the king's devoted wives, whose function is to bring fortune, victory and glory to the king. The comparison also offers a panorama of patrons' expectations regarding the female's role in society. The epigraphical study is employed to understand the textual prescriptions, as prominence is given to the same deities in the *śilpa* texts too. We also noted the importance attributed to these deities in the distribution scheme of temples in rural spaces. It revealed the placement of goddess temples either in the periphery of the settlements or on the outskirts, as opposed to the temples of Śiva and Viṣṇu, which could be located in any part of the settlement, including the centre, which is the place of Brahmā. Thus, we notice the Brahmanical conventions strongly applied to the distribution of temples in a settlement. The governing principles linked with the distribution of temples are also clearly hitched to the objective of procuring auspiciousness and securing benefits for the patrons as well as for the settlement inhabitants. The stereotypical gender notions are even implemented in the prescriptions for the procurement of raw material from the forest or the hill, as the stones used for making of idols are grouped into three gender categories: male, female and neuter.

The divergence from the prescribed norms is linked with negative social consequences.

It is discernible that the authors' perception of an architectural creation was undeniably fastened to the Vedic and Puranic conceptions, as the prescriptions in the *śilpa śāstras* seem to be channelled from the existing expanse of scriptures, especially the Vedic and Puranic literature. The preparation of the site and the special importance given to the introduction of cosmic metaphors in the sculpting of images seem to have been channelled from these sources. A continuous endeavour to maintain the social and cosmological order is conspicuous in the *śilpa śāstras*. Hence, the study makes it explicit that architectural creations were seen not only as physical entities but also as social landscapes, harbouring the existing notions, objectives, prejudices and requirements.

Notes

1 Acharya, Kumar, Prasanna (tr). 2011. *Architecture of Mānasāra: Text with English Translation, Notes and Index*. Delhi: New Bharatiya Book Corporation.
2 Dagens, Bruno, ed. and tr. 2007 (First published: 1994). *Mayamatam: Treatise of Housing, Architecture and Iconography, 2 vols*. New Delhi: Indira Gandhi National Centre for the Arts.
3 Shastri, Panditbhushan V. Subrahmanya, and Vidwan M. Ramkrishna Bhat (tr.). 1946. *Varahamihira's Brihat Samhita*. Bangalore: V.B. Soobbiah and Sons.
4 Ibid., 437.
5 *Architecture of Māṇasāra*, 113.
6 *Architecture of Mānasāra*, 74.
7 The text lists eight kinds of villages, each deemed suitable for a specific class of inhabitants (Table 6.1).
8 *Architecture of Mānasāra*, 129.
9 Ibid.
10 Ibid., 122.
11 Ibid.
12 Gupta, Anand Swarup (ed.), Satyamsu Mohan Mukhopadhyaya, Ahibhushan Bhattacharya, N.C. Nath, and V.K. Verma (tr.). 1968. *The Vāmana Purāṇa*. Varanasi: All India Kashiraj Trust.
13 *Architecture of Mānasāra*, 101–5, 108–38.
14 *Architecture of Mānasāra*, 74.
15 *Architecture of Mānasāra*, 131.
16 Ibid., 112.
17 Ibid., 276–7.

18 Desai, Devangana. 1996. *The Religious Imagery of Khajuraho*. Mumbai: Franco-Indian Research. 167. Desai refers to the text *Īśānaśivagurudeva-paddhati* which designates the Saptamātṛkās as *āvaraṇa* deities.
19 *The Vāmana Purāṇa*, 277–8.
20 The *Varāha Purāṇa*, Part-1. S. Venkitasubramania Iyer, trans. 2003 (1985). In *Ancient Indian Tradition and Mythology*, Vol. 31, edited by J.L. Shastri. Delhi: Motilal Banarsidass Publishers.
21 Ibid., 218.
22 *Architecture of Mānasāra*, 112.
23 *Mayamatam*, 73–81.
24 Ibid.
25 *Architecture of Mānasāra*, 928.
26 Ibid., 929.
27 Ibid., 930.
28 *Pīta* = yellow; *Ambara* = clothes.
29 *Dukūla* = fine silk.
30 *udha* = pure; *sphaṭika* = crystal; *sama* = similar; *kāśa* literally denotes appearance, shine, as well as a white flower. Thus, -the term here can be contextually understood either as the white complexion (of the goddess) or her shine and appearance.
31 *Architecture of Mānasāra*, 934–5.
32 *Vistīrṇa* = wide; *śroṇi* = buttocks.
33 *Architecture of Mānasāra*, 933.
34 Ibid., 934.
35 Ibid., 933.
36 Ibid., 931.
37 Ibid.
38 Ibid., 936–7.
39 Ibid., 937.
40 Hultzsch, E. ed. and tr. 1891. *South-Indian Inscriptions: Tamil Inscriptions of Rajaraja, Rajendra-Chola, and Others in the Rajarajesvara Temple of Tanjavur*, Vol II-Part I. Calcutta & Bombay: Thacker, Spink & Co. 35.
41 Ibid., 92.
42 Hultzsch, E. (ed.), 1979. *Epigraphia Indica*, Vol. III (1894–95). New Delhi: Archaeological Survey of India. 40.
43 Ibid., 57.
44 Ibid., 52.
45 Hultzsch, ed. and tr. *South-Indian Inscriptions*. 84–90.
46 *Architecture of Mānasāra*, 902; *Mayamatam*, 741.
47 *Architecture of Mānasāra*, 294.
48 *Architecture of Mānasāra*, 902; *Mayamatam*, 741.
49 *Mayamatam*, 741–3.
50 Ibid.

51 *Architecture of Mānasāra*, 902, 903, 907.
52 *Mayamatam*, 741, 743.
53 *Architecture of Mānasāra*, 1073.
54 Ibid.
55 Ibid., 1073–4.
56 Ibid., 1074.
57 Ibid.
58 Ibid., 1075.
59 Ibid.
60 Ibid., 1078.
61 Ibid., 1081.
62 Griffith, Ralph H. (tr.). 1917. *The Hymns of the Atharva-Veda*, Vol. II (second edition). Benares: E.J. Lazarus and Co.
63 In the *Atharva-veda*, two different representations of *Vratya* are given: first, he is identified as a supernatural being, the chief *Vratya*, conferred with the status of a deity, and secondly, he is also portrayed as a wandering human, a religious scholar, who appears as a guest at a householder's residence (193). It is instructed that this guest should be highly regarded, for his stay at the house will confer upon the householder the holy realms on earth and in heaven (195).
64 *The Hymn of the Atharva-Veda,* 199.
65 Kramrisch, Stella. 1928. *The Vishnudharmottara: A Treatise on Indian Painting and Image-Making* (Part III). Calcutta: Calcutta University Press. 70.
66 Ibid.
67 Ibid., 71.
68 Marking a circle around the (above mentioned) plot with garlands of flowers; placing on the plot, in the south-west, a pot filled with gold, covered in fine clothes, and adorned with grass at the base; marking a circle on the *vedi* with grain (*śāli*) powder; upon it, marking a plot of twenty-five squares (*upapīṭha* plot) or (*pīṭha* plot); covering the two plots with *kuśa* grass, flowers, and fried rice, and marking them with lines of powdered rice grains; on the plot, placing the pitchers filled with pure water; the pitchers are nine or twenty-five in number, depending on the number of squares in the plot; the pitchers are covered in clothes and strings, and adorned with leaves, fruits and flower garlands; the centre of the plot is furnished with the main pitcher, while other pitchers are arranged on the surrounding squares; placing on the upper altar (*vedi*) eight auspicious things; the architect washing their feet and purifying the images; worshipping Brahmā and other gods with the recitation of *mantras;* Brahmā (lord of the universe), in the vessel placed at the centre, is worshipped by offering incense, a lamp, sandal paste, and flowers; other offerings (optional): clarified butter, corn, milk, molasses, etc.; accompanied by singing, music and dancing, the cow (*dhenu*) and other

signs (*mudrā*) are shown to the deity; performing the sacrifice by the *sthapati* (chief architect) in front of the fire and the vessel; offerings to the fire are made 108 times and consist of *samid* (plant), clarified butter, *caru* (boiled rice) and fried rice; making a concluding offering to the deity (*bimba*) along with the recitation of *the gāyatrī mantra;* placing the idol on the plot for chiselling of the eyes; performing,the purification of jewels; making an offering to the idol consisting of flowers, perfumes and lamps and sprinkling holy water on the idol, accompanied by auspicious sounds; showing the idol the cow figurines (*dhenumudrā*). 1075–8. *Architecture of Mānasāra.*

69 This is with reference to the concept of *Vāstupuruṣamaṇḍala,* discussed in the earlier section.

Part Three

Protection and Power: Manifestations of the Goddess

7

Deities for the Cities: Protector Goddesses of the Kathmandu Valley

Arun Gupto

The chapter maps and analyses the group of protector goddesses called the Vārāhīs, who have sacral-placements at different locations in the Kathmandu Valley. These placements are not only found in temples but also in sacral spaces in the forms of images, energy locations, shrines, mounds, and imaginings. Imaginings are suggestive of mythic awareness, thoughts and beliefs that such divinities do not have particular abodes but are present as soon as the deity is remembered and evoked. Imaginings are as visible in vernacular minds as a temple of a goddess is. The aspect of these imaginings is devotional consciousness. Consequently, the use of the term 'sacral-placements' is not meant to oversimplify divinities in relation to images and temples alone. Such imaginings are universal in the context of the construction of the supernatural. The embodied deities in temples are as significant as the imaginings. Thus, the Vārāhīs are multiple in numbers, not limited to the *Purāṇas* and the Tantra texts, but also found in local prayer booklets, calendars, prayer sheets and the personalized states of devotional minds.

The conceptual purpose here is the analysis of Vārāhīs as protectors in urban locations. These deities have evolved from thousands of years of tradition, transcending anthropocentric features and contradicting the binarism of grotesque and beautiful because they are agreeable and venerable in both human and animal forms, as well as in fearful and tranquil impressions. To limit the mapping and analysis of the goddesses, I have focused on Vajravārāhī, Śvetavārāhī and Raktavārāhī only, so as to avoid a long list of the goddesses who belong to this group. Structurally, I describe the images and surroundings, provide information on mythical narratives, and then discuss their conceptual significance.

The valley, with the capital city Kathmandu, has an overwhelming presence of myth in the forms of arts, narratives, supernaturals, rituals, histories and cognition. This is how myths are realized in the valley. Thus, half of the valley appears as myth in imminence; the valley embodies a culture of immediacy of myth, the spaces of imminence of the gods and goddesses, imaginings and temples. Every nook and corner has temples and energy centres that evolved in the past and travelled into the present. The goddesses of Vārāhī, Mahāvidyā and *Mātṛkā*[1] groups, along with many other male and female deities, are the travelling divinities because they are understood more deeply when one walks tirelessly and discovers that the deity belonging to Vārāhī becomes the mother goddesses or the *Mātṛkā* in other locations. The protector Vārāhīs possess annihilating desires, saving the world from demons[2] and at the same time, they take leave from the city. The Nava Durgā[3] group of goddesses disappears in the month of June. The ceremonies of the nine goddesses, who are placed as masks in the Nava Durgā temple, are enacted from September or October to June, after which they leave the city during *Bhagasti* or *Bhala Bhala Aṣṭamī*[4] when their masks are burned to be recreated anew in the coming year. The Vārāhīs are thus transformed into symbols of death and regeneration. They travel while both retaining and transforming their features and associations with multiple other groups of goddesses.

There are thousands of images, energy locations, shrines and mounds of the protector deities, which can be experienced mainly through walking. Walking evokes sensibilities, gives pleasure and imparts knowledge. Walking is part of rituals associated with the goddesses of multiplicity. It helps the knower understand the mythical essence of the valley in terms of how cities in the valley design myth architecturally and identify them performatively through dance and visual arts. These deities impart various devotional realizations. For instance, the *pīṭha*[5] of the protector deities are located on the outer edges of Bhaktapur, while the inner locations of the same deities are the *mandira* (temple), and at the centre of the city resides the goddess of knowledge, Tripurasundarī. The Temple of Taleju, however, has taken a place of significance in the Durbar Square (Palace Courtyard), probably during the Malla period. Thus, the outer and inner sacral-placements can be realized by stepping into the spaces of the city, which appear complex but are designed as the sacral aspect of urban aesthetics. Furthermore, among the four cities – Kathmandu, Patan, Bhaktapur and Kirtipur[6] – Bhaktapur has multiple Vārāhī temples and energy centres than the other three cities of the valley.

Protectors of the City

Natural disasters, diseases and invasions have inflicted suffering on urban establishments throughout history, which has been narrativized in folk rituals as well as in stories. Protection and security have always been major human concerns. The modern modes of protection and security have their own designs, but the idea of protection has its mythical dimension in the valley. In times of trouble and crises – from the medieval times[7] onward – the mythical belief system has been the most powerful resort for internalizing devotional surrender to the supernatural in mystical, spiritual and aesthetic modes. This internalization may not only be for security but also for solace. During dynastic times, kings and priests maintained societal order through the practice of rituals. Power had to be generated through various levels of emotions: faith and fear functioned as the logic of supernatural power, which was institutionalized by religious orders.

Kathmandu Valley has been the site of transformations, both natural and human, for thousands of years. Supernatural beings have always been necessities, both in symbolic and literal representations, for blessings and protection, as well as for reward and punishment. The mytho-poetic, or poetry-making, imaginations have always needed the supernatural as powerful entities to save and bless humans. Kālī, Tārā, Gaṇeśa and Lakṣmī are among the many such mythical beings loved and feared by people. The boar-faced deities are half-human in form and are internalized as protectors with animalistic, human and divine strength. They are revered despite having non-human forms that may appear grotesque from an anthropomorphic perspective, yet they are accepted and venerated as powerful and loving mothers.

Protection and myth have worked in mysterious ways – as rituals, narratives and dependence on something beyond rational authentication. Almost all gods and goddesses of myth are protector beings. Holding the severed head of enemies by a goddess aligns with the divine palm gesturing to bestow *abhaya*, blissfulness and reassurance. The terrifying deity with the severed heads and the *mudrā* of the hand for blessing go together: one cuts the head and the other gestures to the viewer to be fearless. The sow-head of the protector deity goes with the multiple hands symbolizing knowledge and blessing. The totality of the image is metonymic, and hence the iconography is not merely within the body of the image but also outside, in the premises of the temple or *pīṭha*. Therefore, the description of the images in the section belonging to the three multiple Vārāhīs is about iconography as an image–context relationship, which I will discuss independently while writing about individual Vārāhīs.

Mapping the Goddess

In Kathmandu Valley tradition, Vārāhī is one of the mother-goddesses (*aṣṭamātṛkās* or eight mother goddesses) and is the consort of Unmatta Bhairava, a local form of Śiva, the trinity from the Hindu pantheon. She enters into the Buddhist fold when Vajrapāṇi is incorporated as Vajramukhī.[8] Śvetavārāhī, Nīlavārāhī, Vajravārāhī[9] and Dhanvantarīvārāhī are the prominent[10] protectors. Śvetavārāhī resides in the north, in Bodegaun. In the south is Vajravārāhī, in Chapagaun (both in Lalitpur[11] municipality). Nīlavārāhī is in Bode, Madhyapur municipality, in the east, and in the west is Dhūmavārāhī in Kathmandu metropolitan area. There also are other popular energy seats and temples of the deity in Nepal: Chābdīvārāhī and Ḍhoravārāhī in Tanahun district, Tālavārāhī in Pokhara, Dhanavantarīvārāhī temple in Lalitpur and Dakṣiṇavārāhī temple in Thimi.[12] In the city of Bhaktapur, they are placed as the Vārāhī protecting the west, Bhadrakālī[13] (the southwest), Kaumārī (the south), Māheśvarī (the southeast), Brahmāyaṇī (the east), Mahālakṣmī (the north-east), Mahākālī (the north) and Indrāyaṇī (the northeast). These are the eight mother goddesses who protect the city. The formation adds to the imaginings not only to impart confidence but also to comprehend an architectural-devotional fortification, rare in terms with mythical infusion in urbanism.

These deities guard the cities with a multiplicity of identities and features. Nīlavārāhī is worshipped locally as Takaṭī Ajimā,[14] and her annual chariot procession is held during Pāhā Ratha (car) festival (Piśāca Caturadaśī) in the month of Falguna.[15] The Nīlavārāhī dance starts generally in August at Bode. The performance begins in the night and ends in the morning. The *pīṭha* of this Ajimā is at Taṅkeśvara near Kalimati, and the *dyo-che* as the other form is in Jaisideval area. In Bhaktapur, the Vārāhī is a prominent mother goddess with a *pīṭha* at Vārāhīsthāna adjoining the Arniko Highway. Such formidable characteristics and associations with other deities embolden the devotional mind. The belief in the power of protection unfolds more with the presence of the Vārāhīs per se without their association with the mother goddesses. Thus, Vajravārāhī whose colour is red protects the livestock in the western quarter of the valley. The colour of Nilavārāhī is blue and she protects the east with restraint of dancing deities without food and communication. Śvetavārāhī's colour is white, and she guards the south as a deity of relationality and togetherness. The colour of Dhūmavārāhī is grey who guards the north, and is said to protect the valley from cholera.

The directional situatedness forms a complex structure, which a traveller may, at times, find the shrines in random order. The supernatural in the Newar belief system is immanent, resisting the idea of transcendental divinities. These supernaturals reside in places ranging from temples to trees, houses to burning ghats,[16] roam in dusk and darkness. The profusion of shrines is the envisioning of divine characteristics in the profusion of sacral-placements and therefore the formation of the cities is associated with the presence of the supernatural.

Historical and Textual Sources of the Vārāhīs

D.K. Chakravarty (1968) writes about the origin of the mother goddesses in relation to zoomorphic features:

> The half animal and half human icons like Vārāhī and Nārasiṁhī as conceived in the Puranic mythology perhaps represent a transitional stage of culture in India when zoomorphism began to fade away and anthropomorphism crept in. The terra-cotta vases in the shapes of birds and animals as also the numerous figurines historic and Early Historic sites having the one hand and such figurines collected early historic sites ...
>
> (130–1)

There is archaeological evidence of worshipping mother goddesses in pre-Indus and Indus Valley times. The earth goddess tradition is known through archaeological evidence:

> The practice of worshiping animal-and bird-faced goddesses was a common religious form. The Indus Valley people had their major deity in the forms of mother goddesses who later became the goddesses as Mata or Matrka, Jagatmata, Jagadamba or finally assumed the Hindu cosmic name Mahadevi. These forms of goddesses were related to pregnancy, procreation, creativity and fertility. The popular maternal images from the Indus Valley culture show the prominent breasts and navel, steatophygic display of yoni, the female mark, a well-marked girdle and occasionally an infant on the left side.
>
> (39)

As far as the sexuality and procreation aspects in goddess culture are concerned, it is postulated (Nagar 1998: 2):

> Harappa and Mohenjo-Daro examples of yoni correspond more to the mother goddess image as compared to Shakti aniconic forms. They

> are found in potteries, clay images and stone images. The features of the images found in Harappa and Mohenjo-Daro are nudity, figurines painted over with red slip or wash, ringstones and discs of stone with a variety of former reliefs of decorative and cultic character with the figures of mother goddesses. These fertility or mother images later developed into the goddesses like Prithavi or Aditi and Devi in the Vedic times.
>
> (40)

Along with historical explanations, there are multiple textual sources about the goddesses. *Śloka* 30 of *Śrī Lalitāsahasranāma Stotram* (a part of the *Brahmāṇḍapurāṇa*) mentions Vārāhī as: '*Viśukra prāṇaharaṇa vārāhī vīryānanditā | Kāmeśvara mukhāloka kalpita śrīgaṇeśvarā ||*'[17] The *śloka* connects her identity with the goddess Pārvatī, the consort of Śiva. The text provides thousands of names of the goddess Lalitā,[18] and Vārāhī is one of them. *Vārāhīsaṁhitā* is a resourceful medieval text on astrology from the ninth or tenth century CE by Varāhamihirācarya,[19] though the title suggests a book on Vārāhī, but in relation to the praise of the goddess the focus is on astronomy. Part of the text describes the physical features of women and their traits like marriageable woman, woman who makes the husband prosperous, auspicious women like goddess Lakṣmī, woman who can bless the family with sons, one who can protect, also sinful and inauspicious woman, a woman who is harmful to her husband. The list is as long and descriptive as patriarchal ideology.[20] *Vārāhītantra*, a Tamil text elaborates on the tantric worship practices to evoke the deity.

In *Śrī Vidyāmahārṇava*, Shri Prakashananda Nath and colleagues explain:

> *Vārāhī stotram* brings out a very significant fact relating to the creation of the universe. It addresses goddess Vārāhī as '*Janani*' (mother) and says that had it not been for the edge of her teeth serving as a support how could the earth rise from the hole of a serpent from pātāla? It means the earth was brought out from pātāla by goddess Vārāhī by supporting it by her teeth.[21]

The role of Vārāhī has evolutionary significance in terms of both cosmic and motherly functions. The animal of the mud, in popular visualization, becomes a great goddess. When the boar is, as Spivak analyses, 'cathected in ritual, each small goddess is the great goddess' (1999: 186). Each animal, even insects and bacterial life forms, becomes the goddess if activated as narrative, embodied, and ritualized. The thousand-armed and -legged being, who looks like insects and bacteria, goes through the reconstruction of being life forms to pantheonic greatness. 'the tenacious dog on the mountain path is suddenly the ad hoc god of the socio-ethical bond (Dharma) for Yudhiṣṭhira' (Spivak: 182), the virtuous eldest of the Pāṇḍavas in the epic *Mahābhārata*. This is the divinization of life forms. In cultural history, such great goddess traditions are noticeable in Nepali traditions too. P. Pal (1985) writes:

> In one form or another, the primordial great goddess whether as an individual or group was probably venerated all over the subcontinent and in Nepal. By the fifth century when the *Devīmahātmya* was very likely composed, they were elevated as the manifestation of the Great Goddess, each of the six being considered to be the energy or power (*śakti*) residing in each of the six major gods: Brahmā, Śiva, Viṣṇu, and his *avatāra*, Varāha, Kumāra, and Indra. Thus they came to be known as Brahmāṇī, Māheśvarī, Vaiṣṇavī, Vārāhī, Kaumarī and Indraṇī. To these six was added Cāmuṇḍā, or Kālī… an ancient goddess of dread and death, and collectively, the seven formed the retinue of the Great Goddess in her battle against her enemies in *Devīmahātmya*.
>
> (27)

Vārāhī is thus the warrior among the group of mother goddesses and is also identified as a distinct entity on her own. Both the male (Varāha) and Vārāhī are forms of Viṣṇu; hence, they share the role of protection. As a hog-faced, three-eyed woman, she sits under a Palmyra tree (*tāla* tree)[22]; The goddess, as Caitanya-Bhairavī, serves as an attendant and counsellor to the devī Cittanusārinī. In this form, she appears *mahāghora* (fierce).

Vārāhīs in the Kathmandu Valley

Vajravārāhī protects the valley from the south. Her temple is in Chapagaun, some ten kilometres south of Patan. The complex is near the town and yet keeps its distance among the trees, which were once part of a lush forest that is disappearing rapidly due to ever-increasing human habitation. The temple was probably built in 786 CE. Within the complex, a sow carved in stone looks directly towards the shrine, and behind the image, there is a house with open space to gather and prepare for rituals. The open spaces around the shrine form a courtyard. The temple is surrounded by lions serving as gatekeepers. The two-storied shrine houses three images of the goddess, each in a standing posture, stepping on two sows. The two images on the right and left, representing the yoginis of the central deity, are more visible in comparison. Their right legs are bent, and their left legs are stretched. They have four arms holding a *khaḍga,*[23] a bowl, and an arm raised in *abhaya*[24] *mudrā*. Their waists are girdled by eight human or demon heads along with a human head on thier belly. The yoginis[25] resemble in *mudrās* with the only difference of the position of the bowls, the yogini on the right holds the bowl on her left whereas the yogini on the left hold it on the right. She is considered as the fiercest form of Vajrayoginī who is the consort of Herukā Cakrasaṁvara.[26] She is the deity of pleasure and the destroyer of ignorance, the centre of mediation, the forms of compassion, which various texts characterize with a range of powerful feminine attributes.

There are many temples in the valley dedicated to the goddess. Vajravārāhī's association with the colour red is significant. She guards the valley from the southwest and protects the livestock. In Vajrayana Buddhist tradition, as Vajrayoginī, she is the consort of Cakrasaṁvara, the Buddhist deity of *karuṇā* (compassion) and *upāya-kauśalya* (skilful means). He is depicted in the colour blue, embracing Vajravārāhī, the deity of wisdom, in sexual union. She is also depicted as a twelve-armed Vārāhī, portrayed as a dancing deity. One of the prominent attributes of the dancing deity is *jvālā-mudrā* (flame mudra), posed by one of the pairs of hands. Her feet are upon the *māras.*[27]

In *Vārāhīsaṁhitā,* the five forms of Vārāhī are Svapna, Caṇḍa, Mahi (Bhairavī), Kṛka and Matsya.[28] The *Varāhapurāṇa* narrates that Vārāhī was created by Varāha to fight against a demon called Andhakāsura. Furthermore, Vārāhī, as one of the Mātṛkās, symbolizes jealousy.[29]

In comparison to Vajrayoginī,[30] Vajravārāhī is more formidable in countenance though she is almost similar in mytho-religious identity to Vajrayoginī. The very terrifying is the embodiment of compassion. The deity who fearlessly protects animals and humans is compassionate by inner self and is thus *bhayānaka*[31] in imagery to drive away the dangerous outsiders. She is the mother who stands by the edge of the city. The profundity of her attribute can be understood in *Bhavacakra maṇḍala* (The Wheel of life), the boar is the symbol of ignorance in the centre and the goddess is the one who overcomes ignorance because she is the *vajra*, the adamantine, the indestructible divine centre of the *maṇḍala*.

She has multiple forms and manifestations, but the most recognized one is with Vajrayoginī. Her Vajraghona and Vajravairocanī forms associate her with Tantric Buddhist traditions. Her Tibetan form is Dorje Phagmo. Vajraḍākinī is the one who dances in space; hence, she is called the sky-dancer who cuts across all binaries because she manifests in the liminal space of good and bad, life and death, fearfulness and compassion. She is therefore called *sarvabuddhaḍākinī*, the Ḍākinī of all the Buddhas. The goddess who protects is a supernatural being of purity and nakedness, which leads to all forms of purity, such as fearlessness from worldly attribution, liberation from attachment and the epitome of sublime wisdom.

Svetavārāhī Temple is enclosed in an iron cage in front of a courtyard surrounded by a stretch of office rooms. In Badegaun, it takes a twenty- to thirty-minute drive from the Vajravārāhī Temple to reach the temple complex. The remoteness of the shrine becomes very apparent to a visitor. The villages are scattered along the sides of a narrow road, some paved and some dusty. Parts of the urban valley shimmer in the distance if one visits the place during the summer season.

The deity evolves out of Cakrasaṁvara, who visited the place and took the form of Śvetavārāhī. At the same time, according to local myths, it is the place where the right breast of Sati fell.[32] Śvetavārāhī is a local deity of the valley, who is very exclusive to the imaginary of the locals.

The local deities have significant inter-religious evolutions. On the one hand, she is associated with Saṃvara, who is the manifestation of Hevajra; the god, in association with Prajñā (in terms of both the goddess and her associated symbolism as wisdom), is called Hevajra; the female consort who embraces Saṃvara is Vajravārāhī. On the other hand, her religious significance is realized in the context of the goddess Satī.[33] Such a religious fusion works from the space of the vernacular. Gods and goddesses 'travel' in creeds formed out of institutional religion. But the mythical narrative cordiality is a form of hospitality which accepts or frees the supernatural into multiple belief systems. Deities thus do not belong to any institutionalized fixity of religions. Such unions are the deep structures of faiths where Hindu Kālī and Buddhist Vajrayoginī evolve out of Tantric traditions of the vernacular, out of non-canonical traditions and Buddhist cults related with Mahayāna. Furthermore, a deity of established Hindu pantheon is accepted as a very exclusive local deity as a venerated Ḍākinī. Travelling in this sense is a back and forth devotional movement.

Yaktavārāhī's seat or the *pīṭha* of the deity is located in the southern part of Bhaktapur. The quarter or the areas surrounding the shrine are home to many Newar households. One of the significant visual impressions is the pair of lions guarding the temple from the Malla period.[34] Almost by the side of Mangal Tirtha Ghat, near Hanumanta River, the Vārāhī *pīṭha* is a two-storied pagoda which was renovated by Ananda Deva of the early Malla period, probably in the mid-twelfth century CE. It is believed that he was the founder of the shrines of eight *Mātṛkās*.[35] According to some local accounts, the *pīṭha* was constructed by King Jaya Prakash Malla of the eighteenth century.[36]

The *Śaktipīṭha* of Yaktavārāhī is one of the eight mother goddesses. The vast compendia of the Vārāhī texts in South Asia have pervasive mythical sources. The *Purāṇa*, such as *Devī Bhāgavata*, *Mārkaṇḍeya*, *Skanda*, *Varāha* and *Liṅga* frequently reference the deity as both Mātr̥kās and Vārāhīs. The Indian state of Odisha, along with Assam and Bengal, has strong tantric traditions, and the origin of such Mātṛkā stems from these traditions. The images of the goddess are found in the Vaitāla and Mukteśvara temples in Bhubaneswar, Odisha.[37] In cities like Puri and Cuttack, there are multiple such images. Since goddess worship in the *Śakti* traditions of eastern India is common, Nepali traditions of *Śakti* worship belong to the same span of geo-cultural connectivity. Just as there are multiple goddesses worshipped in eastern India, Nepali traditions exhibit striking similarities with these practices. The aspect of the mother goddesses includes the Ajimā group of deities, who are literally grand mothers. The Vārāhīs are numerous in the valley, to the extent that they are uncountable due to their multiple and cross-ritualistic identifications. It would not be surprising to study Vārāhīs-Ajimās within a specialized discourse. Walks and interactions help one identify Ajimās such as Chhabdivārāhī, Dakṣiṇavārāhī, Talavārāhī, Lativārāhī and many more grand mother deities. These deities are more closely associated with Śiva traditions, which explains their connection to the multiple forms of Śiva from Bhubaneswar to Kathmandu, and from Assam to Bengal.

Such *pīṭhas* and temples are symbolic spaces for fostering a sense of community, taking the religious complex both as the deity of the clan and as the community's cherished one. The towns and cities of the valley have their own deities, which they favour among many other groups of gods and goddesses. The cherished ones, called the *iṣṭa-devatā*, do not merely signify a personal deity but also represent an identity appropriate to be imitated as a symbol of power to be feared, like Kālī or Vārāhī. She can protect herself and also the world. 'She breaks the conventional epitome of the feminine', a student told me.[38] Such attributes are personal for the devotee as well as public. The Vārāhīs look fierce and that is the epitome of power in a double bind of a terrifying being and protecting being. The fierce is the protector, the very grace of the protecting being comes out of the rage of the supernatural; the act of protection carries the attributes of the fearsomeness.

The direction in the urban valley is significant in the context that these deities are spaced at considerable distances, taking into account that when they were built, the valley people had to travel long distances from one end to the other. If Dhūmavārāhī is within Kathmandu, Nīlavārāhī is in Bode, Bhaktapur. The valley is a consortium of cities and towns where the religious sites have cartographic visibility. The protector deities are the deities on the edges of the valley and even on the edges of a particular city. Such placements are not always approachable, and hence the divinities have sacral-placements as temples as well as in the imaginings. The idea of godhood as protection is structured outside of the habitations, and yet they constantly live within the devotional awareness. They are travelling deities identified in one group of goddesses to personal realizations. The valley thus has a tangible and intangible presence of the Vārāhīs. The tangible is in the shrines, and the intangible is in the mind of the devotional city. Half of the valley is myth in such idealization.

Notes

1 Mahāvidyā and *Mātṛkās* group of goddesses are known as goddesses of supreme knowledge and mother goddesses, respectively.
2 Kinsley, David. 1998. *Tantric Visions of the Divine Feminine: The Ten Mahavidyas*. New Delhi: Motilal Banarsidass Publishers. 32.
3 Vārāhī is one of the nine Durgās worshipped in Bhaktapur, Nepal.
4 Aṣṭamī refers to an auspicious day in Hindu-Brahminical ritual calendar.
5 A *pīṭha* is a shrine with a stone image of a deity. They do not have idols as in a temple shrine. During Bisket Jatra and Vijaya Dashmi festivals in Bhaktapur, the idol of a temple is brought and placed in the *pīṭha* of the same goddess.
6 I will use the present names of the cities with occasional references to the vernacular identities popular in the valley. Kathmandu is Kasthamandap, Kantipur; Patan is Lalitpur; Bhaktapur is Khopa, Bhadgaun. There are more vernacular names in the Newari language.
7 The term 'medieval' in the history of the valley suggests the Late Lichhavi to Malla Period. Pratapaditya Pal divides Nepali history into Licchavi (330–879/80), Transitional (879/80–1200), Early Malla (1200–1482), Late Malla (1200–1769) before the coming of the Shah monarchs in 1769; the latter's rule ended in 2008.
8 See English, Elizabeth. 2002. *Vajrayogini, Her Visualization, Rituals, and Forms: A Study of the Cult of Vajrayogini in India*. Boston: Wisdom Publication. 47.
9 She is also known as Dorje Phagmo.
10 See Nepali, Gopal Singh. 2015. *The Newars: An Ethno-Sociological Study of a Himalayan Community*. Kathmandu: Mandala Books. 309.
11 One of the names of Patan, the second largest city of the Kathmandu Valley.

12 Thimi is also a municipality in the valley.
13 Goddess Vaiṣṇavī may have been replaced by Bhadrakālī.
14 Ajimās are grand mother goddesses in Newar belief system.
15 Phālguna corresponds to February and March.
16 A *Ghat* refer to river banks where, along with other religious rituals, the deceased bodies are ritualized.
17 The deity who slayed the demon Viśukra is delighted and she rejoices by her strength. She is the one whose son was created by her look.
18 Lalitā is Tripurasundarī, one of the Māhāvidyā.
19 See Pt. Sukhanand Mishra, trans. 2008. *Vārāhī (Bṛhat) Samhita*. Bambai: Khemraj Shri Krishnadass Publisher.
20 Ibid., '*strīlakṣaṇam*' ('The Nature of Women') in Chapter 70, 246.
21 Shri Prakashananda Nath et al. *Śrī Vidyāmahārṇava*. Baranasi: Shri Vidyabimarsham Pitham. Cited in Haripriya Rangarajan. *Images of Vārāhī: An Iconographic Study.* 2004. Delhi: Sharada Publication House. 66.
22 The famous temple by this name in the Phewa lake in Pokhara, Nepal may suggest *tāla* either as Palmyra tree or a lake.
23 Suggests a sword.
24 The gesture which imparts fearlessness.
25 They are the female deities as the manifestations of *śakti* (group of deities conceived as feminine energies and knowledge) as well as the consorts of Bodhisattvas in Buddhist narratives.
26 A Bodhisattva in Mahayana tradition.
27 Māras are antagonistic to *nirvāṇa* and thus are considered as demons.
28 *Vārāhī (Bṛhat) Saṁhitā* by Varāhamihirācarya. Trans. Pandit Sukhanandamisratmaj and Panditwar Baldevprasadji. 2008. Mumbai: Khemraj Shreekrishnadass.
29 See Mātṛkās for their representations.
30 For an elaborate discourse on the deity, see English, Elizabeth. 2002. *Vajrayogini: Her Visualizations, Rituals, & Forms*. Boston: Wisdom Publications. See I have taken information from Kinsley, David. 1997. *Tantric Visions of the Divine Feminine: The Ten Mahavidyas*. Delhi: Motilal Banarasidass.
31 The literal meaning of the term suggests something frightening in common parlance.
32 See Karmacharya, Basudev. BS 2071 (2014). *Lalitpur Jillaka Prasidha Devidevatako Parichaya* (*Introduction to the Famous Goddesses and Gods of Lalitpur District*). Lalitpur: Shrimati Chandeswari Karmachara.
33 The epic *Mahābhārata* identifies Satī as the daughter of Dakṣa Prajāpati, the son of Brahmā. He gave his daughter to Śiva. Śiva was humiliated by her father and consequently she had committed suicide and Śiva in anger had roamed the cosmos carrying the corpse of the goddess on his shoulder, threatening the entire existence. Viṣṇu to calm him down

had cut the body into pieces. The places where the parts of the body fell became sacred sites.

34 The temple was constructed in the time of King Anandadeva and renovated during the reign of Jagatprakash Malla. See Prajapati, Satyanarayan, 'Yaktiko Varahi Mandir'. BS 2073 (2016). In *Sri Yakti Ajima Smarika*. Kathmandu.

35 *Shri Yakti Pitha Varahi Ajimaya*. Bhaktapur: Samundra Printers, Bhaktapur. 2–3.

36 The book has different page numbers, for Newari, Nepali and English ones. 4.

37 H.C. Das in 'Saptamātrikās in Orissa' writes: Four mātṛkā figures, namely Vaiṣṇavī, Vārāhī, Indrāṇī and Cāmuṇḍā, in chlorite stone (7' × 21'), now preserved in the Orissa State Museum, Bhubaneswar, resemble in style and workmanship the Mātṛkās of Puri and Jajpur. All the figures are in *lalitāsana* pose, with babies in their arms, except Cāmuṇḍā (201). See https://www.jstor.org/stable/44139070.

38 I constantly communicate with a group of students who are working on Nepali art within the conceptual dimension of spatiality, textuality and sexuality. On such matters and their aspects of the aesthetic sensibilities help us understand the ideas behind such images. During such visits we have interacted with locals like priests, community chiefs who are the members of the *Guthis* and elders. A *Guthi* in Newar tradition is a community trust which takes care of cultural heritage. See multiple research on the *Guthis* that is available online.

8

Tantric Modes of Worship of Mother Goddesses in Early Medieval Karnataka

Malini Adiga

Generic references to the worship of mother-goddesses occur from an early period in Karnataka. Ruling dynasties, such as the Kadambas, for instance, have in their introductory profile the statement that they were anointed after meditating on Svāmi Mahāsēna and the assemblage of divine mothers (*svāmi-mahāsēna-mātrgaṇānudhyatābhiṣīktānāṁ*).[1] Similarly, the early Cālukyas too claimed to be protected and promoted by the Saptamātṛkas (*saptamātṛbhir-abhivardhitānāṁ*).[2]

From the eighth century onwards, however, when we begin to have copious numbers of lithic records, we find references to local goddesses who received benefactions for the conduct of worship. Thus, the Honnuḍike inscription (Tumkur taluk, district) of the reign of Śrīpuruṣa Gaṅga mentions his father's younger brother (*kiriyayya*) as making a grant of the income from the harvest (*suggiyuḷ*) in gold to the goddess of Ponriḍuki (modern Honnuḍike).[3] Another inscription of the same period from Meḍutambihaḷḷi refers to the goddess (Bhagavatī) of Puttūr to whom the local ruler Kaṇṇam Gūḷarasa gave five *gūḷas* (a land measure) of paddy land (*kal̲ani*). In both these cases, it is not possible to determine whether these were fully Brahmanical cults with due rites of worship or local cults that were being promoted by local rulers. As B.D. Chattopadhyaya points out, the early medieval period saw the appearance of a number of cults of goddesses because of a linkage between these cults and emergent monarchies.[4] A similar situation can be observed in the ninth-century Marase inscription which records the establishment of a temple of Bhagavatī at Mariyase (modern Marase, Mysore taluk, district). Grants of land were made to the goddess by Permāḍi Gāvuṇḍa, who seems to have been the local headman, along with the local body the Thousand (*sāsirvaru*) and the king's accountant (*śrīkaraṇa*)[5]

In the case of the worship of Kil̲tabāḷ-er̲etti Bhaḷāri (goddess with a sharp, drawn sword), there can be no doubt about the forms of worship. The Manne Plates of Rācamalla I, dated 828[6] record that the temple of this deity was located in the Doḍḍavāḍi village of Mānya viṣaya (around Maṇṇe, Nelamaṅgala taluk, Bangalore district), and the village itself was granted for food offerings (*bali*), incense (*dhūpa*) and lamp (*dīpa*). The grant was entrusted to Dēva Śarman, a Vaikhānasa. Judging from the name, the deity is a fierce form of the mother-goddess and was possibly of tribal origin. However, by the early ninth century, her worship had taken on a Brahmanical form with *upacāras* performed regularly, and she was apparently well-integrated into the Puranic Hindu fold.

The tenth-century shrine of Bhaḷāri in Piriyahoḻma (Nanjanagud taluk, Mysore district) was managed by the Śakti Pariṣe. This was a fully Puranic cult dedicated to the deity Bhaḷāri-Mahādēvar-Bhagavatī, to which the local body and Ayyapa Gāvuṇḍa granted land and contributions from the lands of the tenants.[7] It was entrusted to Kūci Bhaṭārar of the Śakti Pariṣe of the Kālāmukhas which suggests that the worship conformed to the canon.

An inscription from Kuditini (Bellary taluk, district) dated 947 records grants of sixty-two *mattars* of land made by the Mahājanas of Kuruṅgōḍu for the temple of Dēkamma, who seems to have been a local deity. We are told that the land was made tax-free by the Emperor (*Cakravarti*) Kṛṣṇa III Rāṣṭrakūṭa at the request of the pontiff Rudrarāśi Bhaṭārar, who seems to have been the trustee of the temple, though this is not specifically mentioned. In addition, Lōkeyya Gāvuṇḍa, who is described as the *adhipati* of the Svāmi Kārttikēya tapōvana, granted an oil mill to the temple of Dēkamma.[8] Judging from the association of the Kālāmukha pontiff, the deity seems to have been integrated into the Brahmanical forms of worship. The provision of the oil mill suggests the *upacāra* of lighting the lamp before the deity.

Apart from these, we have references to shrines of the mother-goddesses being established in temples of Śiva as subsidiary shrines. Two inscriptions from Suttūr record grants of land to the goddess. In the first instance, an inscription from 1015 mentions the setting up of the subordinate shrine of Durgaiyār at the temple of Stavinnar at Suttūr by Tēvanāḍu Vēḷān and Muñcaḍi Ariyam Cimma, who then endowed the deity with land purchased from the Sabhā of Śrotriyūr (modern Suttūr).[9] In 1032 Doreyya śeṭṭi endowed the goddess Śrōtriyūravve with lands and a goat was also provided for suggesting that the goddess received blood sacrifices.[10] An inscription of 1094 from Chikka Bemmatti (Arkalgud taluk, Hassan district)[11] records the addition of subsidiary shrines of Bhairava, Bhagavatī and Nārāyaṇa to the Pollēśvara temple. The original temple had been constructed by Ahitara Rēci śeṭṭhi to which his granddaughter Caruvakabbe added the subsidiary shrines. We can deduce little of the rites followed in this case.

A mother-goddess shrine at the agrahāra Jayangoṇḍa Śōla Caturvēdimaṅgalam in Kaivāra Nāḍ was recognized as the guardian deity of the nāḍu and the nāṭṭār. The assembly of the nāḍ bound themselves to the provision of a goat per inhabitant every Tuesday to the goddess.[12] This would imply blood sacrifices on a large scale at the shrine which was located in the premises of an agrahāra. This would indicate the existence of non-Brahmanical forms of worship at an agrahāra. This would also apply to the goddess Śrōtriyūravve mentioned in the Suttūr inscription referred to above.

Human sacrifices to goddesses were also known. As Hiltebeitel points out, the Draupadī ratha at Māmallapuram has a relief sculpture of a pair of male figures kneeling by the side of a four-armed goddess, identified with Durgā, holding a sword in one hand and a top-knot of hair in the other. Similar figures are also known from other temples in Tamil Nadu.[13] An inscription from Hecche from the close of the tenth century records the self-sacrifice of a vēlevāḷi Lōkaṭega swore to offer his head to the goddess Guṇḍadabbe of Hayve if his king (*arasa*) Śāntivarma of Herdese had a son. When the king had a son, he had his head cut off. The king thereupon made a grant in his honour of twenty-four hera-drammas (coins).[14] This would point to a similar practice of self-sacrifice before the mother-goddess. Not much is known of this deity who seems to be a fierce mother-goddess who received human sacrifices.

Jaina Yakṣīs as Objects of Worship

Among the Jainas, the Yakṣīs who were attendant deities of the Tīrthaṅkaras, began to be worshipped as independent deities, and some of them became focal points of Tantric cults by the tenth century. Thus, Ambikā, in the Meguti temple at Aihole from the seventh century, is depicted independently of the Tīrthaṅkara and the children who, according to iconographic texts, are meant to be on her lap are instead held by attendants while she sits in state. This suggests her emergence as an independent deity.[15] Similar independent images of Yakṣīs have also been found at Bādāmi.

Of the numerous Yakṣīs who grew to be the foci of Tantric cults, the most prominent were Jvālāmālinī or Jvālinī, the attendant of the eighth Tīrthaṅkara, Candraprabha and Padmāvatī, the Yakṣī of Pārśvanātha. The cult of Jvālāmālinī is said to have been started by a monk of the Drāmiḷa Saṅgha, Elācārya, who invoked the goddess to rid a nun of evil spirits. This seems to have happened around the middle of the ninth century, and by the tenth century, we have the composition of the *Jvālinīkalpa,* which systematized the cult.[16] The centre of the cult seems to have been Kanakagiri tīrtha in Chamrajnagar district which is referred to in the text *Jvālinīkalpa* as Malaya Hēmagrāma. The temple of Pārśvanātha situated here includes idols of Jvālāmālinī, Padmāvatī, Kuṣmāṇḍinī and Brahma Yakṣa in the *sukhanāsi.*[17]

Padmāvatī is the other Yakṣī whose cult was popular and who became the focus of a Tantric cult. Probably adopted from the Vaiṣṇava pantheon,[18] she is associated with the Tīrthaṅkara Pārśvanātha and is depicted with the snake hood above her head. The text *Bhairava Padmāvatīkalpa* was composed around the tenth century and deals with the Tantric rites associated with her worship. By the eleventh century, this cult had become so popular that several Jaina ruling lineages in Karnataka brought in this goddess into their founding legends.

Royal Associations with Jaina Goddesses

The evolution of founding legends in early medieval Karnataka gives us a clear indication of the rising importance of cults of the mother-goddesses. Here, we take up the case of the Gaṅgas, the Hoysaḷas and the Śāntaras. The Jaina Yakṣī Padmāvatī figures in all three, and this occurs early in the second millennium CE.

The Kulagāṇa Copper Plates of Gaṅga Śivamāra I (Chamrajanagar taluk, district) from the early eighth century record the grant of lands to the cēdiya (*caityālaya*) at Kellipusūr in Koḍugūr nāḍu.[19] This Jaina benefaction of the Gaṅgas makes a fragmentary reference to the association of the *śramaṇācārya* with the founding of the Gaṅga kingdom which is further elaborated in the tenth-century Kūḍlūr Plates of Mārasimha II. These name the Jaina ācārya Simhanandi as the saint associated with the founding of the kingdom and his gift of a sword with which Mādhava smote a stone pillar, which seems to symbolize the obstacle to their sovereignty. He is then said to have crowned Mādhava with Karṇīkara blossoms.[20] The standard introduction in Gaṅga Copper Plates states merely that the first ruler of the lineage acquired fame and prosperity by cutting the pillar with a single stroke of his sword (*sva-khaḍgaika-prahāra-khaṇḍita-mahāśilā-stambha-labdha-bala-parākrama*). This holds good even for the Narsapur Plates (Kolar taluk, district) of the reign of Rācamalla II (902 CE)[21] which is also a Jaina benefaction recording a grant to the basadi at Kannamaṅgala of lands and gardens.

Eleventh-century records of their collateral descendants in the Shimoga district add the biruda of '*Padmāvatī labdha-vara-prasāda*' to their titles.[22] But it is in the twelfth-century inscriptions of these collateral descendants that the origin story brings in Padmāvatī and another Yakṣī who are besought for boons. In the first instance, the brothers, Daḍiga and Mādhava, who founded the Gaṅga rule in the south are said to have been born by their father bringing under control the Yakṣī (*śāsanadēvatē*) of Padmaprabha Tīrthaṅkara by means of mantras thereby attaining knowledge of the directions ('*tanage tanūbhavarillade manadoḷu cintisutamirddu Padmaprabhanārppinakaṇi sāsanadēvatēyaṁ pūjisi divya mantradiṁ sādhisidam| sādhisi diśādhītavidyanāgi putrairibbaraṁ paḍedu*').[23] When the brothers reached Gaṅga Pērūr in the south they met the Jaina ācārya Simhanandi of the Kāṇūr gaṇa who took them under his tutelage. After teaching them for some time he summoned Padmāvatī dēvī with due observances and obtained boons, a sword and the kingdom for them. Mādhava then took the sword and cut a stone pillar in two ('*Padmāvatidēviyaṁ vidhipūrvakamāhvānaṁ geydu varaṁ baḍedu khaḷgamumaṁ samastarājyamanavargge māḍe|munipati nōḍalu vidvajjana pūjyaṁ Mādhavaṁ śilāstambhamanārdanugeydu poyyalu puṇmane muṟidudu vīrapuruṣarēnaṁ mādaru||*').[24] On witnessing this act of valour (*ā sāhasavam kaṇḍu*) the Munipati proceeded to crown him with Karṇikara blossoms and bestowed the kingdom, with followers and an army. It is in the eleventh century and later then that the role of the goddess and the use of mantras to bring them under control fully come into focus. It is interesting that Padmanābha, the father of Daḍiga and Mādhava is said to have brought the Yakṣī of Padmaprabha under subjection and gained knowledge of the directions (*diśādhītavidya*). Until then the story focuses on worship of the Jinas and the bestowal of symbols of sovereignty by Indra who was impressed by the devotion of the Gaṅga kings.

Among the Hoysaḷas too, the role of Jaina ācāryas and the blessings of the Yakṣī Padmāvatī are specifically mentioned as part of the founding legend. The role of the Jainas is elaborated in the grants made to the Jaina shrines. Thus, for instance, the Bastihaḷḷi record (Belur taluk, Hassan district) from 1133 provides an elaborate narration of this. This epigraph details grants made by the Hoysaḷa monarch Viṣṇuvardhana to the Jaina shrine Drōhagharaṭṭa Jinālaya, constructed by Boppadēva, the son of Gaṅgarāja, in his father's memory. The inscription states that a Jainācārya, wishing to increase the prosperity of Saḷa (the eponymous founder of the dynasty), was bringing the goddess Padmāvatī of Śaśakapura (the early Hoysaḷa capital) under subjection through mantras when a tiger attacked.

Whereupon, he called out 'Poy saḷa' (Strike, Saḷa), and the prince struck fearlessly, making the tiger his symbol and gaining the name of Poysaḷa. Since the time was spring, the goddess, now renamed Vāsantikādēvi, was worshipped by the king.[25]

While the Gaṅga and Hoysaḷa, founding legends, mention the goddess Padmāvatī being summoned (*āhvāhana*) or brought under subjection by means of spells (*mantradiṁ sādhisi*), the *Śāntara* story of beginnings merely mentions the founder, Jinadattarāya, migrating to the south because he was disgusted by his father taking to cannibalism.[26] En route he is said to have killed the asura Siṁharatha and the (goddess?) Jakkiyabbe, pleased with his valour bestowed the *siṁha lāñchana* (lion symbol) on him. He further is said to have killed the demons Andhakāsura, Kanakāsura of Kanakapura and Khara and Dūṣaṇa thereby pleasing the goddess Padmāvatī. She then took abode in the Lokki tree at Kanakapura, also known as Pombuccha and was henceforth known as Lokkiyabbe. She is said to have bestowed Pombuccha as *rājya sthāna* on him and established the city (*poḷal*).[27] Here, there seems to be no monk-intermediary unlike in the case of the Gaṅgas and the Hoysaḷas. The *Śāntara* founder, Jinadattarāya had direct relations with the goddess. The Humcha inscription in which this legend appears is dated 1077. An earlier inscription dated *c.*950 mentions the establishment of the goddess Lokkiyabbe at the basadi of Pombucchapura by Jinadattarāya and grants to the basadi at Kumsi made by Gāvuṇḍas and śeṭṭis of Kumbasepura (modern Kumsi). The legend itself finds no mention in this earlier record but seems to have developed by the following century. The Lokki tree inhabited by the goddess is still pointed out at Humcha and temple festivities involve staging the *Śāntara* founding legend.

In these founding legends, Padmāvatī is brought under subjection by spells or favours the founder, impressed by his prowess. In any case, she is shown bestowing boons and establishing kingdoms. The Tantric texts composed to systematize their cults give detailed descriptions of the rites observed. If we turn to epigraphic evidence, two inscriptions – one from Kolar and one from Kuldhanūr – give a clear picture of how the goddess was conceived and the rites followed.

The Kolaramma Temple

The Kolaramma shrine dates to the eleventh century and enshrines Durgā (the inscription refers to Cāmuṇḍēśvari in the Mūlasthāna) and the Saptamātṛkas. The inscription in question dates from 1071 CE. It sets down the allocations of revenue for various rites performed within the temple in great detail.[28] A further record probably of the same date continues the allocations for the temple personnel in terms of annual and daily rates of payment.[29] There are references to rituals to be performed on specific days, those to be performed on a weekly, fortnightly or monthly basis. On a daily basis there are arrangements for offerings to each of the deities in the Saptamātṛka group, inclusive of Vīrabhadra and Gaṇapati, Cāmuṇḍēśvari of the Mūlasthāna, Yōgēśvari, Kṣētrapāladēva, Mahāśāsta and Sūryadēva consisting of four nāḷis of rice, two dishes of curry(*? kaṟiyamudu iraṇḍum*), two areca nuts (*aḍaiyakkāyumudu iraṇḍum*), four betel leaves (*ilaiyamudu nālum*). On days of solstice and eclipses, arrangements were made for the sacred bath of the goddess, provisions of paddy and rice for placing below the kalaśā, 1/4 kāśu for buying the necessary materials for the bath (*snapana dravya*), 1/8 kāśu for a cloth to tie around the chief kumbha, for offerings of rice, four dishes of curry, twenty areca nuts and forty betel leaves. It is at this point that the Tantric rituals are first introduced. There is provision for the Yōgini-Yōgēśvara pūja for which intoxicating drinks and a sheep is mentioned specifically. This would indicate at least three of the pañcamakāras – *madya*, *māmsa* and *maithuna* – took place as part of the rituals for the solstice and eclipses. They are mentioned several other times in the course of the record as being part of the general rituals taking place during monthly festivals and during the *śānti* rituals. Here the context seems to be the cakra pūjā of the Kaula mārga.[30] Apart from this, the rituals also include a *kanyā pūja* involving seven virgins (*peṇ-pilaigaḷ eḻuvarkkum*) and a bachelor (*Vikkēśvara māṇi*) to be performed every Tuesday of the year. We do not know much about the details of the *kanyā pūja*, we cannot say if it was Tantric in character. However, the Tuesday rituals also include a burnt offering of a goat (*angāra-balikku nāḷ oṉṟukku āḍ-oṉṟāga nāḷ aimbattiraṇḍukku āḍ-aimbattiraṇḍu*).

Provision of goats is also made for offerings to the Dhvajadēvar on the days of hoisting the flag and taking it down for the festival of Uttarā-nakṣatra in the month of Panguṇi. Other rituals on the occasion show significant continuities with the festival of Draupadī recorded by Hiltebeitel and include sprouting seeds in *pāḷigai*.[31] The ceremony of sprouting seeds apparently coincides with the hoisting of the flag (*ttiru-k-koḍi ēṟugaikku ttiru-muḷaiyaṭṭ–pāḷigaiy-iḍā-kkīḷ-aṭṭa nēṟ-kuṟuṇi-ariśi*). The seeds were probably discarded on the seventh day of the festival where once again the *pāḷigai* were to be placed on a bed of rice (*ēḷanāḷ-tiruviḻav-eḍukka-t-tiru-muḷaiy-aṭṭa-p-pāḷigai – k-kīḷ aṭṭa nel kuṟuṇi ariśi*). Sprouts were also part of the ceremonies for śānti to the goddess and we hear of nine kumbhas flanking the Cāmuṇḍā kalaśa placed on the sacrificial altar which once again recalls the details noted for the Draupadī festival.[32] During the seven days, *hōma* was to be performed to Cāmuṇḍā (probably the main deity of the temple) twice a day for which provisions of ghee, rice and parched rice were made. A burnt offering of a goat was also made for the occasion, once daily (*śāmūṇḍa-hōmattukku..nāl oṉṟukku āḍu oṉṟāga nāḷ ēḻukku āḍu ēḻāga*). Provisions of goat being offered as sacrifice were also mentioned in connection with the seven days of *graha-śānti* and *arputa-śānti*. At the conclusion of the Cāmuṇḍā *hōma* (? *samāptiyil*) we have an additional provision of eight buffaloes (*erumaiy-eṭṭu*) and goats as sacrificial victims (*paśu*).

Alongside these offerings of meat, we have clear references to the presence of Vedic specialists active during the festival. The Brahmā who officiated at the festival, those reciting hymns, a Ṛgvēdi, a Sāmavēdi and a Yajurvēdi are all mentioned in the course of the festival details. They seem to have been paid in cash, with the Brahmā and the hymn reciter receiving 1/4 of a *kāśu* each, and the other Vedic specialists receiving 1/8 *kāśu* each. Those who sang and danced at the festival were also paid in cash.

The supplementary inscription of the same date[33] makes provisions for the annual allocation in kind and cash to various temple personnel. It is significant that the highest-paid person was Kannāṭa Paṇḍita, who conducted the *mādāpaṭṭiyam* (?) in the temple, receiving 180 *kalams* of paddy annually. The next highest-paid individual was the brāhmaṇa Mārasinga Baṭṭā of the Gautama gōtra, who conducted the worship and received 60 *kalams* of paddy annually. Interestingly, the four Yōginis who participated in the Yōgini-Yōgēśvara *pūjā* were paid 60 *kalams* annually, while the four Yōgēśvaras received 90 *kalams*, indicating clear gender discrimination. The participants in the *kanyā pūjā* are not mentioned here and perhaps were not regular employees attached to the temple. However, a *Bhayirava-mudali* (chief Bhairava?) is mentioned as receiving 60 *kalams* of paddy annually, while his three subordinate *Bhayiravas* collectively received 90 *kalams*, individually half of what he was entitled to. It is not clear what their functions were. Seven drummers who played various kinds of drums were to receive 15 *kalams* of paddy each. Washermen and potters serving the temple also received 15 *kalams* annually. The dancing master was allocated 37 *kalams* of paddy as well as 1 *kāśu* in cash, while the 24 dancing girls were to receive 22.5 *kalams* of paddy annually. The astrologer and the lecturer of *vyākaraṇa* were each to receive 30 *kalams* of paddy and 1 *kāśu* in cash. This suggests that the temple might have served as a centre of Brahmanical education on a small scale. These allocations clearly indicate a social hierarchy among the regular service providers and employees of the temple. While it was controlled by brāhmaṇas, there were rituals involving blood sacrifices on a regular basis, as well as Tantric rites involving *madya*, *māṁsa* and *maithuna*, which necessitated having the Yōginis and Yōgēśvaras as regular employees of the temple.

Nupur Chaudhuri and Rajat Kanta Ray, in their study of Sahajiya Buddhist practices and the later continuities derived from them, suggest, based on later Brahmanical Tantra works, that the cult of the Siddhas of the Sahajiya Buddhists was sufficiently influential and popular for orthodox Hinduism to attempt to absorb it. They state, based on later texts, that this absorption was achieved through a ritual compromise, with Vedic rituals being practised during the day and Tantric rituals at night.[34] The *cakras* with a woman in the centre, and couples around her became a practice in the later medieval period. These *cakras* assembled at night where the *pañcamakāras* – *madya māṁsa*, *matsya*, *mudrā* and *maithuna* – were practised without inhibitions and there were no caste barriers. Since these practices would have invited censure, they were performed by night.[35] The Kolaramma inscription gives us no indication of this day/night duality, nor does there seem to be much social censure attached at the time since the royal officer is seen making provisions for the ritual with no attempt at hiding the fact. The fact that only three of the *makāras* seem to be practised here is also noteworthy. These seem to be the core of the Tantric practice as is brought out by Devangana Desai too in her summary of Kaula practices in the early medieval period: '…they believed in the Trikamata which consists of indulgence in meat and drink and worship of Śiva in the company of a female partner sitting on the left during the rites. The Kaula worshipper played the role of Śiva united with Pārvatī and exhibited the yoni-mudrā.'[36] Mother-goddess temples thus seem to have accommodated both Tantric rituals and blood sacrifices even when the rituals and the shrine were brought within the Vedic/orthodox fold in the early medieval period.

A similar blend of the orthodox and the Tantric can be seen in the Sirur inscription (Bagalkot taluk, district) of 1049. The inscription deals with a votary of the goddess Mahālakṣmi of Kollāpura, a Pāśupatācārya named Prabhu Rājavarma. He is said to have descended from a Yōgini named Boppalabbe, and his own line of descent is traced through his daughter, who is described as the chief (*mukhyaste*) among the Yōginis. Her daughter was Indulēkhā, whose children were Gaurabbe, Nayiyaṇṇa and Dhāyiyaṇṇa. Gaurabbe's descendant was Mārasingha Prabhu, who endowed the deity Siddhēśvara at Śrīpura for worship and provision of sandal, incense, food offerings, music and dance. The temple was managed by a celibate order of the Kālāmukhas. The association of the donor with the temple of Mahālakṣmī, who is praised as '*devādidevī*' in and surrounded by sixty-four Yōginis (*catuṣṣaṣṭi Yōginī siddha-sandōha parivēṣṭita*), is noteworthy, as is the fact that the genealogy is mainly traced in the female line, though the main protagonists are male. The Siddhēśvara temple seems to be a regular Śaiva shrine with no hint of Vāmācāra.[37] The Yōginis from whom the donor is descended seem to be related to the Jogatis/ Basavis who were dedicated to the local mother goddesses like Yellamma in Karnataka as posited by Anamika Roy. She points out that while Jogatis were women dedicated to the local goddesses, the Yoginis were local goddesses who were elevated to the forms of the great Mother-goddess herself after assimilation in orthodox Hinduism.[38] The fact that the lineage of Mārasingha Prabhu is traced in the female line is also significant in this regard. Their association with the goddess Mahālakṣmi of Kollāpura and the description of that deity as being surrounded by sixty-four Yōginis is also noteworthy. The usage of Yōginis as applied to individuals in the Sirur inscription however differs from that of the Kolaramma temple record. In the latter they seem to be minor officiants in temple ritual whereas here they seem to be individuals of high status associated with a temple cult and matriarchs of an important family.

The Kukkanūr Inscription

The Kukkanūr record belongs to 1178 CE and is thus a century later than the Kolar record. This is a Kannaḍa inscription belonging to the reign of Kalacuri Sankamadēva, the younger brother of Sōvidēva and son of Bijjalarṇpa. Kukkanūr was a *brahmadēya* in the Bēḷvala *viṣaya* and the Kukkanūr-30 division of Kuntaladēśa. It is compared to Brahmalōka due to the presence of *brāhmaṇasāle, brahmakuṇḍa* and learned *vipras*. We are then told that it was the site of several Svayambhū *liṅgas* and companion *Śaktipīṭhas*, a *kṣētra* noted for its Śiva-Śakti composite shrines, for Siddha-Yōgēśvaras and Sahajā-Yōginī groups.[39] The reference to the Yōgēśvara-Yōginī groups recalls the Kolar record. But this is not as clearly localized in the temple nor is there any clear reference to rituals performed as in the case of the earlier epigraph. There is also a hint of the goddess cults being coupled with the lingas, an association which becomes stronger in the record as we move on. The Goddesses Purāṇidēvi, Cāmuṇḍi, Mahāmāye, Taḍāgadambike, Kāḷyambe, Vasantādēvi and Gupta-Cāmuṇḍi are said to be resident there and made Kukkanūr sacred. Jyēṣṭhādēvi who is described as being superior to them in grandeur and majesty (*mahime*) came to dwell at Kukkanūr among them. It is interesting that she is said to be flanked closely (*aḍaka, sārkeyim*), pressed into a narrow compass by Brahmēśvara on the east, Gaṇēśvara on the south, Mūlēśvara on the west and Mallikārjuna on the north. These we are told are *svayambhū liṅgas* which by that character, closely matched her (*svayambhūtvamam geḍegoṇḍondire*) and she dwelt in their midst.[40] It is possible that the description of the goddess surrounded by these *liṅgas* refers to a *yantra*. The sense of the dangerous power of the goddess being held in check by the *lingas* is clearly conveyed here. This is accentuated further by the statement that the shining, splendid (*bhāsuradēvi*), eternal goddess took residence in regular order (*rēkākāradim*) in the *navamaṭha* attached to the Sōmēśvara *linga* with her Bhairava.[41]

Her terrific character is repeatedly emphasized, her anger was to be avoided at all costs since she stupefied with fear, both by her words and by making the mind dull. She is said to protect those who took refuge in her while destroying the arrogant. She is also said to send down strokes of lightning and the spectre of death. The story of Kumbhakarṇa, who was tricked by the goddess into asking for *nidratva* instead of *nirdaivatva*, is also recounted to underscore how she could destroy the evil ones through stupefaction. Thus, the worship of other deities is useless if her grace is not available.[42] Thus, it was eminently advisable to recollect Kāḷikā (Jyēṣṭhā), bow before her, adopt her vows and take refuge in her for the fulfilment of one's desires.

Then follows an account of various forms of the goddess and the purposes served by each. Thus, we are told that the dark-coloured (*ghanavarṇa*) Kāḷikā Jyēṣṭhe and Kapālīśa could effect *stambhana* (stupefaction); Bhadrakāḷi Jyēṣṭhe, who was dark (*kṛṣṇavarṇa*), and Praḷayāntaka could bring about the removal of poison (*viṣaharaṇa*); the smoke-coloured (*dhūmravarṇa*) Mahākāḷī Jyēṣṭhe and Mahākāḷa could bring about the removal of fever (*jvaraharaṇa*); the extremely dark (*mahākṛṣṇa varṇa*) Nīlā Jyēṣṭhe and Bhadrakāḷa could effect enmity (*vidvēṣaṇam*); the extremely smoky-coloured (*mahādhūmravarṇa*) Nīlapatākinī Jyēṣṭhe and Bhadrabhanjana could bring about control or confinement (*sangrahaṇa*); the blue-coloured Vṛddhakubji Jyēṣṭhe and Nīlagrīva could bring about peace (*śānti*); the dark-coloured (*śyāmavarṇa*) Mahājyēṣṭhe and Mahāgrīva could effect attraction and control (*vaśyākarṣaṇa*) as well as death (*māraṇa*); the blood-coloured Bhanjanī Jyēṣṭhe could bring about the loss of position (*pīṭhaninuccāṭanam*); while the extremely blood-coloured (?*mahārakta varṇa*) Prabhanjanī Jyēṣṭhe could fulfil all desires of a ruler (*pīṭha nāyaka*). This comprises the whole range of dark magic effects, and here again, it is noteworthy that though the goddess in her various forms has primacy, she is always coupled with a form of Śiva.[43] Jae-Eun Shin in her study of the Yōginis, the Mahāvidyas and the Kāmākhya cult points out that the Tantric magical rituals and acts were very popular for their efficacy and presented the rulers with effective means of increasing their power. She quotes the *Yoginī Tantra* as listing the six karmas of magical ritual as comprising *śānti*, *vaśya*, *stambhana*, *vidvēṣana*, *uccāṭana* and *māraṇa*.[44] In this context, the inscription's statement that the goddess could fulfil the desires of a military leader is significant. Indeed, the inscription records grants made at the instance of a military leader whose desires had been fulfilled by worshipping the goddess. It is interesting that among the deities Jae-Eun Shin mentions in the context of the six acts according to the *Yoginī Tantra* are Kālikā and Jyēṣṭhā apart from Durgā, Bhadrakāḷi, Ratī, Vāṇi, Ramā, Mātangi and Kulakāminī.[45]

Having given an account of the goddess and her power, the inscription turns to the management of the shrine where she resided. The *sthānācārya* of the temple of Kāḷikā Jyēṣṭhe was from the pontifical lineage of the temples of Siṅgēśvara, Rājēśvara, Cauṇḍēśvara and Vikramēśvara in the Sinda capital of Erambaravi, who were the Rājagurus of the Sinda Mahāmaṇḍalēśvaras. Kālēśvara Saiddhāntikarāja, who was vested with the responsibilities of the sthānācārya of the temple at Kukkanūr, was also the Rājaguru of Sinda Cāvuṇḍa. He is said to belong to the Sinda Nagarēśvara Kālāmukhānvaya; his immediate preceptors are said to be, in ascending order, Yōgēśvaradēva Rājaguru, Muni Vigrahēśvara and Sōmēśvarācārya. While he is described as a master of all knowledge (*sarvajña*), of *kāvyas* (*kāvyajña*), *śāstras* (*śāstrajña*) and logic (*tārkajña*), special emphasis is laid on his mastery of *mantras*, *tantras* and the drawing of *yantras*, as well as the *siddhis* to be obtained therefrom.[46] The categorization of this pontiff as a Rājaguru reminds us of Bhairavānanda in Rājaśekhara's *Karpūramañjari* who procures by means of his Tantric rituals, the acquisition of sovereign status for the hero.[47] Literature of the early medieval period does show the ambivalence and even acceptability of Tantric rituals to rulers as seen earlier in the case of Assam as well, as a supernatural means of enhancing their power and influence.[48] However, while Bhairavānanda was an out and out Kaula Tantric, this cannot be said of Kāḷēśvara in the Kukkanūr inscription. The epigraph balances his knowledge of the conventional śāstras and literature with that of Tantras, mantras and yantras. Also, the attempt to circumscribe the goddess with lingas and male deities is also noteworthy in this case. We do not see that in Kolar, for instance.

The record introduces us to the family of Dhannugi Camūnātha, the Bēḷvala *nāḍādhikāri*, who traces his lineage through the maternal line, referring to his grandfather, Hariścandra Daṇḍanātha, and his maternal uncles, Kālidāsa, Lakhmidēva and Pṛtunēśā, all of whom served the Kalacuris as Daṇḍanātha and Mahāpradhāna. Together with his mother,

Caṇḍābāyi, and his sister, Lāḷiyādēvi, he is said to have visited the shrine of Kāḷikā Jyēṣṭhe at Kukkanūr to give thanks for the fulfilment of his desires (*mun palavu Sūḷuvādēviyam tammabhīṣṭhitasiddhiyādudaṛim*).[49] He is said to have requested his uncle Lakhmidēvayya to intercede with the Emperor for grants to the temple, whereupon the village of Selagaṛa in Kukkanūr-30 together with the attached hamlet (*anādiyim praviṣṭavāgirda*) Benatūrhāl were given as a *sarvanamasya, sarva-bādhā-parihāra* grant as *pāramēśvara-datti* and were given over to the Sthānācārya.[50] It is interesting that the deity Sōmēśvara and the navamaṭha in whose premises the goddess was set up is said to have been a beneficiary as well. The grant was for the purpose of conducting the daily rites for these deities (in plural), the maintenance of the temples and feeding the ascetics resident there.[51] Thus, the juxtaposition of the lingas with the mother-goddess cult ensured that the Śaiva cult with its sectarian pontiffs also benefitted through the support accrued by the heterodox sect of Jyēṣṭhādēvi.

Thus, the two inscriptions studied here give a contrasting picture of Tantric worship in early medieval Karnataka. While the Kukkanūr inscription provides a detailed description of the deity and the occult effects her worship could have, the Kolaramma inscription offers a depiction of the rituals followed and the temple administration. In any case, we can observe that Tantric rites in the worship of the mother-goddess coexisted with more orthodox forms of worship, and this seems to be a characteristic of goddess cults over time.

Notes

1 Kielhorn. F. 1900–01. 'Two Kadamba Grants'. In *Epigraphia Indica*, Vol VI, edited by E. Hultzsch, 12–20.
2 Fleet, J.F. (ed.), 1878. 'Sanskrit and Old Canarese Inscriptions, No.XLVIII'. In *Indian Antiquary*, Vol VII. 300–3.
3 Ramesh, K.V. (ed.), 1984. *Inscriptions of the Western Gaṅgas*. New Delhi: ICHR. No. 64. 238–9.
4 Chattopadhyaya, B.D. 2005. *Studying Early India: Archaeology, Texts and Historical Issues*. Delhi: Permanent Black. 172–91.
5 Gopal, B.R., et al. (eds.), 1976. *Epigraphia Carnatica*, Vol 5. Mysore: University of Mysore Prasaranga. My186.
6 Settar, S. 1976–77. *Archaeological Survey of Mysore: Annual Reports 1906–12, A study*, Vol 3, Dharwar: Institute of Kannaḍa Studies. 33–4.
7 Gopal, B.R., et al. (eds.), 1974. *Epigraphia Carnatica*, Vol 3. Mysore: University of Mysore Prasaranga, Nj 294.

8 Reddy, Devarakonda (ed.), 1998. *Kannaḍa University Epigraphical Series*, Vol I. Hampi: Kannaḍa University Prasaranga. Bellary No. 39.

9 Gopal, B.R., et al. (ed.), 1974. *Epigraphia Carnatica*, Vol III. Nj 213.

10 Ibid., Nj 215. The goddess is the local deity currently housed in a tin shed at the outskirts of the village with rites akin probably to those of Māriyamman. I visited Suttūr in 2010.

11 Gopal, B.R., et al. (eds.), 1984. EV VIII. Mysore:University of Mysore Prasaranga. Ag 146.

12 Rice, B.R. (ed.), 1905. *Epigraphia Carnatica*, Vol X. Bangalore: Government of Mysore. Kl 26, 25. Incidentally, in Koteshwara where I currently reside, the goddess Māriyamman has a shrine in the main temple car street which is also the Brahmin residential area and she receives blood sacrifices at her annual spring festival. The meat offerings are distributed to her worshippers the next day. Thus, even today, the coexistence of the non-Brahmanical forms of worship in agrahāras continues.

13 Hiltebeitel, Alf. 1988. *The Cult of Draupadī: Mythologies: From Gingee to Kurukṣetra*. Chicago: University of Chicago Press. 318–19. The self-decapitation was preceded by blood-letting from different parts of the body. A similar procedure can be seen in the self-sacrifice of heroes independent of mother-goddess association in the Hoysaḷa period wherein warriors styled lenka or garuda cut themselves in eight different parts before decapitation. Vide EC IX.1990. Bl 268.

14 Rice, B.L. (ed.), 1904. *Epigraphia Carnatica*, Vol VIII. Bangalore: Government of Mysore. Sb 479.

15 Nandi, R.N. 1973. *Religious Institutions and Cults in the Deccan*. Delhi: Motilal Banarsidass. 151.

16 Ibid., 153.

17 https://en.wikipedia.org>wiki>kanakagiri_Jain_tirth.

18 Nandi, *Religious Institutions and Cults in the Deccan*, 155.

19 Gopal, B.R., et al. (eds.), 1975. *Epigraphia Carnatica*, Vol. IV. Mysore: University of Mysore Prasaranga. Ch 347.

20 Ramesh, *Inscriptions of the Western Gaṅgas*. 411–32.ll11–13.

21 Rice, B.L. 1905. *Epigraphia Carnatica*, Vol. X, Bangalore: Government of Mysore Press. Kl 90.

22 Nagaraja Rao, H.M., et al. (eds.), 2006. *Epigraphia Carnatica*, XIII Mysore: University of Mysore Prasaranga. Sh 59 from Taṭṭekere, dated 1085.

23 Nagaraja Rao, H.M., et al. (eds.), 2006. *Epigraphia Carnatica*, XIII, Mysore: University of Mysore Prasaranga. Sh 68 of 1112, ll43–4.

24 Ibid., 50–1.

25 Narasimhamurthy, A.V., et al. (ed.), 1990. *Epigraphia Carnatica*, IX. Mysore: University of Mysore Prasaraṅga. Bl 389: '*ā Saḷa nṛpatiya rājyaśrī saṁvardhanamaneydi māḍuva bageyim Vāsavavandita*

Jinapūjāsahitaṁ sakaḷamantra vidyākuṣalaṁ| mudadiṁ Jaina bratīśam śaśakapurada Padmāvatīdēviyaṁ mantradinādaṁ sādhisalva kriyeyoḷe puli mēlpāye Yōgīśvaraṁ kuñcada kāvinḍāntadaṁ poysaḷa enal abhayaṁ poyvuduṁ Poysaḷāṅkaṁ yadubhūparggādudamdiṁdesedudu seḷeyiṁ lōḷaśārdūlachinhaṁ|| ā sanda Yakṣīvaradoḷ vasantaṁ lēsāgie tātkāḷikanāmadindaṁ Vāsantikādēvateyendu pūjāvyāsaṅgavaṁ māḍidanā nṛpāḷaṁ||' lines 9–13.

26 Rice, B.L. (ed.), 1904. *Epigraphia Carnatica*, VIII. Bangalore: Government of Mysore. Nr 35 '*Sahakūran ātan nara māṁsa bratan āge ātaṅgaṁ śriyādēvige puṭṭida Jinadattan ātana caritrakke pēsi dakṣiṇābhimukhiyāgi baruta*'.

27 Ibid., '*Simharathan embāsuran kondaḍe Jakkiyabbe mecchi Siṁha lāñcchanamam koṭṭaḷ. Andhakāsuran emb asuran kondu Andhāsuranendu māḍida. Kanakapurakke vandalli Kanakāsuran konda| Kundada kōṭiyoḷ karaṇum Kharadūṣaṇam kādiyōḍisidaḍe Padmāvatīdēvi mecchi Kanakapuram enisida Pomburcchada Lokkiya maradaḷ nelasi Lokkiyabbe emb eraḍaneya pesaram tāḷdi Pomburccam ātaṅge rājyasthānavendu poḷalam māḍidaḷ*'.

28 Rice, B.L. (ed.), 1905. *Epigraphia Carnatica*, (henceforth *EC*) Vol. X Bangalore: Government of Mysore, Kolar 108 (henceforth Kl).

29 Ibid., Kl 106d.

30 Mahalakshmi, R. 2011. *The Making of the Goddess: Korravai-Durgā in the Tamil Tradition*. New Delhi: Penguin Books. 10.

31 Hiltebeitel, Alf. 1991. *The Cult of Draupadi: On Hindu Ritual and the Goddess*. Chicago: University of Chicago Press. 59–65.

32 Ibid., 59. The description of the festival at Muthialpet in Chennai has reference to the *pāligai, navadhānya* and additional nine pots representing rivers or the nine planets being involved in the rituals.

33 Rice, B.L. (ed.), 1905. *EC* X:Kl 106d.

34 Chaudhuri, Nupur, and Rajat Kanta Ray. 2007. 'Eros and History: Sahajiya Secrets and the Tantric Culture of Love'. In *Religion in Indian History*, edited by Irfan Habib. New Delhi: Tulika Books, 102–5. 115.

35 Ibid., 115–16.

36 Cited in Chattopadhyaya, B.D. 1984. 'Religion in a Royal Household'. In *The Making of Early Medieval India*. New Delhi: Oxford University Press. 222–32, 227.

37 SII, Vol XI. No. 85.

38 Roy, Anamika. 2015. *Sixty-four Yōginis: Cult, Icons and Goddesses*. New Delhi: Primus Books. 4–5.

39 Reddi, Devarakonda (ed.), 1999. *Kannaḍa University Epigraphical Studies*, Vol. II (Koppala district). Hampi: Kannada University Prasaranga: Ylg 52, '*śivalingangaḷu svayambhū prabhuteyinesevom battenal śaktipīṭham bhuvanastutyangaḷom battenalidu śivaśakti-sphurat-sampuṭa kṣētravenuttam Siddhayōgēśvaraa vara sahajāyōginī vrātavast*

yutsavadindallindavendum tolagarenal-adār baṇṇisar Kukkanūram', ll. 17–19.

40 Ibid., ll. 22–4.

41 Ibid., ll. 25–6 '*sphuradudyannava nābha maṇḍaladoḷirppā Bhadrakāḷyāḍi bhāsuradēvi praḷayāntakādyamara rēkākāradim lingamāgire Sōmēśvara vāsadoḷ navamaṭham samsēvyamendalli yādaradindam praḷayāmbe bhairavayutam śrī Jyēṣṭhe rārājipaḷu*'.

42 Ibid., ll. 37–9, l 42 '*tannane teṛadim Jyēṣṭhēyadēvaḷenduṛadavam tānāva deyvangaḷam maṛevokkum bardukāḍanā kumatiyimpēḷ nungudēm māṇbaḷe*' A rough translation would be: In her own way Jyēṣṭhe will not fail to persecute those whom she decides to punish even if they take refuge in other deities.

43 Ibid., ll. 45–51.

44 Shin, Jae-Eun. 2010. 'Yoni, Yoginīs and Mahāvidyās: Feminine Divinities From Early Medieval Kāmarūpa to Medieval Koch Behar'. *Studies in History*, 26 (1): 1–29. 23.

45 Ylg 52, 23.

46 Ibid., ll. 67–70.

47 Chattopadhyaya, B.D., op.cit., 227–8.

48 Ibid.

49 Ibid., ll. 89–90.

50 Ibid., ll. 92–8.

51 Ibid., ll. 99–100 '*Jyēṣṭhādēviya navalingāḍhīśvara Sōmēśvara devara nitya naimittika pūjegam tapōdhanara āhāradānakkam ā dēvāyatanaṅgaḷa khaṇḍasphuṭita Jīrṇōddhārakkavendu* … '.

9

The Bejewelled Beauties and Kingly Desires: The *Rājapūrvaprayoga* of the *Kāmakalākālīkhaṇḍa* of Ādinātha's *Mahākālasaṁhitā*

Navoneel Ray

The *Mahākālasaṃhitā* (*MKS*) is a Tantric manual dedicated to the forms of Kālī named Guhyakālī and Kāmakalākālī.[1] The text is divided into two *khaṇḍas* namely (i.) The *Guhyakālīkhaṇḍa* (*G*) and (ii.) The *Kāmakalākālīkhaṇḍa* (*K*). The *MKS* is however an incomplete text. The text in its colophon claimed to be of *pañcaśatasahasra* or five hundred thousand, however the manuscripts which have been recovered only number up to thirty *paṭalas* so far. The text claims to be written by one Ādinātha and is framed as a dialogue between Devī and Mahākāla. The latter, like in earlier *Tantras*, is the one who reveals the practices of the text to the former. The reversal here is that the object of devotion is directed towards the Devī and not Śiva or his Bhairava form. The extant chapters indicate that the text comprised of 255 *paṭalas*.[2] The total number of verses is, however, uncertain.

The date of the *MKS* has been assigned by Kishori Nath Jha to the twelfth century CE[3]; the previous editor Kavirāja[4] had declined to date the text. The *G* might have been revised after fifteenth century CE to suit newer developments in matters of Haṭhayoga.[5] The fragmentary nature of the text, however, makes it difficult to posit an accurate end date. The earliest reference to our text comes from the seventeenth century CE, in the form of quotations in the *Tārābhaktisudhārṇava* by Narasiṃha Ṭhakkura of Mithila.[6] Apart from Mithila the reference to the *MKS* comes from two works from Nepal: (i.) the first is a late commentary on the *Kumārikākhaṇḍa* of the *Manthānabhairavatantra* (twelfth century CE) written by one Mukundarāja titled the *Samvartārthaprakāśa*[7] and (ii.) the second being *Puraścāryārṇava* of Pratāpa Siṃha[8] (an eighteenth-century ruler of Nepal). Therefore, we can assume that most additions were finished by the second half of the seventeenth century CE which is the provenance of Narasiṃha.[9] Most manuscripts belonging to the *MKS* come from Bihar, Uttar Pradesh and Nepal.[10] Both Kavirāja and Alexis Sanderson believe that the text reflects the regional characteristics of the historical Mithila.[11] The text blends a variety of systems including *krama*, *kaula* and *yogic* ideas. It is surmised that the elements which are reflected in the *G* dates around the tenth century CE. Whereas the dating of the *K* is later from the thirteenth century CE, definitely after the commentary of Jayaratha to the *Vāmakeśvarīmatatantra*. We believe that our text was composed in the Mithila region, but its prominence rose only after few centuries of its composition; in the neighbouring region of Nepal in the seventeenth century CE.

The aim of the text according to Jha was mainly to establish a Tantric sect which was more in line with the *Purāṇas* and the *Vedas*. This is expected as Maithili *Brāhmaṇa* are connected to the formation of the *Kālīkāpurāṇa*, often leading to this *Veda-Tantra* synthesis. The goddess Guhyakālī in one of her forms is seen arising from the four *Vedas*. The *G* in its twelfth *paṭala* mentions some other Tantric communities like the Kāpālikas about which it is a bit reticent. The chapter focuses on the fifth chapter of the *K*, titled '*Kāmakālīkaprayogasyāvataraṇam*' or the 'Descent of the rite of Kāmakalākalī' and draws connections with the larger developments happening in the context of the Tantric canon. The *K* of the text shows a preference for rites dedicated for *laukika* or worldly goals.

Kaula Tradition and the Provenance of the *Kāmakalākālīkhaṇḍa*

The Kaula strand is the latest of the Tantric Mantramārga form of Śaivism. This tradition was supposed to have flourished from the ninth to the twelfth century CE and is devoted to distinct goddesses who are seen as the head of the pantheon related to the Kaula tradition.[12] Sanderson opines that the Kaula tradition reformed the pre-existing tradition of the Yoginīs within its ritual structure. This system had appropriated the older Kāpālika tradition and made it available for the wider community of followers. The initiation in this tradition was simplified and was more focused on the idea of possession or *āveśa*. The erotic impulses of the earlier tradition were carried on and included the coupling with the *dūtī* (ritual consort).[13] Earlier the ritualized coitus produced mingled fluids which were either offered to the deities or consumed to gain *siddhis*. In Kūlamārga the 'orgasm' produced or experienced in ritual was a means of attaining *siddhi*/*mokṣa*.[14] The use of alcohol and meat was seen as a way to gratify the senses in whom the Yoginīs revelled. The offering of blood (from one's own body) brought down the sky-flying Yoginīs who revelled using the adept as a *paśu* or a sacrificial victim. This revelry within the adept's body was supposed to transform the adept by the Yoginīs fusing with the eternal Kuleśvara[15] resplendent within the adept which leads him to master *siddhis* and attain *mokṣa* finally.[16]

As discussed earlier, the date of the *MKS* as a whole is believed to be from the twelfth century onwards. The text also knows about the existence of the sixfold *āmnāya* division and ascribes them to the faces of Śiva.[17] The systematic treatment of this sixfold division comes from the *Parātantra*, which is noted to be composed in the latter half of the Malla period (1200–1768 CE)[18] and probably after the fifteenth century CE.[19] Our text however does not explain the associate deities or rituals of these *āmnāyas* and there were older systems which did know of the sixfold classification.[20] The *MKS* as a whole also refers to older understanding of Kaula concepts and rites because of which one can presume it was composed in the early period.[21]

The main goal of the *K* is to elucidate the ritual practice of the goddess Kāmakalākālī, who is seen as a manifestation of Kālī. Kālī is described as having ninefold manifestation and is conceptualized as the supreme of such manifestations.[22] In the fourteenth *paṭala* when Nārāyaṇa and Mahākāla receive the theophany of Kāmakalākālī, she claims herself to be the terminal amongst all *ugra* forms of the goddess.[23] This terminal position is to be seen as a form of superiority over all the other terrific forms of the goddess. Similarly, in her *saumya* aspect she is Tripurāsundarī, the final source of all such forms.[24] The purpose of the *MKS* it seems was to promote a syncretic deity who combined the qualities of both Kālī and Tripurasundarī. Her lengthy *dhyāna*[25] in the second *paṭala* describes her as red hued as the clouds attached to the rising sun, as dark hibiscus that is bunched together, with the eyes of an intoxicated koel and luminous as ripe jamun. She is short in stature with well-endowed breasts, naked, with open hair and lustful for the sexual company of her mate, Saṃhārabhairava.[26] The contradiction arises from her ornaments which are made of human bones, garland of heads dripping with blood and other body parts of men and children which become her anklet, waistband etc. The ornaments give rise to quite interesting metaphors such as how the necklace of human fingers make her breasts look prominent or how her hips are wide and she has a thin waist, which is engirdled with 'tinkling' knuckle bones of children. She is portrayed as an *ekavīrā* and has kept a foot on a downward-facing corpse; the other foot is kept as if she is taking a step forward to seek out Saṃhārabhairava.[27] The interesting attributes of hers include holding a poisonous rat-like animal called *lālana* and the cub of a jackal or hyena (*śivāpotaṁ*). The latter also accompany her and are visualized as feeding on brains offered by her. She also takes on the stereotypical function of Kālī as the destroyer of time, terrific, awe-inspiring and the destroyer of *kalpas*. There are two other visualizations in the text, one which conceives her in *nirguṇa* form which is associated with a yogic practice for mastering the *kuṇḍalinī*[28] and the second comes from the *stotra* attributed to Rāvaṇa in the tenth *paṭalaḥ*. There her visualization is, however, akin to Guhyakālī.[29]

The earlier assumption was that the text was written for people who wanted to establish a community of Tantric adherents who are in concordance with Vedic orthopraxy.[30] This, however, is a simplification of the complex scope of the text. First of all, the transgressive elements of the earlier Vidyāpīṭha are still maintained in this text and the emphasis on menstrual and seminal fluids for ritual is retained.[31] We believe that the *K*'s initial purpose was to make a compendium of magical rites[32] for the use of royal elites and the wider communities of the region, i.e., Mithila. The warnings of the text need to be considered as a strategy to open up a range of possibilities which the adepts can adapt according to their needs. This can be seen in the assertion in the tenth *paṭala*, where the exhaustive qualifications of the *śakti*[33] are concluded with the assertion that the steadfast *sādhaka* can have a *śakti* of any *varṇa* or *jāti*.[34]

The *Rājapūrvaprayoga*

The fifth chapter is perhaps the most elaborate ritual described in the *K*. The *Rājapūrvaprayoga* as it is called in text for being the grandest one out of the three which are *rāja*, *madhya* and *laghu*.[35] The first is the one described here. Following the formula this text exhorts the adept to not discredit or make fun of this practice as this will lead to dire consequences. The *prayoga* contains a *maṇḍala pūjā* involving thirty-six sixteen-year-old teenagers belonging to different communities.[36] These *sundarīs* are to be bathed, offered clothes, cosmetics like *kajjalaṃ*, *sindūra* and *alakta*.[37] These rituals are done before the creation of the *maṇḍala* and then they are sequentially invited within the *maṇḍala*.[38] There are four guards assigned to the four cardinal directions. The direction of the *maṇḍala* follows the traditional eight directions of the Brahmanical tradition. There are specific colours associated with specific directions of the *maṇḍala*.[39] Guards are to be posted at the four gates leading inside the yantra. The thirty-seven *sundarīs* are divided into two groups. In the first set eighteen are to be entered in the *maṇḍala* and in the last nineteen. The *yantra* is the same as the goddess's *yantra* described in the second chapter.[40] Then the rituals take place which are the generic staple of Kaulas like *āvāhana* of the main goddess, permission for conducting the *prayoga*, *pīṭhanyāsa* etc. The *sundarīs* are worshipped to their satisfaction.

The matter of the *naivedya* again has a set of restrictions which are carried from the previous chapter. First for the *brāhmaṇa* the offering should be *sāttvika*. Regarding alcohol the *kṣatriya* could offer liquor made of honey, palm, *guḍa*, dates and flower. They should also offer *śāli* rice and meats. The liquor barred for the *kṣatriya* is fermented grain alcohol or *paiṣṭikī*. This, however, is open only to the *śūdra*. There are also restrictions regarding which vessel should be used for milk and other liquids. Coconut water in a brass vessel, a copper vessel for milk, curd and honey are allowed for the *kṣatriya* and the *vaiśya*. A *brāhmaṇa* who does the same will face reduction of his life span. A smaller list of offer of able animals is presented here and matches the one above. The added injunctions for who can offer what is given. This can be summed up as: *kṣatriya* can offer lion, tiger and human being, apart from these they can offer all other animals (as listed) with the exception of the *kṛṣṇasāra*; the *brāhmaṇa* can't offer the three mentioned here and if they sacrifice these animals, they will be considered as *brāhmaṇa* killers. Likewise, the *śūdra* is barred from sacrificing *muṣaka*, *mārjāra* and the *cāṣa*. The implements used to sacrifice are described as *candrahāsa* and *khaḍga*. The one who sacrifices the animal should not kill it himself. If they do it themselves, they will be born as animals.[41] The sacrifice of the animal should be done standing and not while sitting. There are also injunctions for what is fit to be sacrificed. Any bird which is less than three *pakṣa* old, any *mahiṣa* which is less than three years and any animal which is less than three months are unfit. Similarly, old and deformed animals should not be given. The *Kṣatriya* can give his own blood as offering. There is also a description for making animals out of substitutes for sacrifice. The text bans this *prayoga* for the *brāhmaṇa* and gives a list of what type of women is fit for this practice. Also, only the latter three can accept lower *varṇa* women and not the *brāhmaṇa*. Similarly, they can't accept a woman higher than them. The adept is also warned not to be lustful as this will lead to failure. The results of this grand *prayoga* are not revealed in the text. The results are left open to whims of the adept. The *prayoga* also employs the classic strategies of secrecy as one finds in Tantric literature of this kind. The aura of heightened secrecy is nothing more than a strategy of the text to cement its prestige.[42] The list of sacrificial victims which are mentioned here briefly build upon the previous chapter of the *K* titled the *Viśeṣaprayogavarṇanam* which is a reference to the famous *Śivābaliprayoga*. Apart from the above restrictions, there is over all denial to the rite to the *brāhmaṇa* and the logic of the text is that only the other three *varṇas* have the liberty for comingling with women freely.[43] The text is always keen to maintain a dual harmony between purity and impurity. Women for this *prayoga* or any other are selected for their ability to menstruate, a potent symbol of impurity in Brahmanical ideology. This also symbolizes their potential fertility in pre-modern times, and a fertility which this text would like to harness to please the goddess Kāmakalākālī. The text in its third chapter, the one to deal with most sexually explicit rites prescribes for purity (*śuciḥ*) in day and to be impure in night (*aśuciśca*).[44] The careful arbitration of transgression and orthopraxy is shown in the tenth *paṭala*'s *Prasannākalaśavidhi*. After clear demarcation which *śaktī* is fit for which *jāti*,[45] Mahākāla says any *jāti* is open to the most steadfast *sādhaka*.[46] Hugh Urban in the context of the sixteenth-century *sādhaka*, Kṛṣṇacandra Āgamavāgiśa, says these rites were a process to assert the elite power of the *brāhmaṇas* through 'transgressive' rites, when it was threatened by newer religions i.e., Islam.[47] The context for our text's origin can lie on two factors. First is the Karṇāṭa dynasty (*c*. 1097–1324 CE) of Mithila and its wish to record older Śākta practices. The second may be the Oiṇīvāras (*c*. 1353–1526 CE) and their assertion of royal power.[48] Both the dynasties were avid Śāktas and had celebrated the autumn festival (*navarātra*) of the goddess with great pomp.[49] This celebration often contained bloody sacrifice of many kinds to appease the goddess and gain her munificence.[50] Bihani Sarkar posits that during these dynasties, rites that have the patronage of the court were recorded in 'official literature'.[51] Many of these recorded practices were older and might have been around for a few centuries before they were written down.[52] The *prayoga* of the fifth *paṭala* declares the validity of the said rite to be similar to a royal decree.[53] The sixth chapter or *paṭala* in concluding this *prayoga* and describing the other *prayogas* of the goddess cryptically asserts that these are only valid for *rājās* and not for the *dvija*.[54] This warning may be retroactive assertion to cement the patron(s) of the rite to assert their royalty or 'royalness'. The naming of the *prayoga* is reminiscent of the Vedic *rājasūya yajña* especially of the *ratnins* of the *ratninam havimśi*. The *ratnins* in the context of the later Vedic society were seen a 'king makers' or *rājakartṛ*. These *rājakartṛs* represented specific groups which represented the kingdom of the *rājan*. N. N. Bhattacharyya saw these people as 'pressure groups' who checked the king from being an 'absolute despot'.[55] In our ritual the *sundarīs* as described in the appendix belong not to specific occupations but are from different *varṇa-jāti* groups and even from tribal communities. These *sundarīs* are conceived as the *śaktis* of their respective stations in life and the invocations of them in the *maṇḍala* represent the future fief of the *sādhaka*. These can be seen from the *ratnins* as represented in the Vedic sources:

Table 9.1 The *Ratnins* of the *Rājasūya Yajña*.[56]

The Texts	*Ratnins*	Number of *ratnins*	Relation to the royal household	Relation to the royal 'bureaucracy'	Non-royal occupation
Taittirīyasaṃhitā and the *Taittirīyabrāhmaṇa*	*brāhmaṇa, rājanya, mahiṣī, vāvātā, parivṛktī, senānī, sūta, kṣattṛ, saṁgrahitṛ, bhāgadughā, akṣāvāpa.*	11	*rājanya, mahiṣi, vāvātā, parivṛktī*	*brāhmaṇa senānī sūta kṣattṛ saṁgrahitṛ bhāgadughā akṣāvāpa*	
Śatapatha-Brāhmaṇa	*senānī, purohita, mahiṣī, sūta, grāmaṇī, kṣattṛ, saṃgrahitṛ, bhāgadughā, akṣāvāpa, go-vikartana, pālagala, parivṛktī.*	12	*mahiṣī parivṛktī*	*senānī, purohita sūta gramāṇī, kṣattṛ, saṃgrahitṛ, bhāgadughā, akṣāvāpa*	*go-vikartana, pālagala*(?), *sūta*
Maitrāyaṇī Saṁhitā	*brāhmaṇa, rājan, mahisī, parivṛktī, senāni, saṃgrahitṛ, kṣattṛ, sūta, vaiśyagrāmaṇī, bhāghadughāhatakṣa-rathakarau, akṣāvāpa, go-vikarta*	13	*rājan, mahisī, parivṛktī,*	*brāhmaṇa, saṃgrahitṛ, kṣattṛ, sūta, bhāghadughā, akṣāvāpa,*	*sūta, vaisyagrāmaṇī, takṣa-rathakarau, go-vikarta,*

Unlike the Vedic ritual which betrays the prominence of a clan society, our ritual is more concerned with the king and the idea of kingship. The *sundarīs* are just a means to an end; they fulfil their roles as signifiers of an ideal Brahmanic kingdom or any kingdom with the occupations they symbolize. This is further symbolized by the criteria they must fulfil to become a *sundarī* as detailed in the appendix.

Conclusion

Further studies on the whole the *MKS* are a desideratum of this author. The rites or *prayoga* described of the twin goddesses of the text provide details about how the Kaula tradition matured. This also goes to show how Śākta Tantric tradition slowly eschews its ultra-transgressive stance on ritual activity and balances moderate transgressions in the end to strengthen the orthodox order. This text is suspended between early understanding of Tantra and final shape this tradition takes in the early modern period. From becoming a legitimate philosophical tradition and yet vested in visceral rites, the *MKS* documents what the tradition becomes when it is received by John Woodroffe and others in the nineteenth and twentieth centuries. Unlike the Vedic sources, our text does not seek validity of rule through his kinsmen and officials, here the goddess is the source of that authority and the *sundarīs* are the representation of the kingdom as the prize of a successful ritual accomplishment. The ritual thus sanctifies as a symbol of kingly authority and for those who wish to rule, fruit of that desire.

Appendix – The *Sundarīs* of the *Rājapūrvayoga*

i.) The Thirty-Six *Sundarīs* of the *Prayoga* (vv. 5.19–23)
brāhmaṇī, kṣatriyā, vaiśya, śudrā, dāsī, naṭī, mālākāriṇī, kumbhakāriṇī, śaucikī, kuvindī, tantuvā, asimārjikā, rajakī, carmakārastrī, kārikā, śauṇḍikī, nāpitī, tvāṣṭrī, kalādī, kāmbarī, kaivartī, saulvikī, tailakāriṇī, māgadhī, veśyā, kumārī, ābhīrā, puṁścalī, sairindhrī, dūtikā, raṇḍā, prativeśnīkā, svajāyā, jīvanī. And with the addition of *cāṇḍālī* and *rājakanyā* the list becomes thirty-six.

The text also specifies these women should be well behaved (*sādhuśīlāṁ*) and beautiful. When worshipping these beauties, the adept ironically is warned not to be lustful. With the list of proscribed 'beauties' one now comes to the list of prohibited women for this *prayoga*.

ii.) The Women Who Are Unfit for the *Rājapūrvaprayoga* (vv. 145–146) *ṛṣikanyā*, alcoholic (*na cākarṣenmadhyapānāṁ kanyākām*), son's wife (*antyajānāṁ striyaṁ*), observant of a *vrata* (*vratasthānāṁ striyaṁ*), guru's kinswoman and wife (*gurvāṅganāṃ guroḥ patnīṁ*), one's own kin women (*sagotrāṁ*), one who's provided shelter (*śaraṇāgatāṃ*), student's wife (*śiṣyayoṣāṁ*), sinner's daughter (*pāpināṁ vanitāṁ*), one who has not menstruated (*nāpuṣpitāṁ*), one who is pregnant (*gurviṇīṁ*), and finally who has children (*bālāpatyāṁ*).

The bringing of the women for the *prayoga* is described as attraction as one is to understand that the worship of these *sundarīs* will attract the Goddess Kāmakalākālī, who in turn will attract the manifold unimaginable fruits of this *prayoga*.

Notes

1 It belongs to the Kaula strand of Tantric Śaivism and dedicated to the forms of eponymous *khaṇḍas* of the *MKS*.

2 A small summary of the contents of the text will be provided as an appendix in the end of the paper.

3 Jha, Kishoranatha. 1976. '*Prastāvanā* (Introduction)'. In *Mahākālasaṃhitā* of Ādinātha, *Guhyakālīkhaṇḍa* (G), edited by Kishoranatha Jha, Vol. I. Allahabad: Ganganatha Jha Kendriya Sanskrit Vidyapitha, 9.

4 Kaviraja, Gopinatha. 1971. '*Bhūmikā* (Introduction)'. In *Mahākālasaṃhitā* of Ādinātha, *Kāmakalākālīkhaṇḍa* (K), edited by Kishoranatha Jha. Allahabad: Ganganatha Jha Kendriya Sanskrit Vidyapitha, 24.

5 Mallinson, James. 2007. The *Khecarīvidyā of Ādinātha: A Critical Edition and Annotated Translation of an Early Text of Haṭhayoga*. London: Routledge. 172–3.

6 *Mahākālasaṃhitā, G*, Introduction. 7. Narasiṁha Ṭhākkura is a quite interesting figure. He was also famous for promoting the cult of Guhyakālī in Nepal in the court of Pratāpa Malla in 1654 CE. In the founding legend of the Guhyeśvarī (Guhyakālī) and was associated with our text *Mahākālasaṃhitā* as proven by his commentary on the text and also by the legend. This text particularly, the *Guhyakālīkhaṇḍa* is closely associated with the cult of Guhyeśvarī to this day. For more information refer to, Michaels, Axel. 2008. *Śiva in Trouble: Festivals and Rituals at the Paśupatinātha Temple of Deopatan*. Oxford: Oxford University Press. 132–3, 140.

7 Dyczkowski, Mark S.G. 2009. *Manthānabhairavatantram: Kumārikākhaṇḍaḥ*, Vol. 3, ed. and tr. Mark S.G. Dyczkowski. New Delhi: IGNCA. 401–3. The dating of the text is uncertain but the reference

to *Mantramahodadhi* puts the upper limit of the text to 1588 CE. Dyczkowski is of the opinion that from the contents one can reasonably go for a later date.

8 *K, (Kāmakalākālīkhaṇḍa)* Introduction, 7. The appendix (*Pariśiṣṭam*) to this edition has included the portions of Narasiṃha Thākkura and Pratāpa Siṃha's works which allude to the *MKS*.

9 Teun Goudriaan and Sanjukta Gupta, 2020. (1981). *A History of Indian Literature: Volume II, Facsimile 2: Hindu Tantric and Śākta Literature*, 154–5.

10 *Mahākālasaṃhitā, G*, Foreword, ka – jña and *Mahākālasaṃhitā* of Ādinātha, *Kāmakalākalīkhaṇḍa*, Umeśa Mishra's Foreword, Gaṅgānātha Jhā Kendrīya Saṃskṛta Vidyāpiṭha, Allahabad, 1971. i–iv.

11 Sanderson, Alexis. 1988. 'Śaivism and the Tantric Traditions'. In *The World's Religions*, edited by S. Sutherland, L. Houlden, P. Clarke and F. Hardy. Boston: Routledge, 685.

12 Alexis Sanderson, 'The Śaiva Literature'. *Journal of Indological Studies*, (24 & 25) (2012–13): 6–7, although the Kaula tradition was still influential in the early modern period and there were adherents of this system present in colonial India.

13 Sanderson, 'Śaivism and the Tantric Traditions', 680.

14 Ibid.

15 Kuleśvara and Kuleśvarī are the deities who are invoked within the body of the *sādhaka* who aid in the transfiguration of the said *sādhaka*. They are invoked within the body of the *sādhaka* and they are the source for all the other deities whom the adept invokes through *nyāsa*. Ibid.

16 Ibid.

17 *K*, 14.36.

18 Sanderson, 'The Śaiva Literature', 66.

19 Alexis Sanderson, 2003. 'The Śaiva Religion among the Khmers (Part I)'. *Bulletin de l'Ecole française d'Extrême-Orient*, Tome 90–91: 370.

20 Dyczkowski, *The Canon of Śaivāgama*, 67.

21 The *Guhyakālīkhaṇḍa* and by extension the *MKS* is dated by some to the tenth century CE but in light of above details it is hardly tenable. It's not wholly uncommon for some later Tantric texts to follow anachronistic precedents than the period of its composition.

22 These are Dakṣiṇakālī, Bhadrakālī, Śmaśānakālī, Kālakālī, Guhyakālī, Kāmakalākālī, Dhanakālī, Siddhikālī and Caṇḍakālī; *K*, 1.42–44.

23 *K*, 14.31–32.

24 *K*, 14.25–26.

25 *K*, 2.16–49.

26 He is largely absent from the text. He is mentioned as recipient of the first *āhuti* in the thirteenth *prayoga* of the third *paṭala*. His name is also similarly missing in the *ṣoḍānyāsa*, the one dedicated to the fifty-one Bhairavas. The interesting part of this *nyāsa* is that its starts with

Narasiṃha, who is the consort of Guhyakālī according to the *G*. The third *nyāsa* of the *ṣoḍānyāsa*, though titled *Kāmakalā* is dedicated to Kāmadeva. This might point towards Kāma and his association with the Nityās of the earlier tradition. Interestingly in the *Vāmakeśvarīmata*, the consort of Tripurāsundarī is absent and we believe this might have influenced our text. See, Anya Golovkova, 'The Goddess's Forgotten Consort: Desire in the Nityā Cult and the Cult of Tripurasundarī' in *International Journal of Hindu Studies*, 24(1): 93.

27 She seeks him out for sexual union.

28 This is in the second half of the seventh *paṭalaḥ* nearly over 103 verses are dedicated for describing the yogic anatomy of the body and mastery over the six *cakras*. This section is quite interesting as here in five verses (7.175–179) it seems to argue for seeking *mokṣa* over *siddhis*. This, however, is overshadowed by verses 196–200 which talk about the different duration of the *dhyānas*, which lead to *siddhis* again. However, if one meditates for a day and a night, they gain *jīvanamukti*.

29 *K*, 10.1–24. The *stotra* is numbered differently from the latter part as the verses concerning the *prasannākalaśa* and *śaktisāmarasya vidhi* are numbered again from one.

30 *K*, Kishoranatha Jha and Gopinatha Jha eds., Introduction, 5–9.

31 As a representative of this assertion one can look at the thirteen *prayogas* of the third *paṭala*, (3.34–76). But as we will discuss later this worked within a controlled environment.

32 Specific rites of the third *paṭalaḥ* will be dealt with in the appendix. Later in this section we will discuss some rites which pointed towards certain *siddhis*.

33 These prescriptions include that the woman should not be of a *varṇa* higher than one's own. *K*, 10.15–20.

34 *bhaktau dṛḍhāyāṃ jātāyāṃ sarvā sarveṣu śasyate* || *K*, 10.20.b.

35 The difference in the *prayoga* hierarchy arises from the number of *sundarīs*. These numbers are mentioned in the beginning of the sixth *paṭala*. This is mainly based one capability of the adept. For *madhya* it's twenty-four and for *laghu* twelve.

36 They are all women. The list of the same will be provided in the appendix.

37 These are described as generic high-quality clothes and are to one's wish. *K*, 5.33.

38 From the text it seems, there is a temple structure receiving regular worship (*samarhaṇaikamandire viracya tatra maṇḍalamah*, *K*, 5.47a) envisioned where the *maṇḍala* is to be made.

39 The scheme followed in the *paṭalaḥ* are East = White, South East = Red (*aruṇa*), South = Dark blue or Black (*mecaka*), South West = Yellow, West = Pink (*pāṭala*), North-West = Green, North = Tawny or Yellowish brown (*piṅgala*) and North east = Smoky (*dhumalama*). Only East

is referred as *pūrva* and the others are denoted by the Dikpāla of the respective direction. *K*, 5.47b–48.

40 *K*, 2.45–49.

41 In the sense one who beheads the animal.

42 For a discussion on similar strategies of importance through secrecy, look at, Urban, Hugh. 2003. 'The Power of the Impure: Transgression, Violence and Secrecy in Bengali Śākta Tantra and Modern Western Magic'. *Numen*, 50 (3): 269–308.

43 *K*, 5.141–144.

44 *K*, 3.29.

45 Used in similar sense of *varṇa*.

46 *K*, 10.20.b; *bhaktau dṛḍhāyāṁ jātāyāṁ sarvā sarveṣu śāsyate||*.

47 Urban, 'The Power of the Impure', 287–8.

48 For a broader discussion on the Oiṇīvāras refer, Jha, Pankaj. 2019. *A Political History of Literature: Vidyapati and the Fifteenth Century*. New Delhi: Oxford University Press. 26–31. Jha notes that very little is known about this dynasty and the that which is known with certainty is its dynastic succession chart.

49 Sarkar, Bihani. 2017. *Heroic Shāktism: The Cult of Durgā in Ancient Indian Kingship*. Oxford: Oxford University Press. 234–58.

50 Ibid., 248–50.

51 Ibid., 271.

52 Ibid.

53 *K*, 5.14.a.

54 *K*, 6.3.a.

55 Bhattacharyya, N. N. 2005 (1975). *Ancient Indian Rituals and Their Social Contents*. New Delhi: Manohar. 62.

56 Bhattacharyya, N. N. 2005 (1975). *Ancient Indian Rituals*, 61.

10

Confronting the *Aṣṭamahābhaya*: Goddess Tārā as Redeemer and Protector

Megha Yadav

Protector from the eight dangers - lions, elephants and fire,
Serpents, robbers, water, plagues
and piśācas - Homage to You!
In this life and in others,
from the eight fears please protect me![1]

The goddess Tārā manifests herself in multiple universes and has varying interpretations in the Buddhist imagination. She embodies the roles of a *Bodhisattva,* a Buddha, as well as the mother of all the Buddhas. She is venerated through a diverse set of practices and rituals. Sometimes, she has two forms: Green Tārā and White Tārā. On the other hand, she has twenty-one forms, and in yet another manifestation, she is worshipped as Aṣṭamahābhaya Tārā (saviour from eight great fears). The great range of her forms attests to her wide-ranging popularity, starting from Indian Buddhism and travelling to Nepal, Tibet, China, Japan and Southeast Asia. Various materials asserting her worship and practice have been uncovered from all these regions. The origin of the goddess Tārā is surrounded by debates. She is found both in Brahmanical as well as Buddhist texts, which have led to discussions regarding her origin. Despite her unknown origins, she became a prominent Buddhist goddess by the seventh century CE. In the visual landscape of Buddhism, she makes her first appearance in the cave sites of western India. At Nalanda and Kanheri, Avalokiteśvara appears with a pair of female attendants, one of whom bears a lotus, perhaps an earlier representation of Tārā. These representations evolve through the carvings in the western India caves—Ajanta, Aurangabad, Nasik, Kanheri and Ellora. Within these cave sites, the basic iconography of Tārā seems to have come into place by the seventh century CE. Additionally, she also emerged as a prominent figure in the Buddhist textual tradition around the same time. The basic canonical text associated with her is the *Tārā-mūla-kalpa,* composed in the seventh century CE. Over time, her universe expanded multifold and incorporated a varied range of forms, representations, narratives and roles. Despite this multifaceted development over the centuries, one common element to survive was her association with Avalokiteśvara. In later forms of Buddhism, notably Tibetan, she is also associated with many other Buddhas, but the presence of Avalokiteśvara still continues. In Indian Buddhism, she remained strongly associated with Avalokiteśvara in one way or another in her many forms. This indicates the presence of an ever-evolving, interacting and changing mythical universe. This changing universe, in its historical context, can be traced through the textual and visual landscape of the time. Buddhist divinities and their iconography have attracted a great amount of scholarship. Picron argues for the multiplicity of such imagery and identifies at least two different levels of their understanding: some conscious, which he qualifies as 'exoteric', and some unconscious, which he regards as (to a certain degree) 'esoteric'.[2] This chapter is an attempt to enquire into the making of Aṣṭamahābhaya Tārā and locate her (in both forms – exoteric and esoteric) in the textual-visual landscape of the early medieval Buddhist paradigm in the Indian subcontinent.

Conceptualizing *Aṣṭamahābhaya* in the Buddhist Tradition

References to fear and the state of being fearful are rampant in Pāli literature,[3] particularly in the *Sutta Piṭaka*. It is a state to be avoided by both monastics and lay followers. Brekke argues for a paradox of fear in Pāli literature. On one hand, fear is seen as the natural form of *sāṃsārika* existence. The basic facts of life – like birth, sickness, aging and death – cause fear in living beings. On the other hand, fear is a necessary state of mind in the striving to escape from *sāṃsārika* existence and achieve freedom. Thus, fear is both a positive and a negative thing[4]; both immediate and absolute. Absolute fear is needed to aspire for freedom from *saṃsāra* and immediate fears are the obstacles. Hence, it is the immediate/ *sāṃsārika* fear that needs to be removed. The most prominent immediate fear is associated with emotions and danger. Pāli texts discuss emotions, and fear arising out of them and their removal at various locations. *Piyavagga* of the *Dhammapada* in several verses explains the interconnection between pleasant and painful feelings. What is pleasurable (*piya*), affection (*pema*), fondness (*rati*), desire (*kāma*), and craving (*taṇhā*) all lead to grief (*śoka*) and fear (*bhaya*). Hence, overcoming fear is an integral part of a monk's practice to remove worldly attachments.[5] The *sāṃsārika* fears can also be of two kinds: social fears and physical fears. Different sections of the Pāli canon focus on different kinds of fears. For our purpose here, we are restricting ourselves to physical fears. *Bhayabherava Sutta* of *the Majjhima Nikāya* of *Sutta Piṭaka* is one of the early texts that entirely revolves around the idea of fear, particularly of the forest and wilderness. The question of this fear arises out of the need for the monks to stay at such places many times. Here, Buddha says that these fears will not affect those who would be of pure mind, self-awakened and go to the Buddha for refuge.[6] Similarly, the question of a monk's behaviour and troubles arising out of his lonely dwelling in the forest, charnel grounds, mountains, etc. has been raised by Śāriputta to Buddha in the *Sutta Nipāta.* While giving an exposition on the behaviour of a monk, Buddha gives us a list of physical troubles that might create fear in a monk's heart; *daṃsa* (mosquito bites), *adhipāta, siriṃsapa, manussaphassa* (attack by men) and *catuppada* (animals).[7] All these fears correspond with life in the forest/secluded areas. In these situations, one is supposed to calm their mind and 'recollect' Buddha. This 'recollection' will drive the fear away.[8] In the Pāli tradition, Buddha is the dispeller of anguish, terror and fear.[9] As Buddha became more and more deified over time, the fears received their protector deity. This marks the beginning of the emergence of a series of deities protecting their devotees from an array of fears and situations. Early Mahāyāna texts also follow the path of Pāli literature and discussion of fear finds a place in these texts as well.

The Saddharmapuṇḍarīka Sūtra,[10] while talking about Avalokiteśvara gives us a glimpse of various kinds of fears that one may have, particularly mentioning the fears of fire, drowning, snakes, evil spirits, thunderbolts and violence (pushed off/chased down a mountain, bodily harm through spells, curses, etc., evil spirits).[11] In another place, it talks about the fear of bandits and foes.[12] In this text, the role of protector is played by Avalokiteśvara and is known as *Abhayaṃdada*, meaning 'he who gives freedom from fear'.[13] In the earlier list of fears, this text has two new additions; fire and drowning. By the time we have the composition of *Lalitavistāra,*[14] the idea of eight great fears seems to have come into place. Interestingly, in this text, the collection of eight things seems to have prominently emerged such as eight great merits, eight great treasures, eight supreme attributes and so on along with eight great fears. Here, the list of eight fears includes (1) rulers, (2) thieves, (3) malicious beings, (4) starvation in the wilderness, (5) fights, quarrels and disputes, (6) gods, (7) *Nāgas* and (8) *Yakṣas.*[15] A further change in the list of eight great fears happened around the fifth to sixth century CE. In the visual tradition of western Indian and Deccan Buddhist caves, the fears are enraged animals (lions), snakes, elephants, evil spirits (might be a representation of *yakṣas* of *Lalitavistāra*), shipwreck, captivity and slavery, the sword of the enemy, and fire.

While the items in the list of fears seem to have been changing, after *Lalitavistāra*, the number eight becomes the standard number of 'great fears'. The changes in the things to be feared can be attributed to the changing socio-political context in which some new challenges arose, and some older ones became redundant. For example, the addition of rulers to the list of great fears in *Lalitavistāra* does indicate more interaction between the Buddhist monks and the rulers and possibly, a hostile relationship between the two in the region of the composition of the text. In the list of the western caves, the most notable new fear is the fear of the waters or shipwreck which in the visual tradition has been represented by a boat in trouble in the middle of the sea, a clear depiction of the seafaring activities. Many scholars have already shown us the rise of mercantile activities via sea route by the fifth century CE. By the sixth century, we have a fairly worked-upon list of eight great fears which after this acquires a more fixed form. The fears represented in the visual landscape of western cave sites, Deccan sites, as well as eastern sites, follow the same list: lions, snakes, elephants, evil spirits/demons, shipwrecks, captivity and slavery, the sword of the enemy/ruler, and fire.

Aṣṭamahābhaya in the Tārā-Avalokiteśvara Tradition

No study of the goddess Tārā can take place without considering the cult of Avalokiteśvara, particularly when discussing the *aṣṭamahābhaya* form of the deities. The cult of Avalokiteśvara predates the cult of Tārā in early Mahāyāna, but the popularity of Tārā develops to the same status and sometimes even challenges the popularity and authority of Avalokiteśvara. In the Mahāyāna pantheon, Avalokiteśvara makes his first appearance in the *Amitābha Vyūha Sūtra,* popularly known as the longer *Sukhāvatī Sūtra,*[16] as one of the two prominent Bodhisattva attendants of Buddha Amitāyus. Among the early *sūtras*, his cult further developed in texts like the *Avataṃsaka Sūtra* and *Saddharmapuṇḍarīka Sūtra,* and later in texts like the *Lalitavistāra.* The *Avataṃsaka Sūtra*[17] refers to Avalokiteśvara as the wise one, the compassionate one and the guide of all beings on the Bodhisattva path.[18] While the *Saddharmapuṇḍarīka Sūtra* introduces him as a saviour and protector, the role of protector seems to have been a very integral part of the conceptualization of the figure of Avalokiteśvara since its inception. In these early depictions, he is portrayed as having taken a vow to rescue beings from a range of dangers and fears, including calamity, threat, confusion, bondage, attacks on their lives, insufficiency of means to support life, inability to make a living, ill repute, the perils of life, intimidation by the crowd, death, miserable conditions, unknown hardships, servitude, separation from loved ones, living with the uncongenial, physical violence, mental violence, sorrow and depression.[19] This text also refers to Vāsantī (night goddess) as a protector. Similar to Avalokiteśvara, she also has a long list of external as well as internal fears from which she saves beings. This is a very extensive list of fears, clearly made with the idea of encompassing almost every aspect of existence. The cult reached its zenith in the fifth to sixth century CE with the composition of many texts exclusively dedicated to Avalokiteśvara and his prominent position in the visual landscape of Mahāyāna Buddhism. Cave sites (in the western Deccan) of Ajanta,[20] Ellora,[21] Kanheri[22] and Aurangabad[23] attest to the popularity of this figure in the visual landscape. While the literary tradition talks about a varied range of fears and dangers from which Avalokiteśvara protects, it is in the visual tradition that the idea of *eight great fears* acquires greater consolidation along with Avalokiteśvara being the protector from these.[24] The fears vary between the literary depiction and visual terrain, as has been explored in the previous section. With the consolidation of eight great fears, Avalokiteśvara was the first deity to be associated with them and protect devotees from them. Around the sixth - seventh century CE, he remains firmly associated with this role and finds representation as Aṣṭamahābhaya Avalokiteśvara. In this period, along with his popularity, we also see the expansion of mythology related to him.

In the expanding universe of Avalokiteśvara mythology, we find the emergence of the goddess Tārā as his attendant, which is evident from visual material from both the eastern (Nalanda) and western (Kanheri) parts of the Indian subcontinent. There is an abundance of mythology surrounding the origin and functions of Tārā. All origin stories of Tārā locate her genesis with Avalokiteśvara, except for one, which relates her birth to Buddha Amitābha. Most popularly, she is seen as the personification of Avalokiteśvara's compassion (*karuṇā*). It is believed that Tārā comes forth in every age, and in this age, once Avalokiteśvara looked down in compassion on the pain of humanity. He saw suffering everywhere. He saw beings born in suffering, dying in suffering, and afflicted by diseases, wars and famines. He saw beings not obtaining what they desired and obtaining what they did not desire. He also saw that, however many beings he helped to escape from the fruitless round of mundane existence, the overall number grew no smaller – and for this, he wept. The tears streamed down his face and formed a great pond. From the depths of its water sprang a blue lotus, and on the lotus appeared the shimmering form of a beautiful sixteen-year-old girl. Her body was delicate, and its translucent green seemed to hover between reality and non-reality, quivering with an energy that could be seen, heard and felt. She was clad in the silks and jewels of a princess, and her hands, expressing boundless giving and refuge, held deep blue lotuses. Born of Avalokiteśvara's tears of compassion, she was herself the quintessence of compassion. She who is bright, of the beautiful eyes, Tārā, the joy of starlight, had once again appeared in this world.[25] Despite an abundance of popular origin stories, the early history of this cult is not well established. The conception of Tārā as the companion of Avalokiteśvara emerged in the early phase of the development of the cult between the sixth and eighth centuries CE.[26] Tārā appears first in the visual landscape rather than the literary world. Many of the Buddhist sites (particularly, Nalanda and western cave sites) carry the earliest representations of this goddess. Her earliest depiction is believed to be of an attendant of Avalokiteśvara, standing behind him and holding a lotus. In the absence of properly recognizable features, this image can only be presumed to be of Tārā. In other depictions in the caves of Kanheri, Ellora and Aurangabad, her depictions are clearer and more identifiable. Her emergence in Buddhist literature can at best be seen as contemporary to these visual depictions or a bit later in the sixth to seventh century CE.

According to Hiuen Tsang, by the seventh century, there were many statues of Tārā in northern Buddhism,[27] she emerged as a Bodhisattva of her own accord and developed a range of literature, paintings and rituals etc. resulting in the multiplication of her forms and taking over Avalokiteśvara as the protector from the eight great fears. The popularity of Tārā in this role, Aṣṭamahābhaya Tārā is attested by the abundant literary and visual material found in various parts of the Indian subcontinent as well as from other parts of Asia. A relief from cave no 9, Ellora, dated to the middle of the seventh century CE is believed to be the earliest visual representation of Aṣṭamahābhaya Tārā.[28] The relief portrays her in the same manner as Aṣṭamahābhaya Avalokiteśvara of the Aurangabad caves. The goddess stands at the centre with eight small panels depicting the dangers and a small figure of the deity on both sides of the central figure. Although Avalokiteśvara played a definitive role during the formative period of Tārā's cult, he did not continue once Tārā's popularity gained momentum and started to spread beyond the borders of the Indian subcontinent.

From the eighth century CE onwards, Tārā invariably became the protector, in both the visual and literary landscape of Buddhism, across the Indian subcontinent and beyond. In the literary tradition, Tārā first appears in three tantras, *Ārya Mañjuśrī-Mūla-Kalpa* (MMK), *Tārā-Mūla-Kalpa* (TMK), and *Vairocana-Abhisaṃbodhi-Tantra* (VAT). Out of these three, some sections of MMK seem to be the oldest and can be assigned to the sixth century CE. In these sections of MMK, Tārā makes her first appearance. Based on the comparative study of these texts, the composition of TMK has been assigned to the seventh century CE. It was composed concurrently with or subsequent to VAT and the first thirteen chapters of MMK.[29] TMK forms the core of the Tārā worship. The three texts share a very close affiliation in terms of the commonly occurring characters, settings and descriptions of the deities. In fact, many chapters in TMK and MMK are almost the same with the difference in the key deities of Tārā and Mañjuśrī. All of them introduce Tārā in the context of Avalokiteśvara. MMK describes her as being adorned with all kinds of jewellery and wearing a red bodice and brightly coloured silk garments. In her left hand, she holds a blue lotus (*utpala*). Her body colour is golden and her waist is slim, but not overly so. She is neither too young nor too old. Her mind is absorbed in meditation, and she is awaiting an order. Her body is slightly bent forward with her right hand holding the *varada mudrā*. She sits in a cross-legged posture, turning her gaze slightly towards Avalokiteśvara. She is surrounded by a halo of blazing light.[30] Here, among many attributes of the goddess, she is also invoked as a protector.

> The goddess removes all obstacles and is the ultimate destroyer of fear. For the protection of the practitioner, she should be painted as the virtuous granter of boons.[31]

> In order to completely remove practitioner's every obstacle; to ensure protection by the rulers of men, and to bring prosperity, she should be installed on the canvas.[32]

While all these canonical texts, particularly TMK, discuss the representations of goddess Tārā at length and mention her role as a protector, not much about the iconography of Aṣṭamahābhaya Tārā specifically can be found in these texts. The cult of Aṣṭamahābhaya Tārā seems to be more of a result of visual and poetic traditions. Her popularity came to be immortalized in the works of several devotee poets along with visual representations. Between the seventh and tenth centuries CE, several poets like Mātṛceṭa,[33] Candragomin, Sūryagupta, Sarvajñamitra, Dīpaṃkara Bhadra, Nāgārjuna,[34] Candrakīrti and Atiśa Dīpaṃkara Jñānaśrī[35] composed poems in her praise (along with several anonymous works),[36] including her role as the great protector in the form of Aṣṭamahābhaya Tārā (see Table 1). Further, devotee poets from the Tibetan lineage translated and composed more texts in praise of her. The poetic tradition of Aṣṭamahābhaya Tārā flourishes with these devotee poets and forms the premise for the expansion of her cult in this form in other parts of Asia. The details of these devotee poets are found mostly in the later date Tibetan sources[37] and their works have been preserved in the *Tengyur* collection. The identity of many of these scholars has been the subject of many enquiries and debates among the modern scholars of Buddhism. The confusion primarily occurs due to different catalogues having varying reference material and comparatively a later period of sources for the study of these scholars. This chapter will only look at three of these devotee poets, i.e. Mātṛceṭa, Candragomin and Sarvajñamitra, due to the paucity of space. Other poets will be discussed elsewhere.

In the Tibetan collections, two praises of Tārā have been credited to Mātṛceṭa: a short eulogy (explaining her iconography and her name), *Ārya Tārā Stotra,* and a longer, more elaborate praise, *Ārya Tārādevī Stotra Sarvārtha Sādhanā Nāma Stotra Rājā* (*TSSSNSR*). In both poems, the author mentions various attributes and iconographical elements of the goddess. She sits on a lotus and moon pedestal, belongs to the lotus family, saves sentient beings from the misery of this world, and so on. However, it is in the *TSSSNSR* that her role as saviour from the eight great fears finds a place.[38] Although she is not explicitly given the name *Aṣṭamahābhaya*, the list of eight fears is provided. These fears are described as *worldly fears* and include the fear of woe, kings, thieves, fire and water, lions, tigers, *rākṣasas* and snakes. The text further describes her as a saviour from diseases and curses.[39]

Candragomin, dated to the mid-seventh century CE, has been mentioned by I-Tsing in his writings. He is further mentioned in Taranath's account. According to these accounts, he was born in the kingdom of Varendra (now in Bangladesh)[40] and is believed to have been a scholar at Nalanda. Taranath gives him credit for writing 432 works,[41] although this number cannot be corroborated with the available works. But this certainly indicates the popularity of Candragomin in the Tibetan tradition. Both Avalokiteśvara and Tārā are believed to have been his tutelary deities.[42] Taranath places greater emphasis on Tārā as his protector. In one instance, he mentions:

> *Śeṣa-nāga, to avenge the harsh criticisms of the past, sent huge tidal waves in the sea, and his (Candragomi) ship was about to be wrecked. From inside the sea, came the voice: Throw out Candragomi. When he prayed to Tārā, the company of the five- the ārya herself and her attendants-came flying there on the back of Garuga. The Nāgas fled in terror. The ship safely reached Dhanasri.*[43]

This story is particularly relevant for showing Tārā as a protector in the sea and from shipwrecks. Out of all her praises, two are entirely developed around the theme of *aṣṭamahābhaya.* A third poem, *Ārya Tārā Devī Stotra Muktikā Mālā Nāma* (*TDSMMN*), translated into Tibetan by Atiśa Jñānśrī and Nak-ts'o, became the premise for her cult in Tibet in the eleventh century CE. This text enlists safety from all kinds of dangers as one of the benefits of the recitation of this praise.[44] Fear of poison and royal punishment have been explicitly mentioned but others have not been named. While two other poems, *Ārya Devī Tārā Stotra*[45] (*ADTS*) and *Ārya Tārā Mahā Aṣṭabhayōttara Stava* (*ATMAS*), have been entirely composed around the eight great fears. The first, *ADTS*, not only talks about the fears but also about their nature, power and how the goddess helps overcome all these fears. The poem has twelve verses, where the first verse is the homage and from verses 2 to 9, each verse is devoted to one kind of fear: angry lions, elephants, fire, snakes, robbers, prison, shipwrecks and *piśāca.* The next two verses add two more fears, the fear of leprosy and the fear of poverty/hunger. The final verse is a dedication of the merit of composing this poem to the world.[46] The second poem, *ATMAS*, is of ten verses only. The first verse is the homage and the last one is the dedication. Each verse from 2 to 9 has been devoted to one form of the eight fears. The same list as the previous poems has been followed here too.[47] A fourth poem, *Ārya Tārā Stotra Praṇidhāna Siddhi Nāma* (A Praise to Ārya Tārā-Accomplisher of Vows), although devoted to all aspects of the goddess gives a consolidate list of the eight great fears and the iconography of the Tārā. The fears are lions, elephants, fire, snakes, robbers, chains/prisons, the ocean and *piśāca.*[48]

Sarvajñamitra, according to Jinarakṣita, who wrote the commentary on his work, informs us that Sarvajñamitra was born in Kashmir and lived in the late seventh and early eighth centuries CE.[49] The same is also attested by *Rājataraṅgiṇī*[50] and later by Taranath's account of Buddhism in India.[51] In the Tibetan *Tengyur* collection, he has six works credited to his name. All of these works are dedicated to the goddess Tārā with a mention of her as a protector. Further, one work is entirely dedicated to the Aṣṭamahābhaya Tārā.[52] Similar to Candragomin, according to Taranath, Sarvajñamitra was also protected by the goddess Tārā from fire. Taranath gives us a story where Sarvajñamitra along with other 107 men was going to be sacrificed by a king for the attainment of powers. On the burning pyre, seeing the cries of other men, he started praying to the goddess Tārā. Keeping with her characteristics, she immediately appears and showers a stream of nectar from her haṇd on the burning woods; hence, saves Sarvajñamitra along with the other 107 men.[53] This once again manifests one of the elements

Table 10.1 Details of the Devotee-Poets.

Name of the Devotee Poet	Dating	Place	Socio-Political Background	Monastic Association
Mātṛceṭa[54]	Late 7th century CE		Brāhmaṇa	
Candragomin	Mid-7th century CE	Varendra (in Modern Bangladesh)	Born into a Kśatriya family; believed to be Paṇḍita in his previous life.	Nālandā
Sūryagupta	Mid–late 7th century CE / mid-9th century CE	Kashmir		
Sarvajñamitra	Late 7th–early 8th century CE	Kashmir	Born into a royal family	Nālandā
Śāntideva	Late 7th–early 8th century CE	Saurashtra (Western India)	Believed to have been born into a royal family.	
Nāgārjuna	Late 8th–early 9th century CE	Eastern India		Nālandā
Candrakīrti[55]	Early 9th century CE	Eastern India		Nālandā
Atiśa Dīpaṃkara Jñānaśrī	Late 10th–early 11th century CE	Vikramapura (in modern-day Bangladesh)	Born into a royal family	Vikramaśilā, Nālandā, Odantapurī, Somapurī

from the *Aṣṭamahābhaya.* This story with some variations is present in multiple texts. In all his six works, protection from the *Aṣṭamahābhaya* is a recurring theme.

The above table records only a few composers from the Tārā tradition. This list is by no means exhaustive.[56] Nonetheless, it reveals several patterns regarding the development of the Aṣṭamahābhaya Tārā tradition. Geographically, a greater number of scholars are located in the eastern part of the subcontinent, but other regions, except the peninsula, have also witnessed the presence of various such poets. Temporally, it highlights the concentration of these works primarily between seventh and tenth centuries CE, a period marked by a plethora of developments in the religious-cultural realm in the Indian subcontinent. The detailed study of these works reveals a very strong presence of the *bhakti* ideals among the composers of the texts. Bhakti involves focused attention and concentration towards the devotional object through recitation (*kīrtana*) and remembrance (*smaraṇa*). Although the terms *bhakti, kīrtana* and *smaraṇa* are not to be found in these writings, the process reveals the presence of the ideas. These writings were meant to be recited in times of distress and in later Tibetan Buddhism, the copying of the texts became an important method for the collection of merit by both the laity and the renunciate. In these works, great emphasis is laid on the ideals of faith and devotion as opposed to *karma,* which finds a larger place in the works of early Buddhism. These texts do not deny the influence of *karma* but are rather silent on the issue. The development of the ideas of devotion and faith on one hand and the consolidation of the list of eight great fears on the other hand gave birth to the popularity of the tradition of the Aṣṭamahābhaya Tārā.

Tibetan Tradition on *Aṣṭamahābhaya*

The story of Aṣṭamahābhaya Tārā was extensively elaborated within the Tibetan Buddhist tradition. Almost all the poems composed by these devotee poets were translated and preserved in Tibetan collections. Numerous similar poems with later dates form a large part of the Tārā texts in the Tibetan collections. In many cases where these poems were originally composed in Tibetan, information regarding the authorship and precise dating is often missing from the colophon. In later Tibetan developments, it was further added that the eight great fears do not only represent external fears but also correspond to eight internal fears. This theme was solidified with the composition of *The Crowning Ornament of the Wise*[57] (Tib., mKhas-pa'-gtcu ga-rKhyn), a fifteenth-century work written by Gedün-drupa (Wylie, dge-dun grub-pa), the first Dalai Lama, although this title was given to him long after his death. Most of this text takes its inspiration from the earlier work of Nāgārjuna. Many of the verses are almost identical; the unique contribution made by this text is the introduction of eight internal fears, corresponding with the eight external fears in the textual tradition: Lion (Pride), Elephant (Delusion), Fire (Anger), Snake (Envy), Thieves (Wrong Views), Flood (Attachment), Demons (Doubt) and Captivity (Greed).[58] Another popular contributing text in the cult of Aṣṭamahābhaya Tārā is the *Ārya Tārāṣṭaghora Tāraṇī Sūtra* (*Sūtra* of Arya Tārā who protects from eight fears). No extant Sanskrit version of this *Sūtra* has been found so far, nor is there any Chinese version recorded in the *Taishō* Buddhist canon. It is also not found in the Denkarma (*ldan dkar ma*) or Phangthangma (*phang thang ma*) Tibetan imperial translation inventories. The translation has no colophon, so we do not know who the translators were, nor do we have knowledge of any other circumstances surrounding the translation of this work into Tibetan. Fifteenth century onwards, we find an abundance of writing on Tārā following the themes of protection from the eight great external and internal fears; the study of which is beyond the scope of this paper.

Notes

1 *Tārāṣṭaghora Tāraṇī Sūtra*, trans. by Samye Translations. 2023. *Tārā Who Protects from the Eight Dangers*. Available at https://read.84000.co/translation/UT22084-051-001.html (accessed on 25 October 2023). verse 26.

2 Picron, Claudine Baut. 2016. 'Images of Devotion and Power in South and Southeast Bengal'. In *Esoteric Buddhism in Medieval Maritime Asia: Networks of Masters, Texts, Icons*, edited by Andrea Acri. Singapore: ISEAS Yusof Ishak Institute Press, 163–90. 164.

3 These references can be found in the literary composition of various religious traditions in the Indian Subcontinent, predating the Pāli literature. The earliest reference can be traced back to the Vedic literature.

4 Torkel, Brekke. 1999. 'The Role of Fear in Indian Religious Thought with Special Reference to Buddhism'. *Journal of Indian Philosophy*, 27 (5): 442.

5 Ibid. 440.

6 *Majjhima Nikāya: The Middle Length Sayings of the Buddha*, trans. by I.B. Horner. 2020. Available at http://buddhadust.net/backmatter/indexes/idx_downloads.htm#pts_pdfs (accessed on 15 December 2023). chapter 4.

7 *Buddha's Teachings Being the Sutta Nipāta or Discourse-Collection*, edited by Charles Rockwell Lanman. 1932. London: Oxford University Press. Aṭṭhaka Vagga 4, Sāriputta Sutta, verse 958–964.

8 Analayo, Bhikku. 2021. 'Overcoming Fear by Recollecting the Buddha: His Role in Early Buddhist Texts', *Mindfulness*, 12: 594–603, Springer, 600–1.

9 Torkel, Brekke. 1999. 442–3.

10 It is one of the earliest and most influential Mahāyāna texts, particularly among the East Asian Buddhist sects. The exact date of its composition can't be ascertained, but, in 255 CE, the text was translated into Chinese for the first time. Hence, most scholars place the original composition of the text between the first and second centuries CE. For further reading, see Burton, Watson. 1993. *The Lotus Sutra*. New York: Columbia University Press. 3–23.

11 *Saddharmapuṇḍarīka Sūtra*, trans. by Peter Alan Roberts. 2022. *The White Lotus of the Good Dharma*. Available at https://read.84000.co/translation/UT22084-051-001.html (accessed on 25 November 2022). verses 24.22–34.

12 Ibid., verse 24.5.

13 Ibid., verse 24.13.

14 *Lalitvistāra* is a story of an awakening of the Buddha from a Mahāyāna perspective. Although many times, it is considered a biography of Śākyamuni Buddha, the text is much broader in its approach and should not be seen as a historical biography. The earliest translation of this text appeared in Chinese in the fourth century CE by Dharamrakṣa. Hence, the original composition must be placed before that. But this text seems to be later than *Saddharmapuṇḍarīka Sūtra*. For further reading, see *Āryalalitavistāranāmamahāyānasūtra*. 2024. trans. by Dharmacakra Translation Committee, 84000: Translating the Words of the Buddha. Introduction. Available at https://read.84000.co/translation/UT22084-046-001.html#toc.

15 *Lalitvistāra*. Ibid., verse 27.11.

16 Exact date of the composition of the text has not been established. Although, the first translation of the text into the Chinese language seems to have happened in the second century CE which suggests an earlier date of the original composition of the text in the Indian subcontinent. For a detailed discussion, see Paul, Williams. 2009. *Mahāyāna Buddhism: The Doctrinal Foundation*. New York: Routledge. 239.

17 This text was composed between first and second centuries CE.

18 *The Avataṃsaka Sūtra*, trans. by Thomas Cleary. 1993. *The Flower Ornament Scripture*. London: Shambhala, 1275–6.

19 'The Avataṃsaka Sūtra'. Ibid. Chapter 39; *Saddharmapuṇḍarīka Sūtra*. Ibid. Chapter 24.

20 At Ajanta, this figure has been painted in caves no. 2, 4, 11 and 17 and it has been sculpted in caves no. 4, 20 and 26.

21 At Ellora, caves no. 3 and 4 carry the figure of *Aṣṭamahābhaya* Avalokiteśvara.

22 At Kanheri, the image is found in caves no. 2, 41 and 90.

23 At Aurangabad, the figure can be seen in the cave no. 7.

24 At Aurangabad, the following dangers are a part of the eight great dangers: Shipwreck, chains, attack with sword, fire, lions, snakes, elephants and *yakṣa*/evil spirits.

25 This story is recounted to us by Taranath in his *The Origin of Tara-Tantra*, written at the beginning of the seventeenth century. Although the text is fairly late, the legend recounted in this seems to be much older with other earlier works providing reference to these stories. His other work, *The Golden Rosary*, is also a great compilation of popular stories associated with Tārā. Most of these stories are set in the backdrop of the Gangetic belt, possibly indicating the Indian origin of these stories.

26 Landesman, Susan. 2008. 'Goddess Tārā: Silence and Secrecy on the Path to Enlightenment'. *Journal of Feminist Studies in Religion*, 24 (1): 44–59. 53.

27 Getty, Alice. 1914. *The Gods of Northern Buddhism: Their History, Iconography and Progressive Evolution through the Northern Buddhist Countries*. Oxford: Clarendon Press. 105.

28 Shaw, Miranda. 2006. *Buddhist Goddesses of India*. Oxford: Princeton University Press. 318.

29 *Tārā Mūla Kalpa*, trans. by Susan Landesman. 2020. *The Tārā Tantra Part I: The Root Tantra*, Treasury of the Buddhist Sciences Series. Massachusetts: Wisdom publication.

30 Ibid., verse 4.89.

31 Ibid., verse 4.91.

32 Ibid., verses 4.93, 4.94.

33 The identity of Mātṛceṭa varies from being a scholar of Theravāda Buddhism belonging to the second to third century CE to being a devotee of Vajrayāna Buddhism and possibly belonging to the post-seventh-century period. Tibetan collections overall ascribe eighteen works to him. The most popular text out of these, *Śatapañcāśataka,* is believed to be a pre-fourth-century CE work and is believed to be a work of Theravāda tradition. Out of all the works credited to him, two poems are dedicated to the goddess Tārā which are of Tantric nature. The earliest possible date for the composition of Tārā praises cannot be before the seventh century CE. The difference in nature of the works attributed to him presents a problem in the identification of the writer(s) of all these texts as the same person. However, there has not been much discussion on the possibility of multiple Mātṛceṭa, but that does seem to be a possibility. Alternatively, it is possible that by the time these poems reached Tibetan translators, the names of the composers were already lost, and poems were ascribed to an already well-known name to enhance the validity and popularity of the poems. This practice can be seen in the context of many other later date poems in the Tibetan Collections. For further reading on his dating, see Hartmann, Jens-Uwe. 1988. 'The *Triratnastotra* Ascribed to Mātṛceṭa'. In *Proceedings of the 4th Seminar of the International Association for Tibetan Studies*, edited by Helga Uebach and Jampa L. Panglung. Munich: BADW, 177–84; Wilson, Martin. 1996. *In Praise of Tārā: Songs to the Saviouress*. Somerville, Massachusetts: Wisdom Publications.

34 The identity of Nāgārjuna is a matter of debate; his dating, place and even the numbers of Nāgārjunas are not a conclusive matter. For a detailed discussion, see Mabett, Ian. 1998. 'The Problem of the Historical Nāgārjuna Revisited'. *Journal of the American Oriental Society*, 118 (3): 332–46.

35 Atiśa Dīpaṃkara Jñānaśrī was born in 982 CE, in Vikrampura, Bengal. He taught at various monasteries: Nālanda, Vikramaśilā, Odantapurī

and Somapurī. He was invited to Tibet by J'ang-ch'up-ö to spread the teachings of the Buddha in Tibet. In 1040 CE, Atiśa and two Tibetan monks left India for Tibet. It is recorded in several later date texts that Atiśa's tutelary deity, Tārā, played a key role in him deciding to go to Tibet. After receiving the invitation to come to Tibet, Atīśa had a visit by Tārā in his dreams where it was suggested to him that if he goes to Tibet, the age of the Dharma will increase but his own will decrease and if he decides to stay in India, his own age will increase but Dharma's age will diminish. After having this prediction from Tārā about Dharma, Atiśa decided to go to Tibet. For a detailed story of his travels, see Taranath. 1990. '*Dam pa'i chos rinpoche 'aphags-pa'i yul du ji ltar dar ba'i Tshul gsal bar ston pa dgos 'adod*'. In *Taranath's History of Buddhism in India*, trans. by Lama Chimpa, and Alaka Chattopadhyaya. Delhi: Motilal Banarsidass.

36 This chapter includes discussion only on those poems that include the praises for Aṣṭamahābhaya Tārā. Beyond these poets, praises by several other poets are included in the Tibetan collection which do not specifically mention the *Aṣṭamahābhaya* and hence, have not been included in the discussion here.

37 The stories of many of these devotees have been retold in Buston's *History of Buddhism* and Taranath's *History of Buddhism in India*.

38 The name Aṣṭamahābhaya Tārā occurs later in the text in the verse 25.

39 Mātṛceṭa. *Ārya Tārādevī Stotra Sarvārtha Sadhananāma Stotra Rāja*, trans. by Martin Wilson. 1996. *In Praise of Tārā: Songs to the Saviouress*. Massachusetts: Wisdom Publication. 214–21. verse 20.

40 Martin Wilson. Ibid. 223.

41 Taranath. Ibid. 207.

42 Ibid.

43 Ibid. 208.

44 Candragomin. *Ārya Tārādevī Stotra Muktikāmālā Nāma*, trans. by Martin Wilson. 1996. *In Praise of Tārā: Songs to the Saviouress*. Massachusetts: Wisdom Publication. 226–31. verses 38, 40. 230.

45 This poem is a part of the Tengyur collection.

46 Martin Wilson. 1996. 232–3.

47 Candragomin. *Ārya Tārā Mahā Aṣṭabhayōttara Stava*, trans. by Martin Wilson. 1996. *In Praise of Tārā: Songs to the Saviouress*. Massachusetts: Wisdom Publication. 236–7. verses 1–10.

48 Candragomin. *Ārya Tārā Stotra Praṇidhāna Siddhi Nāma*, trans. by Martin Wilson. 1996. *In Praise of Tārā: Songs to the Saviouress*. Massachusetts: Wisdom Publication. 234–5. verse 6.

49 Jinarakṣita. *Sragdharā Stotra Ṭikā*, edited by Satish Chandra Vidyabhusana. 1908. *Bauddha Stotra Saṁgrahaḥ* (1). Calcutta: Asiatic Society of Bengal.

50 Kalhaṇa, *Rājtaraṅgiṇī*, trans. by M.A.Stein. 1900. *Kalhaṇa's Rājtaraṅgiṇī: A Chronicle of the Kings of Kaśmīr*, Vol 1. 1900. Westminster: Archibald Constable & Company Ltd. verse iv. 210. 143.

51 Taranath, 220–3.
52 The list of his works in the Tengyur collection can be found at https://read.84000.co/knowledgebase/EFT-KB-SARVAJNAMITRA.html.
53 Taranath, 221–2.
54 See endnote 33.
55 According to Taranath, he was a disciple of Nāgārjuna.
56 Although, the number of scholars in Tārā lineage is very high, we restrict our discussion here on two accounts: one, only the scholars/works focusing on the *Aṣṭamahābhaya* tradition and two, the popularity of the works in the Tibetan tradition, have been taken here for discussion.
57 The full Tibetan name of the text, *rje-btsun bcom-ldan-'das-ma seng-ldeng-nags gyi sgrol-ma la bstod-pa mkhas-pa'i gtsug-rgyna zhes-bya-ba* (Here lies, The Crown Ornament of the Wise, Praise of the venerable Bhagawati Khadiravani Tara).
58 dge-'dun grub-pa. *rje-btsun bcom-ldan-'das-ma seng-ldeng-nags gyi sgrol-ma la bstod-pa mkhas-pa'I gtsug-rgyna zhes-bya-ba*, edited by Donal La Rocca and Lozang Jamspal. 2008. Available at https://www.academia.edu/44757178/The_Crowning_Ornament_of_the_Wise_and_The_Jewel_that_Increases_Wisdom_and_Longevity (accessed on 10 January 2024). verses 20–27.

Part Four

The Making of a Goddess: Contemporary Iterations

11

The *Avarṇa-Savarṇa* Masculine Goddess: Gender Fluidity and Caste Subversion in the Worship of Māriyammaṉ

Malavika Binny

The worship of Māriyammaṉ as a village goddess in south India dates back to the medieval period, according to textual sources. The fierce deity is worshipped predominantly by Dalit-Bahujan communities but also by Brahmins. Several colonial administrators and travellers have also mentioned Māriyammaṉ worship in south Indian villages. Bartholomäus Ziegenbalg, a Lutheran missionary who was instrumental in establishing the Danish-Halle Mission in Tranquebar, wrote about the multiple ways in which Māri was worshipped by distinct communities in India.[1] Māriyammaṉ is usually considered to be the goddess of the pox disease, but she is also worshipped as the rain-making goddess and as a guardian deity for the village. What is also interesting about the goddess is that she is referred to only as a minor deity within the textual tradition, but in terms of the number of temples and the grandeur of temple festivals, Māriyammaṉ shrines far outnumber those of any other goddess in south India. In fact, she is also the major deity in temples established by the south Indian diaspora, particularly by the Tamils, in countries to which they have migrated.[2] In post-independent India, with the increasing presence of the state's Devaswom Boards (the ministry in charge of the upkeep of temples) and the establishment of new temples by upwardly mobile caste communities, there has been a coalescence of temple traditions, leading to a hybridization of rituals and practices. This chapter engages with the twin issues of hybridization and gentrification, which have been occurring in the last decade in Māriyammaṉ temples in south India due to the popular, primarily *avarṇa,* cult gaining traction with *savarṇa* groups as well. It will also address caste and gender subversion, which are coded into the ritual and liturgical traditions of Māriyammaṉ worship.

In South Asia, goddesses have been associated with misery, misfortune or disease from at least the seventh century CE, one of the earliest references being that of Alakṣmī, depicted as the deity of misfortune, in contrast to Lakṣmī, who was the deity of prosperity and good luck. There are references to several female deities of disease and demonic nature from both the Puranic Hindu and Buddhist traditions, such as Hārītī, Parṇaśabarī and Jyeṣṭhā. While these deities were attributed with 'negative' powers of spreading pestilence, disease or morbidity, it did not prevent their worship by devotees, as these deities were also considered to be the ones who could pacify and resolve the dangers. Several of the 'mother goddess' tropes found among folk traditions also have a great resemblance to these deities within the Brahmanical and Buddhist fold. A classic example of the same is the Śrī Kuṟumpā tradition in Kerala, where Kuṟumpā is described as a playful goddess who controls both pestilence and disease.[3] She is sometimes described as an incarnation of Kaṇṇaki from *Cilappatikāram* and sometimes as Durgā. She is also sometimes fused with the image of Kālī. The Kuṟumpā tradition can be identified with Māriyammaṉ as well because of the great similarity with regard to her hymns and pox mythology. The identification of Kuṟumpā with Durgā seems to be later than the association with Kaṇṇaki or Pattinī, as most of the myths found in the *talapurāṇas* are associated with the later myths of Durgā, such as the Navadurgā myth. However, Kuṟumpā is also fundamentally a young virginal goddess, and her spreading of misery is attributed to her childishness, which contradicts her identification as Pattinī. In the distant past, she must have been a local deity who was worshipped as a goddess of disease and misfortune in the villages of central Kerala. Several such deities, most of whom are female, can be found along the southern coasts of Kerala, Karnataka and Tamil Nadu. D.D. Kosambi's arguments on the existence of a mother goddess tradition, which pre-dated Aryan forms of worship on the subcontinent, might be remembered in this context.[4] Using textual, visual and other sources from the Tamil south, R. Mahalakshmi analyses the coalescing of the goddess of the *Pālai tiṇai* – Koṟṟavai – into the Durgā of the Brahmanical pantheon. She describes how the former, depicted as the goddess of victory and war, was closely associated with divinity and the idea of Aṇaṅku, both of which are associated with power and sexuality in *Caṅkam* literature.[5] What is also interesting in her analysis is that Koṟṟavai is described as possessing a retinue of female attendants who are often described as demonic or malevolent in nature. For instance, the *pēymakaḷ*, who feed on the corpses of those slain in battle are vividly described in *Caṅkam* literature. Goddesses such as Māriyammaṉ and Kuṟumpā are also described using imagery that is strikingly similar to Koṟṟavai, and they too have female attendants who are referred to as the *pēymakaḷ* or are very similar to the *pēymakaḷ*. The trope of the fierce goddess who can cause both good and evil, with an entourage of attendants led by the *pēymakaḷ*, is a recurrent one across south Indian religious geography. We will return to this theme in a later section.

Situating Māriyammaṉ within Goddess Archetypes

South Asian goddess traditions are themselves unique, as pointed out by many scholars, often standing in stark contrast to the social realities faced by women of the subcontinent. The depiction of strong, fierce, blood-thirsty goddesses in South Asia does not directly align with the patriarchal values of the social milieu against which they are set, and often, a study of the same becomes a study of the semantics of contradiction. William Harman argues that 'though history shows that the goddess has assumed many distinctive changes in identity and form, the earlier forms we can isolate recapitulate basic gender issues in Indian society: the extraordinary dependence women experience in relation to men, to the demands of marriage, and to social roles'.[6] However, a closer scrutiny of the nuances of the goddess tradition might yield a different set of insights. A non-anachronistic approach to the study of goddesses would reveal the diverse ways in which they have been constructed, appropriated and understood across time and geographical regions. Goddesses could also be compared to gods from the same pantheon to understand the power dynamics in the construct of gender among deities. Gods tend to draw lines, mark off barriers, confirm hierarchies and legitimate traditional control of social and religious space. Their ritual work often involves exclusion. Goddesses, on the other hand, fierce or not, step across social and psychic barriers, meeting their devotees where they are and often empowering them by bestowing powers earned ritually and charismatically, rather than through concerns for lineage and formal training.[7]

A.K. Ramanujan and Stuart Blackburn have suggested a distinction between 'goddesses of control' and 'goddesses of release'. Goddesses of control are reserved, dependable and unlikely to be depicted as passionate. Goddesses of release are unpredictable, sometimes erotic and sometimes angry, but never conventional.[8] There has also been a tendency among scholars to group South Asian goddesses as belonging to the 'great tradition' (referring to the Vedic-Brahmanical tradition) and the 'little tradition' (usually referring to the folk/village-based tradition), though there is considerable overlap between the two. Another dichotomy that has been suggested by scholars, one that is also seen in missionary accounts, is a binary categorization into vegetarian and non-vegetarian goddesses. Both binaries are inapplicable to the Māriyammaṉ tradition, as one sees the goddess being worshipped by both non-vegetarian and vegetarian communities, with rituals involving animal sacrifices in the case of the former and the same being absent in the latter. Similarly, one can also see Māriyammaṉ shrines being shared by Brahmin and non-Brahmin communities, though the power and caste hierarchies are all but apparent in such situations. Henry Whitehead observed that there are several villages where Māriyammaṉ is not offered any animal sacrifice,[9] while the major temples dedicated to the goddess of disease have offerings of sheep, goats, buffaloes, fowls, pigeons, parrots, cows and calves being made to the goddess.[10]

There is no way to know how long Māriyammaṉ has been worshipped in southern India. The earliest written documents about her came quite late in her history and date from the eighteenth century.[11] There are also some references to Māri, but one cannot be sure that all of those references are to Māriyammaṉ, the deity. The references, language and the syntax used in the *Māriyammaṉ Tālāṭṭu*, a song in praise of the goddess sung in the folk lullaby style, seems to belong to the sixteenth century.

An Argumentative Goddess

Māriyammaṉ is depicted as a young virginal goddess who is the sister of Śiva in the earliest hymns. In later hymns, she is also referred to as Śiva's consort and is often analogized to Pārvatī. Most of the later and present-day hymns dedicated to Māri start with salutations to Piḷḷaiyār or Gaṇeśa. Māri is frequently described as arguing with Yama in the earlier hymns, which might be an allusion to the goddess rescuing her devotees afflicted with pox from the scourge of death. Most hymns also depict her as arguing with other gods, particularly Viṣṇu and Brahmā. Māri, the young, vocal, fierce goddess, having the upper hand in these arguments and squabbles, is also remarked upon. The references to the arguments might also indicate the competing traditions of Vaiṣṇavism and Śaivism within the Tamil religious landscape. She is also mentioned as arguing with Vedic seers and is referred to as both *Siddhānta Māri Mutte* and *Vedānta Māri Mutte,* highlighting her prowess in philosophy as well as Vedānta.[12] The folk lullaby *Māriyammaṉ Tālāṭṭu* thus attempts to bring together contradictory and competing traditions, positioning Māriyammaṉ at its epicentre.

Caste and the Goddess

Traditionally, most temples dedicated to Māriyammaṉ have not been staffed by members of the Brahmin community because the goddess is generally understood to appreciate blood sacrifices. Many of the stories about the goddess specifically associate her with service castes, including barbers, craftsmen and washer folk. In Kerala, she is also closely associated with the Vishwakarma community and certain Nayar sub-castes. The Vishwakarma community, in particular, have a large number of temples and shrines dedicated to the goddess, and quite a lot of prominent Vishwakarma families acknowledge her as their clan deity in the form of Rēṇukā Māriyammaṉ. Ziegenbalg, in the eighteenth century, refers to the Brahmin community as well as oppressed caste communities as worshipping the goddess.[13] In particular, there are references to Paraiya priests in Māriyammaṉ kovils. Scholars have also suggested that women are admitted on par with men in the Māriyammaṉ temples, with those who are menstruating also not prohibited from entry and worship unlike in other temples. Quite a large number of small and simple Māriyammaṉ shrines are being turned into grand temples of the typical Dravidian style in the post-independent period, and this has led to issues of gentrification on the one hand and Sanskritization on the other.[14] A considerable number of Māriyammaṉ shrines in countries such as Singapore and Malaysia have already gone through the process of gentrification, as neighbourhoods have become more upscale and as communities have become more economically mobile.[15] The same process can be observed in south India over the last two or three decades with a large number of traditional Māriyammaṉ sacred spaces, which were more in the nature of groves or small shrines in the homestead of the communities. There is an increase in the presence of Brahmin priests even in the non-Brahmanical Māriyammaṉ temples. In some of the larger temples, Brahmin priests are present on an everyday basis for daily prayer and worship, but in most Māriyammaṉ kovils, the presence of Brahmins is limited to ritual occasions. This has led to a change in the ritual processes particularly in the festivities of the temple. A major shift which can be easily observed in these non-brahmanical temples is the trend towards vegetarianism.[16] There is a substitution of most offerings or rituals which involve animal blood with that of vegetables or vermillion. Rooster sacrifice or buffalo sacrifice which was a very common practice in the non-Brahmanical Māriyammaṉ tradition[17] has almost ceased in Kerala, though it continues in parts of Tamil Nadu during temple festivals.[18] There is also a larger use of Sanskrit hymns from the *Devī Māhātmyam* being used in daily prayers. Though on the surface, the process seems to have the appearance of 'Sanskritization' or Brahmanical appropriation, there seem to be more complex processes at work involving an intricate power-play between the various communities involved. Two Brahmin priests who were interviewed argued that the non-Brahmanical shrines which they had started officiating in the late 1990s have become more prosperous and more sacred after the deity started to be worshipped through Sanskritic rituals and hymns. They also claimed that the worship of Māriyammaṉ in the form of Pārvatī who is a far more benevolent form of the goddess is more beneficial for the devotees as she has the nature of a 'mother' in the latter form.[19] The priests did not show any aversion to animal sacrifices and mentioned that both vegetarian and non-vegetarian traditions have coexisted in Māriyammaṉ worship, and non-vegetarian practices and rituals are performed by the devotees themselves. At the Pazhormattom Māriyammaṉ temple at Irumpanam, Ernakulam, the Vishwakarma priests and trustees of the temple claimed that the goddess was more pleased with the animal sacrifices, and they conduct the sacrifices replacing the roosters, goats and buffaloes with ash gourds, pumpkins and melons. They also argued that the fundamental nature of the goddess was fierce whose heated temperament could only be cooled with sacrifices. They also argue that Māriyammaṉ in her form as a young fierce goddess is easier to please and would be more inclined to grant wishes (*kṣipra prasādinī*) than in other forms such as Durgā or Sarasvatī.

Māriyammaṉ is, true to her name, a changing goddess; *māri* being the term used for 'change' in Malayalam. Her temples are appearing more frequently in larger cities, and her worship has developed an increasingly respectable, high-caste, Sanskritic character, with a de-emphasis on blood sacrifices and an increasing emphasis on her character as benign, gracious and generous. She continues to cause and cure illnesses involving fever, especially tuberculosis, cholera and typhoid.[20] In a post-pandemic world, her temples are attracting even more devotees than in the past, according to informants from the districts of Ernakulam, Thrissur and Trivandrum, and her festivals are becoming more and more elaborate, extending from three days to a week, with several local shop owners sponsoring many of the events.

The Festivals of the Masculine Goddess and Caste-Gender Subversions

During the course of the survey, it was realized that the 'festival' to re-install the idol in the Irumpanam Māriyammaṉ temple at Tripunithura, Ernakulam in Kerala was underway in May 2017. The present author spent two weeks documenting the temple festival and, over two subsequent years, also spent time being an observer at the festival. The initial re-installation festival in 2018 lasted nine days and featured a large set of rituals. The subsequent temple festival in the post-Corona period lasted six days, with one of the days dedicated to commemorating the day on which the re-installation was performed. The festival rituals range from *brahma-kalaśa* (filling of the holy pitcher) and *koṭiyeṭṭaṁ* (hoisting of the ritual flag) on the first day, followed by *ūru cuttal parayeṭuppu* (the ritual procession where the temple priests or trustees visit homes in the neighbourhood, and accept food grains from them). On the second day, *Kuṅkumābhiṣekam* (vermillion-bath) is performed, followed by *agni karakam* (fire-pot dance) on the third day. On the fourth day, *ūru cuttal parayeṭuppu* continues, followed by *agni karakam* (dancing with pots that have fire or flames on the top). The fifth day witnesses the *satya karakam,* during which offerings are brought from another temple, the Perunnakulam Śiva temple, to the Māriyammaṉ temple. On the fifth night, an *agni praveśa* (fire-walking) is also organized where a group of devotees and priests walk over a flaming charcoal and ember-filled trail in the precincts of the temple. On the last day of the festival, the temple committee conducts the *mañcaḷ nīrāṭal* (the turmeric bath of the deity), followed by a grand feast that is open to all.

Though there are minor variations in the order of events in most other Māriyammaṉ temples, the vermillion and turmeric baths of the deity, *karakams* and the fire-walking rituals are staples of Māriyammaṉ festivals across South and South East Asia. The festival days feature almost all these rituals being performed with a fairly large throng of people in attendance, particularly during the nights on which the *Kuṁkumābhiṣekam* and the *mañcaḷ nīrāṭal* take place. What is also of peculiar interest among the ritual festivities is the fact that these days see the presence of both Brahmin and non-Brahmin priests, as well as the performance of both Brahmanical and folk-based rituals in the temple. An example of the latter is the *guruthi,* which is performed outside the structure of the temple, where an ash-gourd or wax gourd is cut open by the non-Brahmin priests. The priests provided the information during the interviews that, before the Prevention of Cruelty to Animals Act was implemented in 1970 (and strictly enforced from 1975 onwards), a rooster was sacrificed instead of the ash or wax gourd to satiate the goddess. What is also fascinating is that a short survey of the *guruthi* practice in five temples in the Ernakulam district of Kerala revealed that informants—who were non-Brahmin priests, oracles or shamans—felt that the festival was 'incomplete' without the *guruthi* and that the goddess would not be satisfied or pleased without the sacrifice, as it was an ancestral practice. Thus, while the sacrifice could be modified, it could not be completely discarded. The *guruthi* would be performed without much public notice by non-Brahmin priests, though Brahmin priests in Kerala also perform *guruthi* in Bhadrakālī temples. The temple trustees, with whom the present author spoke, and who belonged to the Vishwakarma community, mentioned that Brahmin priests were invited to officiate in the temple, particularly after the temple was renovated, to 'help' devotees from other castes offer sacrifices and rituals to the goddess, as these devotees might find it more appropriate to have Brahmin priests performing the rituals.

In fact, most of the rituals and festivities involve a complex negotiation between the Brahmin and non-Brahmin priests. Usually, the day-time rituals, such as the *Gaṇapati-hōma* and the hoisting of the ritual flag, are performed by the Brahmin priests, whereas the night-time rituals are officiated by the Vishwakarma or other non-Brahmin priests. Recently, Brahmin priests have also been spotted at night time festivities, but their role is largely limited to lighting the sacred fire and chanting, while it is the other set of priests who perform all the other rituals. During the occasions of the vermillion consecration and turmeric bath of the goddess, the non-Brahmin priests are 'transformed' into the attendants of the goddess or the goddess herself. They wear red- coloured skirts as well as the *pūṇūl,* or sacred thread, and dance (Figure 11.1). There is considerable caste and gender ambivalence during the ritual occasions. The wearing of the sacred thread by members of the non-Brahmin community is indicative of their ritual transformation into the priests of the goddess. It is also interesting to note that they have chosen the sacred thread – an indicator of Brahmin status—to denote their transformation into priests. The wearing of the sacred thread is an important step in the rituals, but it does not require the sanctioning authority of the Brahmin priests and is done by the Vishwakarma priests themselves under the leadership of a head priest from their own community, who oversees the ritual (Figure 11.3).

The sacred thread is only worn during ritual occasions and is disposed of in the nearby river once the festivities are completed. Karin Kapadia's observation regarding the dynamics between the oracles belonging to oppressed castes and the Brahmin priests during festivities in Tamil Nadu, and the subversion of the idea of purity, becomes significant in this context.[21] Kapadia claims that devotees believe the goddess chooses to inhabit the bodies of 'lower caste' devotees because their faith is considered more pure. In the case of the Māriyammaṉ temple festival rituals, there is also an occurrence of caste subversion, as the non-Brahmin priests officiate the rituals and adorn themselves with the *pūṇūl* without any initiation from Brahmin priests; their legitimacy is directly derived from the goddess and their devotion to her. The priests further purify themselves by walking over embers during the *agni praveśa* rituals, where they fire-walk with the *karakam* pots on their heads while wearing skirts (Figure 11.2).

Figure 11.1 Non-Brahmin priests wearing red skirts and sacred threads during the festival.

Figure 11.2 Karakam and fire-walking.

Figure 11.3 Offerings to the goddess and rituals performed by non-Brahmin priests wearing the sacred thread, *pūṇūl*.

Gendering the Goddess

In the celebration of Māriyammaṉ's festival, there is considerable gender ambivalence to the extent that the bodily form of the devotees, and particularly the priests, is fluid. During the *Kuṅkumābhiṣekam* (vermillion bath), the priests, belonging to a non-Brahmanical background, wear skirts of red silk with anklets on their feet, smear themselves with vermillion, and dance with copper and brass pots called *karakam* on their heads. They refer to themselves as female attendants of the goddess, chide each other and behave like the 'friends of the goddess'. During the *mañcaḷ nīrāṭal*, a huge vat of water with turmeric is boiled, and male priests dance in a frenzied manner in skirts of yellow silk, carrying pots of holy water with mango or margosa leaves on the rim of the pot (Figure 11.4). On both occasions, the attendants also wear the *pūṇūl*. In recent times, this may be done in the presence of Brahmin priests, but the wearing of the sacred thread can also occur without their presence. The *mañcaḷ nīrāṭal* is considered a purificatory ritual, and the final step of the ritual process involves the priests and attendants taking a bath in the boiling water. In fact, the entire set of rituals, spanning five to seven days, can be thought of as a cleansing exercise. Almost all the significant aspects of the most important rituals have an element of cleansing in them—be it walking over charcoal embers, smearing oneself with vermillion, or bathing in hot turmeric water. There is considerable gender as well as caste fluidity in the rituals, with men

Figure 11.4 The procession before the ritual turmeric bath (*mañcaḷ nīrāṭal*).

wearing skirts, acting as female attendants of the goddess and embracing their 'feminine side'.[22] Particularly during the *mañcaḷ nīrāṭal*, there is an exchange of coy smiles and playful remarks between the priests and the attendants, 'as if a bunch of girls or women are taking a bath in a pond together'. The entire ritual is set in an ambience of playfulness as well as holiness, which do not cancel each other out but are enmeshed in one another. R. Mahalakshmi, when tracing the emergence of the Koṟṟavai tradition, argues that the goddess is followed by a company of female attendants who engage in gory acts of revelry. The smearing of vermillion on the bodies of the priests, the fire-walking and the frenzied dancing that accompanies the *mañcaḷ nīrāṭal* are highly reminiscent of Koṟṟavai and her attendants.

The priests and the attendants thus engage in a process of self-cleansing by subverting both caste and gender norms. One can also discern a third intersectional aspect in the ritual festivities, which is that of age. While the men who participate in the rituals are middle-aged, the persona they adopt during the ritual occasion is that of the young goddess and her young female attendants.

Queering the Goddess

William Harman talks about a particular Māriyammaṉ temple in Chennai at Melmaruvathur, where a certain man called Pankaru Atikalar, referred to as 'she' and 'her', is regarded as the incarnation of the goddess.

> Twice a week, Pankaru is possessed by the Goddess. Holding a neem branch (which almost all traditional possessed worshippers of Māriyamman throughout the South carry during their trance possession states) s/he appears twice a week, Tuesdays and Fridays (with special pronouncements on holidays), to channel communications from the goddess. During these oracular pronouncements, Pankaru's demeanor completely changes. S/he walks like, acts like, and talks like a woman.[23]

Though we do not see such direct gender ambivalence in the deity in Kerala, there are several occasions, like the one mentioned in the last section, where identities are merged together and status markers such as gender and caste are succinctly challenged and subverted. But it is not only the devotees of the goddess who engage in gender ambivalence; the goddess herself can be thought of as possessing androgynous qualities. There are frequent references to the goddess as 'Āṇaḻaki' – as possessing masculine beauty – along with her being represented as an argumentative goddess. She is also referred to as 'Ardhanārīśvarī', which is a feminine term denoting her status as a goddess, as opposed to Śiva being referred to as 'Ardhanārīśvara', a masculine term.

In a probing of Tamil myths about divine marriage, Shulman states, 'The virgin goddess's persona is split into golden and black parts, leading to Śiva's non-erotic, androgynous marriage with the "tamed" golden one, and marginalization of the erotic and "dangerous" black goddess.'[24] In the Malayalam version of the *Māriyammaṉ Pāmālai* (a set of hymns in Tamil dedicated to the goddess), simply referred to as the *Māriyammaṉ Mālai* in Kerala, there is a simplified version of the myth about the fight between Śiva and Māriyammaṉ where upon being bestowed with the pearls of pox by Śiva, the goddess tries out the pearls on Śiva himself. In the ensuing tussle between the god and the goddess, Śiva consents to give half of his body to Māriyammaṉ, a proposal which the goddess is not too happy about, so she agrees to merge into Śiva's body, and thus the goddess becomes Ardhanārīśvarī, maintaining her status as a goddess and thus not becoming or assuming a male status.

One can thus argue that both in the ritual aspects of the worship of the goddess and in textual and liturgical references to her, Māriyammaṉ continues to defy the contours of gender, challenging the normative definitions of the conventional goddess image in South Asia. A close investigation of the tradition will also reveal how it is negotiating with the increasing tendencies of Sanskritization and savarṇa-ization, including the presence of Brahmin priests even in temples of oppressed caste communities. The ritual occasion of the festival becomes a heterotopic space where both gender and caste are subverted, with middle-aged men from non-Brahmin castes performing as young female attendants of the goddess, administering priestly duties and mediating on behalf of the goddess. The fluidity in terms of both caste and gender during the ritual occasions is contained within the time frame of the festival and does not spill over into the daily worship patterns of the goddess in the contemporary period. Thus, her worship also reveals how oppressed caste communities respond to and negotiate with the modern challenges of gentrification and Sanskritization.

Notes

1 See Gross, A., V.V. Kumaradoss, and H. Liebau. 2006. *Halle and the Beginning of Protestant Christianity in India*, Vol. I-II, Halle: Verlag der Franckeschen Stiftungen zu Halle.

2 Amrith, S.S., 'Tamil Diasporas across the Bay of Bengal'. *The American Historical Review*, 114 (3): 547–72.

3 Gentes, M.J. 1992. 'Scandalizing the Goddess at Kodungallur', *Asian Folklore Studies*, 51 (2): 295–322. Also see, Menon, D.M., 1995. 'From Pleasure to Taboo: Drinking and Society in Kerala', *India International Centre Quarterly*, 22 (2/3): 143–56.

4 Kosambi, D.D. 1985. *Myth and Reality: Studies in the Formation of Indian Culture*. Delhi: Sangam.

5 Mahalakshmi, R. 2011. *The Making of the Goddess: Ko<u>r</u><u>r</u>avai-Durgā in the Tamil Traditions*. Delhi: Penguin.

6 William Harman, 'From Fierce to Domesticated: Māriyamma<u>n</u> Joins the Middle Class'. *Nidān: International Journal for the Study of Hinduism*, University of Heidelberg Press, 24(1): ii.

7 Ibid., iii.

8 The first mention to the dichotomy was referenced in Srinivas, M.N.,1952. *Religion and Society among the Coorgs of South India*, Oxford: Clarendon Press and this was later developed into an argument by Singer, Milton. 1972. *When a Great Tradition Modernizes: An Anthropological Approach to Indian Civilization*. UK: Pall Mall Press.

9 Whitehead, H. 1921. *The Village Gods of South India*. New York: Oxford University Press. 91.

10 Ibid., 106.

11 Harman, 'From Fierce to Domesticated', 46.

12 *Māriyamma<u>n</u> tālāṭṭu*, Translated by R. Ramachander, Kannabiran Ravi Shankar and Dr Sankar Kumar. For the text and translation, see http://stotrarathna.blogspot.com/2009/07/Māriamman-thalattu-tamil.html.

13 Ziegenbalg, B. 1713. *Genealogy of the* South-Indian Gods*: A Manual of the* Mythology *and* Religion *of the People of Southern India*. Madras: Higginbotham & Co.

14 Sinha, Vineeta. 2010. 'Unraveling "Singaporean Hinduism": Seeing the Pluralism Within'. *International Journal of Hindu Studies*, 14 (2/3): 253–79. Also, Xavier, S. 2010. 'An Analytical Study on Sanskritisation of the Deities of Folk Tradition with Reference to Tamil Nadu'. In *Proceedings of the Indian History Congress*. IHC: Delhi.

15 Sykes, Jim. 2015. 'Sound Studies, Religion and Urban Space: Tamil Music and the Ethical Life in Singapore'. *Ethnomusicology Forum*, 24 (3): 380–413.

16 Interview with Mr. Srinivasan, priest at Palaormatton Irumpanam Māriyammaṉ Kovil, April 2023. The same information was given also by Mr. Vasu and Mr. Sadasivan, temple committee members, Chandana Māriyammaṉ Temple, Ernakulam, April 2023.

17 Ziegenbalg, B. 1713. *Genealogy of the South-Indian Gods: A Manual of the* Mythology *and* Religion *of the People of Southern India*. Madras: Higginbotham & Co. 137–40.

18 Deccan Herald, 2024. Ritualistic sacrifice of roosters prevented in Kerala following animal rights organization complaint. *Deccan Herald*, Kozhikode, 20 January. https://www.deccanherald.com/india/kerala/ritualistic-sacrifice-of-roosters-prevented-in-kerala-following-animal-rights-organisation-complaint-2858146.

19 Interview with Mr. N.Vasudevan and Mr. K. Ramakrishnan, priests at Punnapuram Māriyammaṉ Kovil, Thiruvananthapuram, May 2023.

20 Harman, 'From Fierce to Domesticated', 50.

21 Kapadia, K. 2019. *Siva and Her Sisters: Gender, Caste and Class in Rural South India*. Delhi: Taylor and Francis. See especially chapter 6. 'Dancing the Goddess: Possession, Caste and Gender'.

22 The term was used by a middle-aged informant who takes part in the rituals himself.

23 Harman, 'From Fierce to Domesticated', 59.

24 Shulman, D.D. 2014. *Tamil Temple Myths: Sacrifice and Divine Marriage in the South Indian Śaiva Tradition*. Princeton: Princeton University Press. 140–1.

12

Death and the Making of a Goddess

Twinkle Siwach

The acquisition of divinity is a historical phenomenon. One such phenomenon in recent history is the acquisition of the divine status of '*satimata*' in a village in Rajasthan, embedding the contextual social and cultural ideals. The example of how Roop Kanwar, in the village of Divrala in Rajasthan, acquired the status of *satimata* in a short period of time suggests both the cultural and material ways in which the social milieu works to attribute divinity. As D.D. Kosambi and other scholars have pointed out, we have historical evidence of goddess cults emerging in local milieus.[1] Additionally, as Susan Wadley has argued, femaleness in Hindu ideology is often understood in terms of *shakti* (energy/power) – the act of *sati* only amplifies her powers.[2] The characterization of womanhood is built around the roles of a good, benevolent, dutiful, controlled wife and mother. The *sati*, therefore, approximates, in some sense, the ideal form of womanhood, where one transcends into a goddess: she not only becomes the ideal but, in some instances, also becomes the village guardian.[3] This chapter, by narrativizing the context that prompted the ascendance of Roop Kanwar to the status of *sati*, offers an insight into the making of a goddess within a historical framework.

Deification of Women

Scholars have theorized three stages of acquiring *sat*, namely, '*pativrata*' (a woman taking ritual vows in a marriage ceremony to protect and serve her husband), '*sativrata*' (when the moral or ascetic heat that a woman builds up while holding her vow as a *pativrata* explodes into flames – it is her 'purifying heat' that immolates her) and '*satimata*' (a woman becoming a transcendent being in the process of dying – an auspicious figure since she remains wedded to her husband eternally).[4]

In this manner, she becomes a symbol of 'a deified female condition' of power, purity, fertility and protection, which leads to 'an institutionalization of this deification'.[5] She becomes a goddess of the village and even beyond.

Drawing from the three stages discussed above, one also understands how the social location of a woman is defined by patriarchal norms: her husband, the idea of marriage or virginity, and how societal norms are imputed onto her and her status even in her death. The story of Roop Kanwar brings to us the social phenomenon that facilitated the making of a goddess, *Satimata*. The act of becoming *Sati* and embodying divine power (*sat* = truthfulness, goodness) has, in this sense, drawn the attention of scholars. Sree Padma, for example, has extensively worked on *gramdevatas* and argues that in such cases, there is collective guilt arising from the feeling that a woman has died due to 'patriarchal proclivities in village society' and therefore, in her deification, she is 'transmogrified' as a goddess.[6]

However, the social context of the attribution of divinity is fraught with contestation and struggle. In the case being studied here, where a young woman protagonist is said to have ascended to the funeral pyre of her husband and the process culminated in her being accorded the status of *sati*, there are strong proponents who argued that the act was involuntary and contrary to contemporary legal and social norms. There were others, however, who believed that it was a voluntary act, performed in accordance with the age-old practice sanctified by religious norms. The invocation of sacred powers and rules of purity that accompanied the historical example of the phenomenon of *sati* made the act sacred, and once this was done, the arguments of contravention of legal provisions and norms seemed to be overwhelmed.

Thus, a social projection of a person sitting calmly and joyfully on a pyre, embracing the movement towards the final end of the body with hands raised to bless, fulfilling people's wishes and curing their ills, was also a way to synchronize the cultural with the social, and the social with patriarchal norms.[7] The phenomenon of *satimata* was such a powerful spectacle, especially in its modern recording, that it soon became a social and cultural phenomenon. Visitors, as often happens in a socially produced spectacle, felt they were 'in the vicinity of a supernatural occasion'.[8] They believed they were cured of diseases like polio and eye problems. Sree Padma has discussed how devotees perceive the *sati*'s role 'as a protector of the family', who fulfils their wishes, takes care of their overall well-being and acts as a guardian.[9]

The Prehistory of Divinity: Historical Framework of a Debate

The process of attributing divine status has been quite complex and contested, as is the case with any historical phenomenon. One of the most powerful narratives has been the one which, from the beginning, considered the process in terms of the legal and juridical angle and found the pre-history of the phenomenon of *sati* to be a history of a legal issue involving homicide. That history required legal adjudication of a criminal act resulting in death. From this perspective, it was found to be difficult to accept the idea of someone setting themselves on fire of their own volition. It is argued that there must have been external pressure—familial, social, etc. or force, which made the act subject to criminal investigation and juridical processes. This further necessitated the identification of the human agency involved in the entire act.[10]

As debated intensely since the nineteenth century, the issues ignited fresh intellectual and social criticism, and all the details that surrounded the debate in the past resurfaced. This included the issues of women's sexuality, familial loyalty and the idea of being inauspicious. It was, therefore, as debated earlier, easier to sentimentalize loyalty to the husband in a society based on patriarchal norms. The social reality of the process required the primacy of those facts to be studied, scrutinized and adjudicated. This emphasis made the establishment of the act as homicide a prolonged legal process.[11]

The second version, emerging over time, had by now taken quite strong socio-political roots. It was an act of self-volition, with putative reports suggesting that the women, including Roop Kanwar, sat on the pyre in a majestic manner, chanting the *Gayatri mantra*.[12] The elders in the village reportedly believed and narrated how the subject herself sat on the pyre and, while burning in the natural heat, her 'eyes glowed red' as she 'raised her hands' to bless the people who had gathered to witness her sacrifice.[13]

Mediation and Processes of Acquisition of Divinity: Social and Material

The process of the making of the goddess, as indicated in the emergence of other goddesses by R. Mahalakshmi in this volume, in the case of Roop Kanwar, too, began socially.[14] Multiple stories emerged from the field that coloured the spectrum of media coverage and public knowledge. The dynamic media reporting attracted heavy crowds to the village. Moreover, the media's intervention began to frame knowledge of the case, which ultimately traversed the public sphere, i.e., outside the village and the state. The news of the *sati* broke out soon in neighbouring villages through bus drivers and vendors en route to Divrala. The tea stalls became the ideal Habermasian 'public sphere', where people heard about the case from each other and discussed different aspects of it. These discussions amplified the size and scale of the information, which eventually led to people's influx into Divrala in large numbers to offer their prayers to Roop Kanwar. The *chunri* (glorification) ceremony, in particular, demonstrated a large assembly of people.

In the days that followed, the state government issued a ban on all public transport heading towards the village. Despite the ban, the buses kept coming in, with people sitting on the tops of the buses and hopping onto the sides of taxis and jeeps on the way to Divrala.[15]

The religious concept of *sati* embodies the ideal wife, who adheres to the notion of a perpetual union between husband and wife that persists even after death, an act they perform together to achieve unity. Some people in the village also propagated the belief that religion and ritual are closely intertwined, creating a nexus where 'dying together' in a 'joint funeral' represents efforts towards forming an 'inseparable bond'– 'reuniting the living with dead'.[16] For this reason, later visual depictions portray her sitting on the funeral pyre, comforting and protecting her husband – depicted as alive despite being deceased – from direct flames. Simultaneously, she is shown as someone who has transcended feelings of pain or discomfort, entering the realm of the divine. Such ideas also resonate in certain ritual practices wherein married women observe fasts to pray for the longevity of their husbands' lives on various occasions throughout the year, such as *Karwachauth, Vat Savitri Vrata, Teej* and others. Widows are not only prohibited from participating in these rituals but even their physical presence during these events is considered 'profane'. Over the years, the romanticized portrayal of these practices in many Indian Hindi films and daily television soap operas has captured the ethos of middle-class aspirations. Social media platforms have further amplified this trend, with many celebrities and influencers popularizing how women come together to perform 'collective effervescence'.

Thus, the idea of Roop Kanwar's *sati* travelled a long road in a short duration. It reinforces the notion of a loyal wife who, due to her pure chastity, rose above other ordinary beings. Otherwise, she was an educated and modern woman who mostly grew up in an urban environment and yet died (wilfully or forcefully) by burning herself, wearing her bridal attire to serve and protect the honour and pride of her husband and his family. It also reflects the journey of her transformation from a young girl into a married woman (*pativrata*), the one who traditionally wears all signifiers of marriage (vermilion, bangles, *bindi*, *mangalsutra* etc.). In her death, the transformation from a human into a divine being (*sativrata*) is reflected, as she joins her husband in his death and their bodies are burned together.

In the aftermath, she becomes a sacred being (*satimata*), wherein powers are manifested in her. The figure of motherhood is highlighted as she enacts her role as a protector of earthly beings from another world (somewhere in between the world of humans and gods). It is in her transition from being a *sativrata* to a *satimata* that she is considered powerful, as she is looked upon as someone who has progressed beyond life and now possesses supreme powers with the blessings of Brahma, Vishnu, and Shiva, as demonstrated in the images sold around the glorification ceremony. Hence, she becomes a transcendental being – one who is capable of blessing or cursing. Likewise, her act of raising her hands and crying for help, as reported, is interpreted by the villagers as an act of showering blessings, while others pointed out that even if they wanted to, they could not stop her because they feared that, at that moment, she possessed the power to curse. The woman's image as a goddess is then materially translated, not just through a collection of images as part of a collective memory, but also through unequal patriarchal social relations.

Becoming Divine: Material Manifestation

In the aftermath of the event of Roop Kanwar's *sati*, it was recorded that a temporary shrine was erected at the site; a photo collage was installed, and visitors offered coins for the construction of a temple in her honour.[17] In addition, the site of the funeral pyre was transformed into a '*sati-sthal*'; reports indicate the building of an elevated platform where a red veil braided with gold thread was hung on a trident (*trishul*), symbolizing the goddess figure. The trident here takes on 'an anthropomorphic shape of the goddess'.[18] The site also functions as a physical space where 'techniques of the exhibition' are employed to attract devotees – such as placing her embodied symbolic figure on an elevated platform, creating a distinct space for her (separating the sacred from the profane), positioning her on a higher pedestal, and finally, creating an aura around the space through the use of sacred objects like incense sticks, a trident, a red veil and *sindoor* (which is exchanged after offering prayers in Hindu custom).[19] All of this contributes to the symbolic process of elevating her to the status of a goddess, positioned above the realm of ordinary things. Consequently, even the village became an epitome of religion, with Divrala being referred to as '*Devgaon* (Village of God), *Devbhumi* (Land of God), *Dham* (Shrine)', etc.

For people worshipping at the *sati-sthal*,[20] it was a site for performing public religion, where everyone had access on the one hand, and different sensory organs were being activated on the other. For instance, touching the ground signifies touching the feet of *satimata* and taking her blessings.[21] The incense sticks activated a smell that differentiated the *sati-sthal* as a sacred space from the common ground; one can relate this to the aura of sacredness and purity. For the same reason, the worshippers venerate her positioning on the elevated platform and come in proximity to the space with bare feet.[22] These everyday practices helped in creating patterns of devotion and the 'paraphernalia of *puja*'.[23]

An interesting element is the commercial fall-out: the huge influx of people from neighbouring villages had alerted the Revenue Officer because the site attracted significant commercial transactions. For instance, around 70 lakh rupees was reported to have been collected within a year, and there was an approximate footfall of around two lakh people.[24] One can also see how social relations played a critical role in promoting *sati,* as was witnessed in this case with the involvement of groups like *Dharm Raksha Samiti.*[25]

The process of such spectacle creation also involves the reinforcement of messages through mass-disseminated props like wall and pocket calendars, posters, cassettes and photo collages.[26] The process also offered commercial opportunities for selling posters and photo collages, pictures of the couple – in this particular case from their wedding day – ribbons and toys. Alongside, prayer sessions were organized, and people were encouraged to contribute large amounts of donations.[27] Even before the *chunri* ceremony, placards were sold in large numbers for seven rupees, and eventually, the price spiked to Rs. 25 per piece.[28] Observing the sale of many such odd little artefacts, the Women and Media Committee report that had been constituted argued that 'the alliance of religion, community, and commerce was very much evident'.[29] Guy Debord also provides insight into the linkages between spectacle and capitalism; the spectacle being enacted here was more in terms of a reassertion of patriarchal norms legitimized through the ideas of myth and religion.

The community celebrations, too, came up in the process as one witnessed slogans supporting Roop Kanwar, such as '*desh dharm ka nata hai, sati humari mata hai*' (it is a relation between the state and religion, sati is our mother). The spectacle here, thus, was mediating between the existing social relations through this performance, where the people not merely watched the performance but hailed it and, in the process, reaffirmed their faith in community, religion and country.

The absence of pain, grief or any kind of physical suffering in the visual depictions of the historical protagonist – the actual person who was acquiring this new found divinity – is striking. This not only strengthened people's belief in her sacrifice, but it also signified sacrifice as a feeling of happiness and comfort. The power of *sati* is brought into focus through Roop Kanwar's glowing face and expression of a smile while sitting alive on the pyre in these images. Such a depiction aligns with people (mainly her devotees) or those who viewed the act of *sati* as a symbolic performance in the restoration of *dharma*, honour and pride.

There were images that enhanced the attributes of divinity by attaching material objects to it: a large amount of gold jewellery was added, she was shown holding a book in her left hand and the height of the flames rising from the pyre was increased. In these images, she was now seen to be blessed by well-known goddesses, which symbolically depicted her attainment of powers. They were separated by clouds in between them, which depicted how she was distanced from her fellow beings, and there was further distancing from the Supreme Being. Here, her stages of transcendence were depicted: the ordinary woman transforming into a Supreme Being.

The images are utilized in everyday ritual practices, such as worship. They also play a functional role in maintaining collective memory. Here, we also examine Christopher Pinney's ethnographic work to understand the consumption patterns of images among rural consumers in the last two decades of the twentieth century. He presents an argument that villagers are not much interested in 'producers or publishers' but in the 'content, efficacy and praxis that surrounds the acquisition and ongoing maintenance of pictures'.[30] He brings out a pattern in ownership of these images by individual households, in the ways deities are chosen for daily worship, as it reflects also the caste and community hierarchies.[31] He also talks about the idea of '*darshan*' – to see and to be seen by the deity, since it is this idea of 'exchange of vision that lies at the heart of Hindu worship'.[32] Therefore, the images in circulation, as seen in the pictures related to the Roop Kanwar *sati* as a sample selection, portray a *darshanic* relationship that engages the eye as an important sensory organ of the devotees.[33] It is through the *darshan* of the deity in the public space that the devotees' desire emerges for holding the divine closer to their eye in the form of posters, placards, calendar, photo collage etc. The devotee, then, creates a need in the market for such a product – to install it in the private space. The use of 'corpothetic extension' moves the image closer to the devotee – as the images are customized with the 'application of glitter, brocade, plastic flowers or adhesion of the paper'.[34] Moreover, it is interesting how the sacredness of these images is suspended in their market relation but returns immediately outside the realm of circulation.[35]

In a short historical framework, the phenomenon of goddess-making is seen as a social and political phenomenon, as the act which was socially and legally contested is overwhelmed by cultural and social conventions, and the attributes of divinity are mediated to human beings to make the historical protagonist a female goddess. All material and legal entanglements get overshadowed in the process, indicating the power of both tradition and patriarchal norms working to invoke the social and cultural repertoire of the goddess to reiterate their dominance. The legal course that the case took increasingly confined itself to the criticism of the glorification of *sati* rather than the breach of legal and civic norms. The question of agency and the possibility of alternative decisions by women in a patriarchal society were completely ignored.

Notes

1 Kosambi presents accounts of *sati* monuments from different regions, that are of two kinds – *sahagamana*, that is the presence of two breast-like humps on top of a sati stone meaning that the widow immolated herself on the same pyre with her husband's corpse; and *anugamana*, that is presence of a single hump meaning that she followed her husband into the next world some days after the cremation on a separate pyre. See, Kosambi, D.D. 1962. *Myth and Reality: Studies in the Formation of Indian Culture*. Accessed online: https://archive.org/details/MythAndReality/mode/1up?view=theater.
2 Wadley, Susan. 1977. 'Women and the Hindu Tradition'. *Signs*, 3 (1): 113–25.
3 Ibid., 117.
4 Sree Padma. 2013. *Vicissitudes of the Goddess: Reconstruction of the Gramdevata in India's Religious Traditions*. Oxford: Oxford University Press. 222.
5 Ibid.
6 Ibid. 3.
7 See, Jennifer M. Bushaw. 2007. Suicide or Sacrifice? An Examination of the Sati Ritual in India. Dissertation submitted to the Centre for Middle Eastern Studies, The University of Chicago.
8 Ibid.
9 Sree Padma. 2013, 219.
10 Ibid.
11 For a detailed treatment of the whole case, see, Siwach, Twinkle. 2021. FIR and Media: Informational Universe of Crime and Violence in Contemporary India. Unpublished PhD Thesis: Centre for Media Studies, JNU, New Delhi.
12 Menon, Meena, Geeta Sheshu and Sujata Anandan. 1987. 'Trial by Fire'. Bombay: Women and Media Committee, *Bombay Union of Journalists*, 5.

13 Similar claims were made in the case of Om Kunwar (1981); the woman possessed by *sat* is believed to have special powers to bless and curse, the mundane activity is presented as a miracle, 'in this state, she comes in direct contact with God'. See, Vaid, Sudesh, and Kumkum Sangari. 1991. 'Institutions, Beliefs, Ideologies: Widow Immolation in Contemporary Rajasthan'. *Economic and Political Weekly*, 26 (17): 2–18. 4.

14 Tanaka Masakazu visited the village in 1988; there was a checkpoint at the village entrance where she was asked to leave her camera. See Tanaka Masakazu (no date). 'Defying blessings of the goddess and the community: Disputes over sati (widow burning) in contemporary India'. 9. Available at: http://www.zinbun.kyoto-u.ac.jp/~shakti/en/suttee.html.

15 Vishal Mangalwadi, 'Making a Carnival of Murder', *Indian Express* cited in Sen, Mala. 2001. *Death by Fire: Sati, Dowry Death and Female Infanticide in Modern India*. London: Weidenfeld & Nicolson. 9.

16 The ritual allows a woman to cleanse her as well as her family's evils by performing *sati*, an act that demands courage and the will to sacrifice herself on the pyre of the husband. The place where *sati* is performed also becomes sacred. See, Bushaw, 2007.

17 For this purpose, over 30 lakhs rupees were collected and a group of trustees was elected by the village panchayat. See, Mala Sen, 2001, 6–7.

18 Sree Padma 2013, 215.

19 Jacques Ranciere. 2013. *The Politics of Aesthetics*. UK: Bloomsbury Publications. 111–12.

20 Durga Prasad Panda. 2019. 'Thirty-two Years after Roop Kanwar's Death, Blind Faith Still Overshadows Reason', *Outlook*, 18 October.

21 See, Pinney, Christopher. 2004. 'What Pictures Want Now: Rural Consumer of Images, 1980–2000'. In *Photos of the Gods: The Printed Image and Political Structure in India*. London, UK: Reaktion Books, 197. The author discusses about the literal significance of '*pair ankh se lagana*' which means looking at the feet with respect and touching the feet is to 'physically express one's obeisance'. It indicates at the hierarchical relationship between the devotee and the goddess in which the devotee submits the body, through the eyes, to the feet of the deity.

22 There is often a tap or running water at the entrance of the pilgrimage site to wash the hands and feet which is a gesture to wash off dirt and separate the sacred and profane by maintaining purity. Emile Durkheim talked about the bipartite division of things into sacred and profane and about the distinguishing traits between them from which he also derived the definition of religion. See, Durkheim, Emile. 1995. *The Elementary Forms of Religious Life*. trans. Karen E. Fields. New York: The Free Press.

23 Christopher Pinney 2004, 197.

24 Susan Abraham 1997, 9.

25 Based in Jaipur, the group was run by young educated Rajput men. The convenor, Narendra Singh Rajawat, belonged to a family of lucrative leather export business.

26 Guy Debord, whose work has been influenced by the writings of Walter Benjamin, gives us an idea about how everything that has directly lived moves away into a representation and the modern conditions of production create 'an immense accumulation of spectacles'. See Debord, Guy. 2014. *Society of the Spectacle*. trans. & annot. Ken Knabb. Canada: The Bureau of Public Secrets. 24.

27 As mentioned earlier, Tanaka Masakazu was made to leave her camera at the checkpoint at the village entrance.

28 Mala Sen, 2001, 7.

29 See, *Trial by Fire*, 11 December 1987.

30 Christopher Pinney 2004, 190–1.

31 Ibid., 183.

32 Ibid., 193.

33 Ibid.

34 Ibid., 197.

35 Jain, Kajri. 2007. *Gods in the Bazaar: The Economies of Indian Calendar Art*. London: Duke University Press. 226.

13

Goddesses in the Diasporic Imagination: Political and Cultural Issues

Anisha Saxena

On 20 January 2021, Kamala Harris became the first woman vice president of the United States. The 2020 US presidential elections were the fifty-ninth presidential elections and were held on 3 November 2020. The United States currently has a two-party system where the 'liberal' Democratic and 'conservative' Republican Parties dominate the political universe of the country.[1] For the 2020 elections, former vice president of the United States, Joseph R. Biden, Jr. (or Joe Biden), secured the nomination ticket for the Democratic Party and his running mate was Kamala Devi Harris, a junior US senator from California. Harris was the first African American, first Indian American and the third female vice presidential nominee on the Democratic Party ticket.[2] Tensions in the United States were high, and the voters were deeply polarized. Some major issues that concerned the voters included the mishandling of the Covid-19 health crisis by the Trump administration, Supreme Court appointments, the economy, gun control, race and ethnic inequality, and abortion.[3] While the Republican voters and politicians stressed the economic stability of the country, the Democrats expected voter advantage on issues like climate change, Covid policies, the Supreme Court nominations and abortion.[4]

Within this tense political and social electoral environment in October 2020 on the first day of *Navaratri*, Meena Harris, niece of the former vice president of the United States Kamala Harris, tweeted a morphed image of Durga slaying the demon, Mahisha.[5] Based on a common popular image of goddess Durga (see Image 1), through the superimposition of faces, the image envisioned Kamala Harris as Durga, Joe Biden, the former president of the United States, as her *vahana*, the lion, and Donald Trump, the president of the United States from 2016 to 2021 (who is also currently president) as the demon Mahisha. The image became viral and was criticized on social media by a section of the Hindu diaspora settled in the United States. They argued that the image was disrespectful, and Meena Harris was forced to delete the image and for a few months she also deactivated her Twitter [I am aware that recently the social media platform has been rebranded as X. For the purposes of the present chapter I will refer to it with its previous name, Twitter] account.[6] In this chapter, I mention Hindu diaspora as individuals who are residing in the United States and publicly identify themselves as Hindus. These individuals also support political or social causes for benefits of the larger Hindu community.

Given the recent surge of the Hindu diaspora in the political and public life of the United States, the chapter attempts to understand the processes of creation and consumption of images of the South Asian goddess and its varied forms in the United States. Further, the chapter examines the role of social media platforms like Twitter in the circulation and the expression of reactions to these images. The omnipresence of social media in the twenty-first century human life means that historians can no longer ignore the significance of this medium in shaping historical events, public opinions and reactions.[7] While in the United States and Europe, studies on the interactions between social media and religion have been explored since the early 2000s, it is still a developing field in South Asian studies. The existing scholarship on South Asia and social media is restricted to the study of social media and rise of Hindu extremism in India, role of social media in perpetuating religious violence in South Asia, and digital religion including studies on online religious rituals and *darshan*.[8] This chapter lies within the intersections of social media, religion and diaspora studies.

Kamala Harris as Goddess: Caution May Cause Harm!

On the morning of 18 October 2020, Meena Harris tweeted 'I am actually speechless, other than to say that the first day of Navaratri was LIT'.[9] Her short tweet was followed by three fire emoji symbols. 'LIT' in her tweet meant excited or excellent. The image that Meena Harris tweeted instantaneously became viral, attracting mixed reactions from the Hindu diaspora and Hindus living in India and the United States. The reactions included both wrath and support. Meena Harris was forced to temporarily deactivate her twitter account because of the online hate and harassment she received. This left a gap in my research, and to examine the patterns of dissemination of the image and reactions towards it so I have focused on the Twitter account of Suhag Shukla, executive director of Hindu American Foundation (henceforth HAF).[10]

On its website, HAF describes itself as an American Hindu human rights and advocacy group.[11] Founded in 2004, the group has its roots in the Vishwa Hindu Parishad and its students wings in various universities in the United States.[12] On her Twitter handle, Shukla identifies herself as a Hindu and executive director of HAF. Currently Shukla has over thirty-four thousand (34.1K) followers on Twitter. In her response to Meena Harris's tweet and the image of Kamala Harris as Durga, Shukla tweeted:

> Dear @meenaharris, by now you know that your tweeting a caricature of the feminine divine, Maa Durga, with faces superimposed, deeply aggrieved many Hindus globally. To avoid such an error in judgement, for future reference, please refer to HAF guidelines on commercial use of Hindu Images.[13]

Shukla in her tweet, did not include the image of Kamala slaying Trump, but instead included HAF's guidelines on commercial use of Hindu images.[14] The detailed guidelines that are available on their website state:

> In the past several years we've seen Ganesh toilet seats, Kali underwear, Krishna bathmats, Om flip flops, and countless other items displaying Hindu sacred imagery in ways that many Hindus find disrespectful at best or downright offensive at worst. Though Hindu imagery is regularly used in a commercial context to market many domestic items, both in India and the United States, there are certain guidelines that are generally observed. In India, there is an often-unspoken understanding on what is and is not appropriate usage of images of deities and of sacred symbols. Intent also matters. Often sacred iconography is used in advertising or placed on Indian products and businesses to invoke blessings for the endeavor. Outside of India, however, these standards may well not be known and any intent to invoke blessings isn't necessarily at play.[15]

Further the guidelines proposed by HAF are divided into three broad categories – first, 'Don't do it, will cause offense', second – 'Caution-may cause offense' and third – 'Less likely to cause offense'.[16] The first category of objects that according to HAF should not have images of Hindu gods and goddesses includes – bathmats, toilet seats or seat covers; underwear, socks, pants or shorts; footwear, of any type and material; swimwear; door mats, rugs; alcohol, meat; yoga mats, skateboards, anything where the image is likely to be destroyed through normal intended usage, intended to be stepped upon; anything intended to be placed in spaces reserved for defecation, or placed on or near bodily organs of reproduction and elimination.[17] Under Caution-may cause offense HAF suggests not printing of Hindu images on bath towels, shower curtains, dish towels; mouse pads;

leather items; any item with significant material modification of a deity (placing non-traditional items in the hands of Nataraja, for example); any item that is likely to get regularly dirty through normal intended usage.[18] Under acceptable or less likely to cause offense were objects including shirts, hats, pins, stickers; magnets; shawls; wall hangings, decorations and decals; phone covers, laptop covers; tote bags; vegetarian food products. The website also warns the readers that it should be kept in mind that eggs are not traditionally considered a vegetarian food by many Hindus.[19] Furthermore, the website encourages businesses to submit their products for review to HAF. This review may guarantee the businesses that their products will not cause religious offense to the Hindus living in the United States and abroad.

The image that Meena Harris tweeted was not meant for commercial use but clearly fell in to second category of guidelines issued by HAF 'Caution-may cause offense', as it was modification of deities' image through superimposition of faces, and as predicted by HAF the image did cause offense. The tweet by Shukla was originally retweeted one hundred and ninety times and had thirty replies.[20] A detailed analysis of the replies revealed that nine users did not find the image offensive; eight users found the image tweeted by Meena Harris offensive and demanded an apology from Harris for disrespecting an image of the female divinity, Durga. Other replies on the tweet I categorized as 'out of context' as they did not directly engage with Suhag's tweet or the image of Kamala Harris as Durga. What is interesting about the debate that ensued over Twitter was that some users shared morphed images of Indian politicians as Hindu gods, including Indian Prime Minister Narendra Modi, and pointed out that those images were not found offensive.[21]

The creation of Kamala Harris's image as Durga and the reactions towards the image must be examined within the political and social space that the Hindu diaspora occupies within the United States. In the nationwide survey of Asian Americans, 10 per cent recognized themselves as Hindus, 87 per cent of these identified themselves as immigrants, 9 per cent as second generation and 4 per cent as third or higher generation.[22] The individuals who identify as Hindu Americans are increasingly choosing to deploy their political and social influence through organizations like HAF or political groups like the Republican Hindu Coalition, a political lobby group whose chairman, Shalabh Kumar, has stated that '[American] conservative values are Hindu values'.[23] YouGov conducted an empirical study on Indian Americans and concluded that religion plays a central role in the lives of Indian Americans.[24]

According to the 2020 census out of a total population of 331,449,28, only 0.5 per cent identified themselves as Hindus.[25] While a religious minority, Hindus are one of the fastest growing populations in the United States and exert significant political and economic influence. In large part due to their education and wealth[26] the Hindu diaspora in the United States is largely engaged with the growing IT sector in the Silicon Valley in California.[27] They have firmly established themselves in what are called the FAANG and WITCH companies.[28] In terms of politics and political representation, currently there are five Indian Americans (all Democrats) in US Congress and almost fifty in US State Legislatures.[29] Lately Indian American politicians have begun publicly embracing their Hindu roots. For example, Vivek Ramaswamy, a businessman turned politician, in 2023 announced his candidacy for the Republican Party's nomination for 2024 presidential elections. Ramaswamy publicly acknowledges his Hindu roots and calls himself a proud vegetarian Hindu.[30]

The Hindu diaspora, like other migrant groups, remains closely tied with their home country and social media has provided them with a platform to retain ties and express opinions on political and social issues that they deem important. Members of the Indian American diaspora, including those who publicly identify as Hindus, are also overly active on social media platforms, including Twitter and Facebook. Community groups like the *Indian Expats* (Facebook) and *SOS Global India* (Facebook) act as community support platforms for Indian migrant groups.[31] Hiller and Franz, who have studied the use of the internet among the diaspora in Newfoundland, found out that when migrant groups engage with each other on the internet, they are linked by 'common interest in their location of origin and a foundational identity that is rooted in that place which defines an in-group, in spite of the fact that people may or may not have ever personally interacted with one another in real time'.[32] They further argue that the online world of social media provides the diaspora with a community with people who have the same common experience of leaving their homeland. According to Julia Gittinger, social media has provided communities with a 'cultural regrouping' platform.[33] She claims, 'When native culture is no longer confined to a single geographical place of the motherland, digital space presents itself as an ideal site for the recovery of and connection with other members of the diasporic community.'[34] This is true for the Hindu diaspora and was observed in their collective response towards the image of Kamala Harris as Durga. Both, the supporters and the critics of the image used a common online platform –Twitter – to share their opinions about the image. By expressing their opinions about the image, they were bound by their common experience as a Hindu immigrant.

Kamala Harris as Durga: Politics of the Image

While examining the image that was tweeted by Meena Harris one is bound to pose questions associated with the genesis of this image. Who was the creator of the image? What was the purpose of its creation? And finally, who was the potential audience for the image? In the absence of a clearly identified creator, one can only speculate about the aims behind the creation and circulation of the image.

While rooted in the religious iconography of the South Asian goddess, the image has a clear political message. Created and circulated before the 2020 presidential elections in the United States. The message of the image was simple: the then former president Trump and his administration represented the evil forces in the United States and the team of Kamala Harris and Joe Biden were going to defeat 'evil' or Republican forces in the upcoming elections and United States will be led by the 'good' or 'divine' Democrats. While examining the iconography of the image, it is safe to conclude that the image was produced to be circulated among the younger, liberal-leaning, Democratic members of the Hindu diaspora. The image is almost a caricature, or a meme catered to their Indian-Hindu religious backgrounds. The creation and circulation of the image were a clear attempt to gain support from the younger demographic for Harris and Biden in the upcoming elections.

It should be noted here that while the image was inspired from a sacred tradition, its circulation among the liberal-democratic leaning members of the Hindu diaspora meant that there was less risk of people taking offence to the reimagined image. This is further validated by the fact that Meena Harris tweeted the image on the first day of *Navaratri*. Meena Harris a lawyer and an author, publicly identifies herself as a millennial and a Democrat. In her tweet, she reminded the Twitter platform users that it is the first day of *Navaratri*, beginning nine days of a religious festival that invokes the South Asian goddess and her various forms. Furthermore, she invokes her aunt, Kamala Harris, as Durga, the destroyer of evil. She celebrated the image for both its political and religious message of goddess Durga killing the demon Mahisha or Harris defeating Trump in the upcoming elections and hence, victory of good over evil.

For the Republicans-supporting devout Hindu members of the diaspora, the image was sacrilegious. Even before Donald Trump became the president of the United States, he had amassed a large support base among the Hindu diaspora in the United States and in India.[35] In October 2016, when Trump was a presidential nominee, he was invited to attend an India-American charity event *Humanity United Against Terror* in Edison, New Jersey.[36] The event was organized by the Republican Hindu Coalition (henceforth, RHC). Founded in 2015 the RHC claims that they represent all Hindus living in the United States.[37] According to their website, RHC is modelled on the Republican Jewish Coalition and aims to bridge the gap between the Hindu American community in the United States and the Republican policymakers.[38] The group claims to represent Hindu Americans from India, Sri Lanka, the Caribbeans, Indonesia, Bangladesh, New Zealand, Australia, Africa and Europe.[39] They also claim that 'Hindus include all faiths like Sikhs, Jains, and Buddhists'.[40] Inspired by the pro-Modi election slogan from the 2014 Indian general elections *Ab ki baar Modi Sarkaar* [This time Modi's Government], the coalition spearheaded the slogan *Abki Baar Trump Sarkar* [This time Trump's government].[41] During the *Humanity United Against Terror* event, the participants were photographed holding placards with slogans 'Trump for Hindu Americans'.[42] The group also circulated '#Hindus for Trump' on Twitter and other social media platforms.[43]

In terms of numbers, according to a 2016 National Asian American Survey, 53 per cent of Asian Indians identify with the Democratic Party and 14 per cent as Republicans and the rest remained undecided.[44] Further, a Pew Research study found out that among the Hindu diaspora in the United States, 13 per cent of those who identify as Hindus vote Republicans and 61 per cent align with the Democratic Party.[45] Considering these statistics and the public display of support from Hindu diaspora for the then former president Donald Trump, the Republican-leaning members of the Hindu diaspora perceived the image as disrespectful. It should be also mentioned here that many Hindus living in the United States do not see Kamala Harris as a 'true' Hindu. She is often accused of betraying her Hindu roots.

Harris is a daughter of immigrant parents, Shyamala Gopalan and Donald Harris. She was born and raised in California.[46] Her mother was a Hindu, who had migrated from India, and her father was from Jamaica. Harris is currently married to Douglas Emhoff, a Jewish man. In many ways, she represents true American multiculturalism. During her swearing-in ceremony as the vice president of the United States, Harris used a Bible. This, for many, became a public act of her embracing her American roots rather than 'Hindu' or 'Indian' roots. This was also in sharp contrast to her peers. For example, former congresswoman from Hawaii,

Tulsi Gabbard, a non-Indian who identifies as Hindu, had used Bhagavad Gita to take her official oath.[47]

While Kamala Harris's personal life has no direct connection with the image discussed here, it contributes to the reactions of the Hindu diaspora to the image. The members of the diaspora do not see her as a true Hindu and hence her image as Durga was even more unacceptable.

Other Controversies over Images of Goddesses

The dispute over the image of Kamala Harris as Durga was followed by another controversy when in November 2020, the American rapper Cardi B appeared on the cover of *Footwear News* magazine apparently posing as a South Asian Goddess. In the photograph, Cardi B appeared with multiple arms, showing off her tattoos and holding a bright red shoe in her hands. The image was promoting her first line of sneakers with the company Reebok.[48]

Inspired by the multi armed iconography of the South Asian goddesses, in the photograph – Cardi B appeared with ten arms and hands.[49] On social media platforms, Cardi B was accused of cultural appropriation.[50] Social media users argued that it was inappropriate for her to use sacred imagery of the South Asian goddess for a shoe advertisement since Hindu worshippers remove their shoes before entering Hindu temples.[51] Later, Cardi B apologized for the image on her Instagram account; she wrote that she was not trying to be disrespectful to anyone's culture and 'Maybe she should've done her research … can't change the past but I'm gonna do more research for the future'. [*sic*][52]

In 2014, the Hindu diaspora in the United States opposed the exhibition *Barbie-The Plastic Revolution*.[53] The exhibition featured a goddess Kali Barbie doll. Designed by Argentine artists Marianela Perelli and Pool Paolini, the plastic doll stood on a plastic skull holding a severed head in one of its hands. The artists for the exhibition had produced many sacred and secular versions of the popular Barbie doll.[54] The Kali doll was not produced for commercial purposes, and only one version of the doll was created to be included in the exhibition. Rajan Zed, an Indian immigrant, and an interfaith leader released a statement against the doll saying, 'Hindus welcome the art world to immerse in Hinduism but taking it seriously and respectfully and not for refashioning Hinduism concepts and symbols for personal agendas. Barbie-fication of Kali is simply improper, wrong, and out of place.'[55]

Prema Kurien in her work has argued that 'the process of migration and the experience of marginalization intensify the emotional attachment to the homeland and increase the importance of religion and religious institutions'.[56] This is clearly indicated in the reactions of the Hindu diaspora towards the images of South Asian goddesses created and circulated in the United States. Additionally, the Hindu diaspora residing in the United States are attempting to exclusively claim and strictly codify the Hindu religious imagery generated and circulated in the United States. Further, the social media platforms like Twitter and Facebook have provided these individuals and groups like HAF with a platform to express and circulate their opinions, anger or support for the images inspired by Hindu religious iconography.

Figure 13.1 Early 1900 print depicting Durga riding a lion defeating Mahishasura.

credit: Wikimedia Commons

Though historically, the South Asian goddess and her iconography have been used to spread political and social messages, the representation of Kamala Harris as Durga was unacceptable to many members of the Hindu diaspora.[57] In a myriad of ways, the image of Kamala Harris as Durga represents the experiences, dichotomies and lives of Hindu diaspora settled in the United States. The creation of the image and it being further shared on Twitter by Meena Harris represent the rise of the Hindus from India within the political landscape of the United States. It also exemplifies how religion plays a significant aspect for Hindus, and the support and criticism towards the image exposes the divisive and complex character of the Hindu diaspora settled in the United States.

Notes

1 Disch, Jane Lisa. 2002. *The Tyranny of the Two-Party System*. New York: Columbia University Press.

2 Murray, Laura K. 2022. *Kamala Harris First Female US Vice President*. Minnesota: Abdo Publishing.

3 PEW Research Center. 13 August. Available at: https://www.pewresearch.org/politics/2020/08/13/important-issues-in-the-2020-election/#:~:text=For%20Trump%20supporters%2C%20the%20economy,very%20important%20to%20their%20vote. (accessed on 13 July 2023).

4 Ibid.

5 Scroll Staff. 2020. 'Hindu Groups Express Anger over Tweet by Kamala Harris' Niece Showing Her as Goddess Durga'. Available at: https://scroll.in/latest/976307/hindu-groups-express-anger-over-tweet-by-kamala-harris-niece-showing-her-as-goddess-durga (accessed on 17 July 2023).

6 Ibid.

7 Moberg, Marcus, and Sofia Sjö (eds.), 2020. *Digital Media, Young Adults, and Religion an International Perspective*. Oxon and New York: Routledge.

8 Ahmed, Imran, Zahid Shahab Ahmed, Howard Brasted, and Shahram Akbarzadeh (eds.), 2022. *Religion, Extremism and Violence in South Asia*. Australia: Springer. Xenia, Zeiler (ed.), 2020. *Digital Hinduism*. London and NY: Routledge, Scheifinger, Heinz. 2013. 'Hindu Worship online and Offline'. In *Digital Religion Understanding Religious Practice in New Media Worlds*, edited by H. A. Campbell. London and New York: Routledge.

9 Scroll Staff. 2020. 'Hindu Groups Express Anger over Tweet by Kamala Harris' Niece Showing Her as Goddess Durga'. Available at: https://scroll.in/latest/976307/hindu-groups-express-anger-over-tweet-by-kamala-harris-niece-showing-her-as-goddess-durga (accessed on 17 July 2023).

10 Shukla, Suhag A. @SuhagAShukla on Twitter (now X).
11 https://www.hinduamerican.org (accessed on 17 July 2023).
12 Kurien, P. 2007. *A Place at the Multicultural Table*. NJ: Rutgers University Press.
13 Shukla, Suhag A. @SuhagAShukla. Dear @meenaharris, by now you know that your tweeting a caricature of the feminine divine, Maa Durga, with faces superimposed, deeply aggrieved many Hindus globally. To avoid such an error in judgement, for future reference, please refer to HAF guidelines on commercial use of Hindu Images. 18 October 2020. Tweet.
14 Ibid.
15 Hindu American Foundation. Guidelines for Commercial Use of Hindu Images. Available at: https://www.hinduamerican.org/projects/commercial-use-hindu-images-guide (accessed on 17 July 2023).
16 Ibid.
17 Ibid.
18 Ibid.
19 Ibid.
20 The number of retweets, likes, replies on a tweet varies depending on members leaving and adding themselves to the social media platform.
21 Praneeth Rao @praneeth_rao. 20 October 2020. 'lol, u will find images of ram with faces superimposed of modi advani etc created by by the hindu parties there are people claiming to be durga avtar, no one gets offended but lol the most tolerant u got offended.' Tweet.
22 Pew Research Report. 2021. 'Asian Americans: A Mosaic of Faiths'. Available at: https://www.pewresearch.org/religion/2012/07/19/asian-americans-a-mosaic-of-faiths-overview/ (accessed on 30 July 2023).
23 Rajghatta, C. 10/162016. 'Donald Trump Pledges Even Better Ties with New Delhi, says 'big fan of India and Hindus' in Times of India'. Available at: https://timesofindia.indiatimes.com/us-elections-2016/donald-trump-pledges-even-better-ties-with-new-delhi-says-big-fan-of-india-and-hindus/articleshow/54878649.cms (accessed on 30 July 2023).
24 Orth, T. 2022. 'Americans' Views on 35 Religious Groups, Organizations and Belief Systems'. Available at: https://today.yougov.com/topics/society/articles-reports/2022/12/23/americans-views-religious-groups-yougov-poll (accessed on 30 July 2023).
25 US Census. Available at: https://www.census.gov/programs-surveys/decennial-census/decade/2020/2020-census-results.htm (accessed on 27 July 2023).
26 Kurien, Prema. 2004. 'Multiculturalism, Immigrant Religion, and Diasporic Nationalism: The Development of an American Hinduism'. *Social Problems*, 51 (3): 362–85.
27 Dave, Pares. 'Indian Immigrants Are Techs New Titans'. Available at: https://www.latimes.com/business/la-fi-indians-in-tech-20150812-story.html#:~:text=There%20are%2089%2C000%20Indians%20living,into%20

the%20start%2Dup%20economy (accessed on 8 March 2023) *Los Angeles Times*. 11 August 2015.

28 In the world of IT and Technology companies the acronym FAANG refers to the five tech giants of the United States – Facebook, Amazon, Apple, Netflix, and Google. WITCH stands for the Indian tech companies – Wipro, Infosys, TCS, CTS and HCL.

29 12 January 2023. Press Release from the office of Congressman Ro Khanna. Available at: https://khanna.house.gov/media/press-releases/representatives-khanna-bera-jayapal-krishnamoorthi-and-thanedar-celebrate (accessed on 28 June 2023) and Astor, M and Cowan, J. 27 February 20203. *The New York Times. Indian Americans Rapidly Climbing Political Ranks* https://www.nytimes.com/2023/02/27/us/politics/indian-american-politicians.html.

30 Graham, Ruth. 'Vivek Ramaswamy Leans Into His Hindu Faith to Court Christian Voters'. *The New York Times.* 9 July 2023. Available at: https://www.nytimes.com/2023/07/09/us/vivek-ramaswamy-hindu-republican-christianj.html (accessed on 28 July 2023).

31 Facebook group *Indian Expat* has 100 K members and *SOS Indian Global*, which is registered as US Solutions and Networking for Indians in the United States currently has 259,773 members.

32 Hiller, H.H and Franz, T.M. 2004. 'New Ties, Old Ties and Lost Ties: The Use of the Internet in Diaspora' *New Media and Society, Vol 6.*

33 Gittinger, Julia L. 2020. 'Cultural Regrouping in the Diaspora Mediating Hindu Identity Online' In *Digital Hinduism*, edited by Zeiler, Xenia. London and NY: Routledge.

34 Ibid.

35 Brown, Lee. 2020. 'Indian Man Prays to Life-Size Statue of Donald Trump, His "God"'. *New York Post*. Available at: https://nypost.com/2020/02/19/indian-man-prays-to-life-size-statue-of-donald-trump-his-god/ (accessed on 2 August 2023).

36 Schreckinger, B. 2016/10/15. 'Trump Goes Bollywood'. Available at: https://www.politico.com/story/2016/10/donald-trump-bollywood-india-hindus-new-jersey-229848 (accessed on 1 August 2023).

37 Republican Hindu Coalition Website. Available at: https://rhc-usa.org/about/ (Accessed on 1 August 2023).

38 Ibid.

39 Ibid.

40 Ibid.

41 Kaushika, P. 11/09/2017. 'Ab ki baar, Modi Sarkar slogan was born in BJP's Election War Room'. Accessed at: https://theprint.in/report/ab-ki-baar-modi-sarkar-slogan-born-bjps-election-war-room/10684/ (accessed on 1 August 2023). And https://rhc-usa.org/about/.

42 Gajjar, Saloni. 24 October 2016. 'Donald Trump Attends "Humanity United Against Terror" Event in New Jersey' Available at: https://www.

india.com/lifestyle/donald-trump-attends-humanity-united-against-terror-event-in-new-jersey-1604268/ (accessed on 8 March 2023).

43 Ibid.

44 2016. 'Report on Registered Votes in Fall'. Report submitted to National Asian American Survey. Available at: https://naasurvey.com/wp-content/uploads/2016/10/NAAS2016-Oct5-report.pdf (accessed on 1 August 2023).

45 Pew Research Centre. 2024. 'Indian Americans: A Survey Data Snapshot', Washington. Available at: https://www.pewresearch.org/2024/08/06/indian-americans-a-survey-data-snapshot/ (accessed on 4 August 2025).

46 Murray, L.K. 2022. *Kamala Harris: First Female US Vice President*. Minnesota: Abdo Publishing.

47 Basu, Tanya. 'Hindus Are Thriving in America, But There Is Only One in Congress'. *The Atlantic*. Available at: https://www.theatlantic.com/politics/archive/2015/03/hindus-in-american-politics/386941/ (accessed on 8 April 2023) 5 March 2015.

48 'Cardi B Apologizes for Goddess Durga Look on Magazine Cover'. Available at: https://www.thehindu.com/entertainment/cardi-b-apologises-for-goddess-durga-look-on-magazine-cover/article33083388.ece (accessed on 3 March 2023).

49 Ibid.

50 'Cardi B Apologizes for Goddess Durga Look on Magazine Cover'. Available at: https://www.thehindu.com/entertainment/cardi-b-apologises-for-goddess-durga-look-on-magazine-cover/article33083388.ece (accessed on 8 March 2023).

51 Ibid.

52 Cardi B Instagram account @iamcardib MISSING.

53 Bell, Venessa. 'Controversial Religious Barbie Doll Exhibition Opens in Buenos Aires'. *The Guardian*. 21 October 2015. Available at: https://www.theguardian.com/travel/2015/oct/21/barbie-and-ken-religious-art-exhibition (accessed on 8 April 2023).

54 Ibid.

55 Wheaton, Oliver. 'Barbie-fication of Kali Is Wrong': Outrage at Artists' Barbie Doll of Hindu God'. Available at: https://metro.co.uk/2014/09/27/barbie-fication-of-kali-is-wrong-outrage-at-artists-barbie-doll-of-hindu-god-4883933 (accessed on 8 March 2023). 27 September 2014.

56 Kurien, Prema. 2004. 'Multiculturalism, Immigrant Religion, and Diasporic Nationalism: The Development of an American Hinduism'. *Social Problems*, 51 (3): 362–85.

57 Sen, Atreyee. 'The Hindu Goddess in Indian Politics'. Available at: https://politicaltheology.com/the-hindu-goddess-in-indian-politics-atreyee-sen/ (accessed on 8 March 2023). 29 May 2015.

Bibliography

Primary Sources

Ādinātha. *Khecarīvidyā*. ed. and trans. by James Mallinson. 2007. *The Khecarīvidyā of Ādinātha: A Critical Edition and Annotated Translation of an Early Text of Haṭhayoga*. London: Routledge.

Ādinātha. *Mahākālasaṁhitā: Kāmakalākālīkhaṇḍa*. ed. by Kiśoranāth Jhā. 1986 (1972). Allahabad: Gaṅgānāth Jhā Kendrīya Saṁskṛta Vidyāpīṭha.

Ādinātha. *Mahākālasaṁhitā: Kāmakalākālīkhaṇḍa: With the Jñānavatī Hindi Commentary*. ed. & comm. by Radheshyam Chaturvedi. 2013. Varanasi: Chaukhamba Surbharati Prakashan.

Aṅgavijjā. ed. by Muni Punyavijaya. 1957. Benaras: Prakrit Text Society.

Aṅgavijjā Prathama Khaṇḍa. trans. by Rajendra Ratnesh. 2016. Jaipur: Prakrit Bharati Academy.

Avataṃmsaka Sūtra. trans. by Thomas Cleary. 1993. *The Flower Ornament Scripture*. London: Shambhala.

Bhagavatī Sūtra Vol. ed. by K.C. Lalwani. 1973. Calcutta: Jain Bhawan.

Bhattacharya, D. C. 1991. *Pratimālakṣāṇa of the Viṣṇudharmottara*. New Delhi: Harman Publishing House.

Candragomin. *Āryatārāmahāṣṭabhayōttarastava*. trans. by Martin Wilson. 1996. *In Praise of Tārā: Songs to the Savioress*. Massachusetts, MA: Wisdom Publication, 236–7.

Candragomin. *Ārya Tārādevī Stotra Muktikāmālā Nāma*. trans. by Martin Wilson. 1996. *In Praise of Tārā: Songs to the Savioress*. Massachusetts, MA: Wisdom Publication, 226-31.

dge-'dun grub-pa. *rje-btsun bcom-ldan-'das-ma seng-ldeng-nags gyi sgrol-ma la bstod-pa mkhas-pa'I gtsug-rgyna zhes-bya-ba*. ed. by Donal La Rocca and Lozang Jamspal. 2008. Available at: https://www.academia.edu/44757178/The_Crowning_Ornament_of_the_Wise_and_The_Jewel_that_Increases_Wisdom_and_Longevity (accessed on 10 January 2024).

Gopal, B.R. and et al., eds. 1976. *Epigraphia Carnatica*, Vol. V. Mysore: University of Mysore Prasaranga.

Griffith, Ralph H. trans. by. 1917. *The Hymns of the Atharva-Veda*, Vol. II (second edition). Benares: E.J. Lazarus and Co.

Hultzsch, E., ed. and trans. 1891. *South-Indian Inscriptions: Tamil Inscriptions of Rajaraja, Rajendra-Chola, and Others in the Rajarajesvara Temple of Tanjavur*, Vol. II, pt. I. Calcutta & Bombay: Thacker, Spink & Co.

Hultzsch, E., ed. 1979 (1894–95). *Epigraphia Indica*, Vol. III. New Delhi: Archaeological Survey of India.

Jamison, Stephanie W., Joel P. Brereton, trans. 2014. *The Rigveda – The Earliest Religious Poetry of India*. Oxford: Oxford University Press.

Jinarakshita. *Sragdharā Stotra Ṭikā*. ed. by Satish Chandra Vidyabhusana. 1908. *Bauddha Stotra Saṁgrahaḥ (1)*. Calcutta: Asiatic Society of Bengal.

Kālikāpurāṇa. B. N. Shastri, ed. and tr. 1991–1992. Delhi: Nag Publishers.

Kielhorn, F. 1892. 'Kālañjara Stone Inscription of Kīrtivarman'. In *Epigraphica Indica*, Vol. I. Calcutta: Superintendent of Government Printing India.

Kielhorn, F. 1900–01. *Epigraphia Indica* VI. Calcutta: Superintendent of Government Printing India.

Kramrisch, Stella. 1928. *The Vishnudharmottara: A Treatise on Indian Painting and Image-Making*. Part III. Calcutta: Calcutta University Press.

Majjhima Nikaya. trans. by. I.B. Horner. 2020(1954). *Majjhima Nikāya: The Middle Length Sayings of the Buddha*. Available at: http://buddhadust.net/backmatter/indexes/idx_downloads.htm#pts_pdfs (accessed on 15 December 2023).

Malliṣeṇasūri, *Syādvādamañjari*. trans. by F. W. Thomas. 1968. *The Flower-Spray of the Quodamodddo Doctrine: Śri Malliṣeṇasūri's Syādvādamañjari*, Delhi: Motilal Banarsidass.

Manthānabhairavatantram. ed. and trans. by Mark S.G. Dyczkowski. 2009. *Manthānabhairavatantram: Kumārikākhaṇḍah*, Vol. 1–14. New Delhi: D.K. Printworlds.

Mātṛceṭa. *Ārya Tārādevī Stotra Sarvārtha Sadhananāma Stotra Rāja*. trans. by Martin Wilson. 1996. *In Praise of Tārā: Songs to the Saviouress*. Massachusetts, MA: Wisdom Publication, 214–21.

Mayamatham. ed. and trans. by Prasanna Kumar Acharya. 2011. *Architecture of Mānasāra: Text with English Translation, Notes and Index*. Delhi: New Bharatiya Book Corporation.

Mayamatam. ed. and trans. by Bruno Dagens. 2007 (1994). *Mayamatam: Treatise of Housing, Architecture and Iconography*, Vol. I & II. New Delhi: Indira Gandhi National Centre for the Arts.

Mukhopadhyaya, Sujit Kumar, ed. 1954. *The Śārdūlakarṇāvadāna*. Santiniketan: Viśvabharati Publishing Department.

Nagaraja Rao, H.M., et al. eds. 2006. *Epigraphia Carnatica*, Vol. XIII. Mysore: University of Mysore Prasaranga.

Narasimhamurthy, A.V., et al. eds. 1990. *Epigraphia Carnatica*, Vol. IX. Mysore: University of Mysore Prasaranga.

Paṇṇavaṇasuttaṁ. Punyavijaya, Muni, Malvania, Dalsukh and Amritlal Mohan Bhojak, eds. 1971. Bombay: Shri Mahavira Jaina Vidyalaya.

Ramesh, K.V. 1984. *Inscriptions of the Western Gaṅgas*. New Delhi: ICHR.

Reddy, Devarakonda ed. 1998. *Kannaḍa University Epigraphical Series*, Vol. I. Hampi: Kannaḍa University Prasaranga.

Rice, B.R. ed. 1905. *Epigraphia Carnatica*, Vol. X. Bangalore: Government of Mysore.

Samantabhadra. *Ratnakaraṇḍaka Śrāvakācāra, Ācārya Samantabhadra's Ratnakaraṇḍaka Śrāvakācāra*. ed. Vijay K. Jain. 2016. Dehradun: Vikalpa Printers.

Settar, S. 1976–77. *Archaeological Survey of Mysore: Annual Reports 1906–12, A Study*, Vol. III. Dharwar: Institute of Kannaḍa Studies.

Suttāgame. ed. by Phulchandji Maharaj. 1954. Gurgaon Cantt: Sūtrāgamaprakāśaka Samiti.

Tārāmūlakalpa. trans. by Susan Landesman. 2020. *The Tārā Tantra Part I: The Root Tantra, Treasury of the Buddhist Sciences Series*. Somerville, MA: Wisdom publication.

Taranath. *'Dam-pa'i-chos-rin-po-che-'aphags-pa'i- yul-du-ji-ltar-dar-ba'i-tshul-gsal-bar-ston-pa-dgos-'adod'*. trans. by Lama Chimpa and Alaka Chattopadhyaya. 1990. *Taranath's History of Buddhism in India*. Delhi: Motilal Banarsidass.

Tārāṣṭaghoratāraṇī Sūtra. trans. by Samye Translations. 2023. *Tārā Who Protects from the Eight Dangers*. Available at: https://read.84000.co/translation/UT22084-051-001.html (accessed on 25 October 2023).

Trivedi, H.V. 1989. *Corpus Inscriptionum Indicarum: Inscriptions of the Paramāras, Candellas, Kachchhapaghātas and two Minor Dynasties*, Vol. VII, pt. 2. New Delhi: ASI.

Umāsvāmi. *Tattvārtha Sūtra, Ācārya Umāsvāmi's Tattvārtha Sūtra: With Explanations in English from Ācārya Pūjyapāda's Sarvārthasiddhi*. ed. by Vijay K. Jain. 2018. Dehradun: Vikalpa Printers.

Vāmanapurāṇa, eds. Anand Swarup Gupta, Satyamsu Mohan Mukhopadhyaya, Ahibhushan Bhattacharya, N.C. Nath, and trans. V.K. Verma, 1968. Varanasi: All India Kashiraj Trust.

Varahamihira. *Bṛhatsaṁhitā*. ed. by V. Subrahmanya Sastri and M. Ramakrishna Bhat.1997. *Varahamihira's Brihat Samhita: with an English Translation and Notes*. New Delhi: Ranjana Publications.

Varahamihira. 2008. *Vārāhī(Brihat)Samhita*. Bambai: Khemraj Shri Krishnadass Publisher.

Varāhapurāṇa. trans. S. Venkitasubramania Iyer. 2003 (1985). *Ancient Indian Tradition and Mythology*, Vol. XXXI, pt. I, ed. by J.L. Shastri. Delhi: Motilal Banarsidass Publishers.

Whitehead, H. 1916. *Village Gods of South India*. London: Oxford University Press.

Ziegenbalg, B. 1713. *Genealogy of the South-Indian Gods: A Manual of the Mythology and Religion of the People of Southern India*. Madras: Higginbotham.

Secondary Sources

Abraham, Susan. 1997. 'The Deorala Judgement Glorifying Sati'. *The Lawyer's Collective*, 12 (6): 4–12.

Agarwala, P.K. 1984. *Goddesses in Ancient India*. New Delhi: Abhinav Publications.

Ahmad, Salik. 2019. *Thirty-Two Years after Roop Kanwar's Death, Blind Faith Overshadows Reason*. Outlook India.

Ahmed, Imran, Zahid Shahab Ahmed, Howard Brasted and Shahram Akbarzadeh, eds. 2022. *Religion, Extremism and Violence in South Asia*. Australia: Springer.

Aiyappan, A. 1931. 'Myth of the Origin of Smallpox'. *Folklore* 42 (3): 291–3.

Analayo, Bhikku. 2021. 'Overcoming Fear by Recollecting the Buddha: His Role in Early Buddhist Texts'. *Mindfulness*, 12: 594–603.

Astor, M., & Cowan, J. (2023). *New York Times*. 27 February. Indian Americans rapidly climbing political ranks. https://www.nytimes.com/2023/02/27/us/politics/indian-american-politicians.html.

Babb, Lawrence A. 1988. 'Giving and Giving Up: The Eightfold Worship among Śvetāmbara Mūrtipūjak Jains'. *Journal of Anthropological Research* 44 (1): 67–86.

Bakker, H.T. 2016. *The World of Skandapurāṇa: Northern India in Sixth and Seventh Centuries*. Leiden and Boston: Brill.

Banerjea, J.N. 1956. *Development of Hindu Iconography*. New Delhi: Munshiram Manoharlal Publishers.

Bernard, Elizabeth and Beverly Moon, eds. 2000. *Goddesses Who Rule*. New York: Oxford University Press.

Bhattacharya, B.C. 1939. *Jaina Iconography*. Lahore: Motilal Banarsidass.

Bhattacharyya, N.N. 1964. *Indian Mother Goddess*. Calcutta University: R.D. Press.

Bhattacharyya, N.N. 1999. *The Indian Mother Goddesses*. Delhi: Manohar.

Bhattacharyya, N.N. 2005 (1975). *Ancient Indian Rituals and Their Social Contents*. New Delhi: Manohar.

Binny, Malavika. 2023. 'Towards an Iconography of Disease: Exploring the Gendered Worlds of the Goddesses of Epidemics'. *Studies in History*, 39 (1): 12–28. https://doi.org/10.1177/02576430231184535.

Bithoo, Virendra Singh. 2018. *Science and Society in Varāhamihira's Jyotiṣaśāstra*. Unpublished Doctoral Thesis: Centre for Historical Studies, Jawaharlal Nehru University, New Delhi.

Boyce, Mary, ed. and tr. 1984. *Textual Sources for the Study of Zoroastrianism*. Chicago: The University of Chicago Press.

Bushaw, Jenny. 2007. 'Suicide or Sacrifice? An Examination of the Sati Ritual in India'. Dissertation submitted to the Centre for Middle Eastern Studies, University of Chicago. Available at: https://www.academia.edu/1963554/SUICIDE_OR_SACRIFICE_An_Examination_of_the_Sati_Ritual_in_India (accessed on 2 May 2023).

Butler, J. 1990. *Gender Trouble: Feminism and the Subversion of Identity*. London: Routledge.

Chakravarty, D.K. 1968. 'The Antiquity and the Evolution of the Saptamatrika Worship in Bengal'. *Proceedings of the Indian History Congress* 30: 129–38. Available at: https://www.jstor.org/stable/44141463.

Chatterjee, Asim Kumar. 1978 (Reprint 2000). *A Comprehensive History of Jainism: Vol. I*. New Delhi: Munshiram Manoharlal.

Chattopadhyaya, B.D. 2016 (2003, 2005, 2008). *Studying Early India: Archaeology, Texts and Historical Issues*. Delhi: Permanent Black.

Chattopadhyaya, B.D. 1984. 'Religion in a Royal Household'. In *The Making of Early Medieval India*. New Delhi: Oxford University Press: 222–32.

Chaudhuri, Nupur and Rajat Kanta Ray. 2007. 'Eros and History: Sahajiya Secrets and the Tantric Culture of Love'. In *Religion in Indian History*, ed. by Irfan Habib. New Delhi: Tulika Books. 102–25.

Chopra, Radhika. 2022. 'Curating Divinity: Religious Souvenirs, Shopkeepers and Bazaar Curation'. *Journal of Multidisciplinary International Studies* 18 (1/2): 111–24.

Coburn, Thomas B. 1988. *Devī-Māhātmya: The Crystallization of the Goddess Tradition*. Delhi: Motilal Banarsidass.

Coburn, Thomas B. 1992. *Encountering the Goddess: A Translation of the Devī Māhātmya and a Study of Its Interpretation*. New York: SUNY.

Connell, R. W. and J.W. Messerschmidt. 2005. 'Hegemonic Masculinities: Rethinking the Concept'. *Gender and Society* 19 (6): 829–59.

Colley, Frederick C. 1978. 'Traditional Indian Medicine in Malaysia.' *Journal of the Malaysian Branch of the Royal Asiatic Society* 51 (1): 77–109.

Cort, John. 2001. *Jains in the World: Religious Values and Ideology in India*. Oxford: Oxford University Press.

Crooke, W. 1919. 'The Cults of the Mother Goddesses in India.' *Folklore* XXXIX: 133–42.

Daniel, E. Valentine and F.P. Judy. 1984. *South Asian Systems of Healing*. Leiden: E. J. Brill.

Das, H.C. 1977. 'Sapta Matrakas in Orissa'. *Proceedings of the Indian History Congress* 38: 197–204. Available at: https://www.jstor.org/stable/44139070.

de Beauvoir, Simon and C. Borde and S.M. Chevallier, trans. 2011. *The Second Sex*. New York: Vintage Books.

Deborah, Davis and Elizabeth F. Loftus. 2012. 'Inconsistencies between Law and the Limits of Human Cognition: The Case of Eyewitness Identification' in *Memory and Law*, ed. Lynn Nadel and Walter P. Sinnott Armstrong. New York: Oxford University Press: 29–58.

Debord, Guy. 2014. *The Society of the Spectacle*. trans. by Ken Knabb. Canada: The Bureau of Public Secrets.

Desai, Devangana. 1996. *Religious Imagery of Khajuraho*. Mumbai: Project for Indian Cultural Studies Publication.

Diesel, Alleyn 2002. 'The Suffering Mothers: The Hindu Amman Goddesses as Empowering Role Models for Women.' *Journal for the Study of Religion* 15 (1). With Special Thematic Section 'Religion and Rhetoric': 39–62.

Disch, Jane Lisa 2002. *The Tyranny of the Two-Party System*. New York: Columbia University Press.

Dube, Leela. 2001. Caste and Women. *Anthropological Explorations in Gender: Intersecting Fields*. Delhi: Sage Publication: 154–73.

Dubois, J.A. 1906. *Hindu Manners, Customs and Ceremonies*. Oxford: Clarendon Press.

Dundas, Paul. 2002. *The Jains*. London: Routledge.

Durga, Panda Prasad. 2019. 'Thirty-Two Years after Roop Kanwar's Death, Blind Faith Still Overshadows Reason'. *Outlook*. https://www.outlookindia.com/national/india-news-thirty-two-years-after-roop-kanwars-death-blind-faith-still-overshadows-reason-news-302221.

Durkheim, Emile. 1995. *The Elementary Forms of Religious Life*. trans. by Karen E. Fields. United States: The Free Press.

Elayath, Kunjikttan. 2003. *Kodungallor Kshetra: Itihasam*. Sringapuram, Kodungallor: Devi Bookstall Publication. Reprint 2017.

Ellingson, S. 2002. 'Introduction'. In *Religion and Sexuality in Cross-Cultural Perspective*, ed. by S. Ellingson and M. Christian Green. London: Routledge.

Emmerick, Ronald E. and M. Macuch, eds. 2009. *The Literature of Pre-Islamic Iran*, Companion Volume I to A History of Persian Literature Volume XVII. London: I.B. Tauris.

English, Elizabeth. 2002. *Vajrayogini: Her Visualizations, Rituals, & Forms*. Boston: Wisdom Publications.

Erndl, Kathleen M. 2000. 'Is Shakti Empowering for Women? Reflections on Feminism and the Hindu Goddess'. In *Is the Goddess a Feminist? The Politics of South Asian Goddesses*, ed. by Alf Hiltebeitel and Kathleen M. Erndl. New York: New York University Press. 91–103.

Eschmann, A. 2014. 'Hinduization of Tribal Deities in Orissa: The Śākta and Śaiva Typology'. In *The Cult of Jagannātha and the Regional Tradition of Orissa*, ed. by Eschmann, A., Hermann Kulke, G.C. Tripathi. Delhi: Manohar. 79–98.

Fleet, J.F. 1878. 'Sanskrit and Old Canarese Inscriptions. No. XLVIII'. *Indian Antiquary* VII: 300–3.

Foucault, Michel. 1989. *The Order of Things: An Archaeology of the Human Sciences*. New York: Routledge.

Galeano, Eduardo and Mark Fried, trans. 2009. *Mirrors: Stories of Almost Everyone*. New York: Nation Books.

Getty, Alice. 1914. *The Gods of Northern Buddhism: Their History, Iconography and Progressive Evolution through the Northern Buddhist Countries*. Oxford: Clarendon Press.

Gittinger, Julia L. 2020. 'Cultural Regrouping in the Diaspora Mediating Hindu Identity Online'. In *Digital Hinduism*, ed. by Xenia, Zeiler. London and New York: Routledge. 68–88.

Golovkova, Anya A. 2020. 'The Goddess's Forgotten Consort: Desire in the Nityā Cult and the Cult of Tripurasundarī'. *International Journal of Hindu Studies* 24 (1): 87–106.

Goffman, Erving. 1956. *The Presentation of Self in Everyday Life*. Edinburgh: University of Edinburgh.

Goudriaan, Teun and Sanjukta Gupta. 2020 (1981). *A History of Indian Literature: Volume II, Facsimile 2: Hindu Tantric and Śākta Literature*. Wiesbaden: Otto Harrassowitz.

Gupto, Arun. 2018. *Goddesses of Kathmandu Valley: Grace, Rage, Knowledge*. 2nd ed. London: Routledge.

Hambly, Gavin R.G, eds. 1999. *Women in the Medieval Islamic World: Power, Patronage, and Piety*. New York: St. Martin's Press.

Hart, George. L. 1975. *The Poems of Ancient Tamil, Their Milieu and Their Sanskrit Counterparts*. Berkeley: University of California Press.

Hartmann, Jens-Uwe. 1988. 'The *Triratnastotra* Ascribed to Mātṛceṭa'. In *Proceedings of the 4th Seminar of the International Association for Tibetan Studies*, ed. by Helga Uebach and Jampa L. Panglung. Munich: BADW. 177–84.

Hatley, Shaman. 2019. *The Brahmayāmala and Early Saiva Cult of Yoginīs*. Unpublished Doctoral Thesis. Department of Religious Studies, University of Pennsylvania., Pennsylvania.

Hazra, R.C. 1963. *Studies in the Upapurāṇas*, Vol. I & II. Calcutta: Sanskrit College.

Hazra, R.C. 1987. *The Puranic Records on Hindu Rites and Customs*. Delhi: Motilal Banarsidass.

Hiller, H.H. and T.M. Franz 2004. 'New Ties, Old Ties and Lost Ties: The Use of the Internet in Diaspora', *New Media and Society* 6 (6): 731–52.

Hiltebeitel, Alf. 1988. *The Cult of Draupadī: Mythologies: From Gingee to Kurukṣetra*, Vol. I. Chicago: University of Chicago Press.

Hiltebeitel, Alf. 1991. *The Cult of Draupadī: On Hindu Ritual and the Goddess*, Vol. II. Chicago: University of Chicago Press.

Humphrey, Caroline. 1984. 'Some Aspects of the Jain Puja: The Idea of "God" And the Symbolism of Offerings'. *The Cambridge Journal of Anthropology Journal of Anthropology* 9 (3): 1–19.

Jain, J.C. 2004. *History and Development of Prakrit Literature*. New Delhi: Manohar.

Jain, K.C. 2001. *Mahāvīra and His Times*. Delhi: Motilal Banarsidass.

Jain, Kajri. 2007. *Gods in the Bazaar: The Economies of Indian Calendar Art*. London: Duke University Press.

Jaini, Padmanabh S. 1998 (Reprint). *The Jaina Path of Purification*. Delhi: Motilal Banarsidass.

Jha, D.N, ed. 2020. *Drink of Immortality: Essays on Distillation and Alcohol Use in Ancient India*. New Delhi: Manohar.

Jha, Pankaj. 2019. *A Political History of Literature: Vidyapati and the Fifteenth Century*. New Delhi: Oxford University Press.

Kapadia, K. 2019. *Siva and Her Sisters: Gender, Caste and Class in Rural South India*. Delhi: Taylor and Francis.

Karmacharya, Basudev. BS 2071 (2014). *Lalitpur Jillaka Prasidha Devidevatako Parichaya (Introduction to the Famous Goddesses and Gods of Lalitpur District)*. Lalitpur: Shrimati Chandeswari Karmachara.

Kinsley, David. 1997. *Tantric Visions of the Divine Feminine: The Ten Mahavidyas*. Delhi: Motilal Banarasidass.

Kishwar, Madhu and Ruth Vanita. 1987. 'The Burning of Roop Kanwar'. *Manushi* 42/43: 15–25.

Kosambi, D.D. 1962. *Myth and Reality*. Mumbai: Popular Prakarshan.

Kosambi, Damodar Dharmananda. 1962. *Myth and Reality: Studies in the Formation of Indian Culture*. Accessed online: https://archive.org/details/MythAndReality/mode/1up?view=theater.

Kurien, Prema. 2004. 'Multiculturalism, Immigrant Religion, and Diasporic Nationalism: The Development of an American Hinduism'. *Social Problems* 51 (3): 362–85.

Kurien, Prema. 2007. *A Place at the Multicultural Table*. New Jersey: Rutgers University Press.

Landesman, Susan. 2008. 'Goddess Tārā: Silence and Secrecy on the Path to Enlightenment'. *Journal of Feminist Studies in Religion* 24 (1): 44–59.

Lerner, Gerda. 1968. *Creation of Patriarchy*. New York: Oxford University Press.

Mabett, Ian. 1998. 'The Problem of the Historical Nāgārjuna Revisited'. *Journal of the American Oriental Society* 118 (3): 332–46.

Mahmood, Saba. 2006. 'Agency, Performativity, and the Feminist Subject', In *Bodily Citations: Religion and Judith Butler*, ed. by E.T. Armour and Susan M. ST. Ville. New York: Columbia University Press. 177–224.

Mahalakshmi, R. 2011. *The Making of the Goddess: Koṟṟavai-Durgā in the Tamil Tradition*. New Delhi: Penguin Books.

Mahalakshmi, R. 2016. The Sacred Geography of *Devī Kṣetras*: Integrative Networks, Cultic Assimilation and Marginalization. Paper presented at the Indian History Congress.

Mahalakshmi, R. 2018. 'Gods, Rituals and Religious Ideas: An Exploration of the Avesta and the *Ṛgveda*'. *Studies in People's History* 5 (2): 127–42.

Masakazu, Tanaka. n.d. 'Defying Blessings of the Goddess and the Community: Disputes over Sati (Widow Burning) in Contemporary India'. Available at: http://www.zinbun.kyoto-u.ac.jp/~shakti/en/suttee.html.

Meister, M.W. 2007. 'Image Iconopraxis and Iconoplasty in South Asia'. *RES: Anthropology and Aesthetics*, 51: 13–32.

Menon, Meena, Geeta Sheshu and Sujata Anandan. 1987. '"Trial by Fire". Bombay: Women and Media Committee'. *Bombay Union of Journalists*. Available at: http://www.unipune.ac.in/snc/cssh/HumanRights/07%20STATE%20AND%20GENDER/06.pdf (accessed on June 2024).

Mirza, H.K. 1971. 'On Avesta, Pahlavi and Persian Sources'. In *Indian Civilization: The First Phase Problems of a Sourcebook*, ed. by S.C. Malik. Simla: Indian Institute of Advanced Study.

Moberg, Marcus and Sjö, Sofia, eds. 2020. *Digital Media, Young Adults, and Religion: An International Perspective*. Oxon and New York: Routledge.

Monier-Williams, Monier. 1960 (1899). *A Sanskrit-English Dictionary*. Oxford: Clarendon Press.

Monier, Williams and C.C. Henry. 1880. 'Indian Mother-Worship.' *The Folk-Lore Record* 3 (1): 117–23.

Murray, Laura K. 2022. *Kamala Harris First Female US Vice President*. Minnesota: Abdo Publishing.

Nandi, R.N. 1973. *Religious Institutions and Cults in the Deccan*. Delhi: Motilal Banarsidass.

Nepali, Gopal Singh. 2015. *The Newars: An Ethno-Sociological Study of a Himalayan Community*. Kathmandu: Mandala Books.

Oldenburg, Veena Talwar. 1994. 'The Roop Kanwar Case Feminist Responses and the Continuing Invention of the Sati Tradition'. In *The Blessing and the Curse: The Burning of Wives in India*, ed. by J.S. Hawley. New York: Oxford University Press. 101–30.

Omvedt, Gail. 2003. *Buddhism in India – Challenging Brahmanism and Caste*. New Delhi: Sage.

Orth, T. 2022. 'Americans' Views on 35 Religious Groups, Organizations and Belief Systems'. Available at: https://today.yougov.com/topics/society/articles-reports/2022/12/23/americans-views-religious-groups-yougov-poll (accessed on 30 July 2023).

Padma, Sree. 2014. *Vicissitudes of the Goddess: Reconstruction of the Gramdevata in India's Religious Traditions*. United Kingdom: Oxford University Press.

Pal, Pratapaditya. 1985. *Art of Nepal*. Berkeley: University of California Press.

Pandey, K.C. 1954. *An Outline of the History of Śaiva Philosophy*. Delhi: Motilal Banarsidass.

Paul, Williams. 2009. *Mahāyāna Buddhism: The Doctrinal Foundation*. New York: Routledge.

Picron, Claudine Baut. 2016. 'Images of Devotion and Power in South and Southeast Bengal'. In *Esoteric Buddhism in Medieval Maritime Asia: Networks of Masters, Texts, Icons*, ed. by Andrea Acri. Singapore: ISEAS Yusof Ishak Institute Press. 163–90.

Pinney, Christopher. 2004. 'What Pictures Want Now: Rural Consumer of Images, 1980-2000'. In *Photos of the Gods: The Printed Image and Political Structure in India*. London: Reaktion Books.

Pingree, D. 1981. *Jyotiḥśāstra: Astral and Mathematical Literature*. Wiesbaden: Harrassowitz.

Pintchman, T. 2014. *Seeking Mahadevi: Constructing the Identities of the Hindu Great Goddess*. New York: State University of New York.

Puniyani, Ram. 2016. 'Durga, Mahishasur and Caste Politics'. *The Forward Press*. Available at: https://www.forwardpress.in/2016/03/durga-mahishasur-and-caste-politics/ (accessed on 27 July 2018).

Ranciere, Jacques. 2013. *The Politics of Aesthetics*. United Kingdom: Bloomsbury Publications.

Reuther, Rosemary Radford. 2005. *Goddesses and the Divine Feminine – A Western Religious History*. Berkeley: University of California Press.

Roy, Anamika. 2015. *Sixty-Four Yoginis: Cult, Icons and Goddesses*. New Delhi: Primus Books.

Roy, K. 2002. 'Goddesses in the Ṛgveda'. In *Invoking Goddesses: Gender Politics in Indian Religion*, ed. by Nilima Chitgopekar. Delhi: Shakti Books. 43–61.

Sanderson, Alexis. 2009. 'The Saiva Age'. In *Genesis and Development of Tantricism*, ed. by Shingo Einoo. Tokyo: Institute of Oriental Culture, University of Tokyo. 41–350.

Sarkar, Bihani. 2017. *Heroic Shāktism: The Cult of Durga in Ancient Indian Kingship*. London: Oxford University Press.

Scheifinger, Heinz. 2013. 'Hindu Worship online and Offline'. In *Digital Religion Understanding Religious Practice in New Media Worlds*, ed. by Cambell, Heidi A. London and New York: Routledge. 1–21.

Sen, Mala. 2001. *Death by Fire: Sati, Dowry Death and Female Infanticide in Modern India*. London: Weidenfeld & Nicolson.

Sharma, R.S. 2014. *Early Medieval Indian Society – A Study in Feudalism*. Delhi: Orient Blackswan.

Shin, Jae-Eun. 2010. 'Yoni, Yoginīs and Mahāvidyās: Feminine Divinities from Early Medieval Kāmarūpa to Medieval Koch Behar'. *Studies in History* 26 (1): 1–29.

Shrimali, K. M. 2022. *The Religious Enterprise: Studies in Early Indian Religions*, Vol. I–II. Delhi: Aakar Books.

Shulman, David. 1976. 'The Murderous Bride: Tamil Versions of the Myth of Devī and the Buffalo-Demon'. *History of Religions* 16 (2): 120–46.

Shulman, David. 2014. *Tamil Temple Myths: Sacrifice and Divine Marriage in the South Indian Saiva Tradition*. Princeton: Princeton University Press.

Singer, Milton. 1972. *When a Great Tradition Modernizes: An Anthropological Approach to Indian Civilization*. United Kingdom: Pall Mall Press.

Sinha, Vineeta. 2010. 'Unraveling "Singaporean Hinduism": Seeing the Pluralism Within.' *International Journal of Hindu Studies* 14 (2/3): 253–79.

Sontheimer, Günther-Dietz. 2004. 'The Vana and the Kṣetra: The Tribal Background of Some Famous Cults'. In *Essays on Religion, Literature and Law*, ed. by Heidrun Brückner, Anne Feldhaus, Aditya Malik. New Delhi: Manohar. 353–60.

Spivak, Gayatri Chakraborty. 1999. 'Moving Devi'. In *Devi the Great Goddess: Female Divinity in South Asian Art*, ed. by Vidya Dehejia. Washington, DC: Arthur M. Sackler Gallery. 165–204.

Srinivas, M.N. 1952. *Religion and Society Among the Coorgs of South India*. Oxford: Clarendon Press.

Stietencron, Heinrich von. 2005. *Hindu Myths, Hindu History: Religion, Art, and Politics*. Delhi: Permanent Black.

Strauss, Claude - Lévi. 1955. 'The Structural Study of Myth'. *The Journal of American Folklore* 68 (270): 428–44.

Sunder Rajan, Rajeswari. 1998. 'Is the Hindu Goddess a Feminist?' *Economic and Political Weekly* 33 (44): WS-34–WS-38.

Sykes, Jim. 2015. 'Sound Studies, Religion and Urban Space: Tamil Music and the Ethical Life in Singapore'. *Ethnomusicology Forum* 24 (3): 380–413.

Taylor, M.C. 2013. 'Purāṇic Masculinities and Transgender Adventures in the Garden of the Goddess', *International Journal of Hindu Studies* 17 (2): 153–79.

Thapar, Romila. 2001. 'Perceiving the Forest: Early India'. *Studies in History* 17 (1): 1–16.

Tiwari, J.N. 1985. *Goddess Cults in Ancient India (With Special Reference to the First Seven Centuries A.D.)*. Delhi: Sundeep Prakashan.

Torkel, Brekke. 1999. 'The Role of Fear in Indian Religious Thought with Special Reference to Buddhism'. *Journal of Indian Philosophy* 27 (5): 439–67.

Urban, Hugh. 2003. 'The Power of the Impure: Transgression, Violence and Secrecy in Bengali Śākta Tantra and Modern Western Magic'. *Numen* 50 (3): 269–308.

Vaid, Sudesh and Kumkum Sangari. 1991. 'Institutions, Beliefs, and Ideologies: Widow Immolation in Contemporary Rajasthan'. *Economic and Political Weekly* 26 (17): 2–18.

Wadley, Susan. 1977. 'Women and Symbolic Systems' in Women and the Hindu Tradition'. *Signs* 3 (1): 113–25. Doi: 10.1353/jowh.2010.0003.

West, M.L. 2007. *Indo-European Poetry and Myth*. Oxford: Oxford University Press.

Wilson, Martin. 1996. *In Praise of Tārā: Songs to the Saviouress*. Massachusetts, MA: Wisdom Publications.

Xavier, S. 2009-2010. 'An Analytical Study on Sanskritisation of the Deities of Folk Tradition with Reference to Tamil Nadu'. *Proceedings of the Indian History Congress* 70: 621–34.

Yang, Anand A. 1989. '*Whose Sati?* Widow Burning in Early 19th Century India'. *Journal of Women's History* 1 (2): 8–33. Doi: 10.1353/jowh.2010.0003.

Younger, Paul.,1980. 'A Temple Festival of Māriyammaṉ.' *Journal of the American Academy of Religion* 48 (4): 493–517.

Zeiler Xenia, ed. 2020. *Digital Hinduism*. London and NY: Routledge.

Newspaper/Online Articles

Basu, Tanya. 'Hindus Are Thriving in America, But There Is Only One in Congress'. *The Atlantic*. Available at: https://www.theatlantic.com/politics/archive/2015/03/hindus-in-american-politics/386941/ (accessed on 8 April 2023).

Bell, Venessa. 2015. 'Controversial Religious Barbie Doll Exhibition Opens in Buenos Aires'. *The Guardian*. 21 October. Available at: https://www.theguardian.com/travel/2015/oct/21/barbie-and-ken-religious-art-exhibition (accessed on 8 April 2023).

Brown, Lee. 2020. 'Indian Man Prays to Life-Size Statue of Donald Trump, His "God"'. *New York Post*. Available at: https://nypost.com/2020/02/19/indian-man-prays-to-life-size-statue-of-donald-trump-his-god/ (accessed on 2 August 2023).

Dave, Pares. 'Indian Immigrants Are Tech's New Titans'. *Los Angeles Times*. 11 August 2015. Available at: https://www.latimes.com/business/la-fi-indians-in-tech-20150812-story.html#:~:text=There%20are%2089%2C000%20Indians%20living,into%20the%20start%2Dup%20economy (accessed on 8 March 2023).

'Donald Trump Pledges Even Better Ties with New Delhi, says "big fan of India and Hindus" in Times of India'. 16 October 2016. Available at: https://timesofindia.indiatimes.com/us-elections-2016/donald-trump-pledges-even-better-ties-with-new-delhi-says-big-fan-of-india-and-hindus/articleshow/54878649.cms (accessed on 30 July 2023).

Gajjar, Saloni. 2016. 'Donald Trump Attends "Humanity United against Terror" Event in New Jersey'. 16 October. Available at: https://www.india.com/lifestyle/donald-trump-attends-humanity-united-against-terror-event-in-new-jersey-1604268/ (accessed on 8 March 2023).

Graham, Ruth. 2023. 'Vivek Ramaswamy Leans into His Hindu Faith to Court Christian Voters'. *The New York Times*. 9 July. Available at: https://www.nytimes.com/2023/07/09/us/vivek-ramaswamy-hindu-republican-christianj.html (accessed on 28 July 2023).

Hindu American Foundation. 'Guidelines for Commercial Use of Hindu Images'. Available at: https://www.hinduamerican.org/projects/commercial-use-hindu-images-guide (accessed on 17 July 2023).

The Hindu. 2023.'Cardi B Apologizes for Goddess Durga Look on Magazine Cover'. Available at: https://www.thehindu.com/entertainment/cardi-b-apologises-for-goddess-durga-look-on-magazine-cover/article33083388.ece (accessed on 3 March 2023).

Kaushika, P. 2017. 'Ab ki baar, Modi Sarkar Slogan Was Born in BJP's Election War Room'. *The Print*. 11 September. Accessed at: https://theprint.in/report/ab-ki-baar-modi-sarkar-slogan-born-bjps-election-war-room/10684/ (accessed on 1 August 2023).

Pew Research Centre. 2024.'Indian Americans: A Survey Data Snapshot', Washington. Available at: https://www.pewresearch.org/2024/08/06/indian-americans-a-survey-data-snapshot/ (accessed on 4 August 2025).

Praneeth Rao @praneeth_rao. 2020. Pew Research Report. 2012. 'Asian Americans: A Mosaic of Faiths'. Available at: https://www.pewresearch.org/religion/2012/07/19/asian-americans-a-mosaic-of-faiths-overview/ (accessed on 30 July 2023).

Press Release from the office of Congressman Ro Khanna. 12 January 2023. Available at: https://khanna.house.gov/media/press-releases/representatives-khanna-bera-jayapal-krishnamoorthi-and-thanedar-celebrate (accessed on 28/6/2023).

Report on Registered Votes in Fall 2016. National Asian American Survey. 2016. Available at: https://naasurvey.com/wp-content/uploads/2016/10/NAAS2016-Oct5-report.pdf (accessed on 1 August 2023).

Republican Hindu Coalition Website. Available at: https://rhc-usa.org/about/ (accessed on 1 August 2023).

Schreckinger, B. 2016. 'Trump Goes Bollywood'. 15 October. Available at: https://www.politico.com/story/2016/10/donald-trump-bollywood-india-hindus-new-jersey-229848 (accessed on 1 August 2023).

Scroll Staff. 2020. 'Hindu Groups Express Anger over Tweet by Kamala Harris' Niece Showing Her as Goddess Durga'. Available at: https://scroll.in/latest/976307/hindu-groups-express-anger-over-tweet-by-kamala-harris-niece-showing-her-as-goddess-durga (accessed on 17 July 2023).

Sen, Atreyee. 2015. 'The Hindu Goddess in Indian Politics'. 29 May. Available at: https://politicaltheology.com/the-hindu-goddess-in-indian-politics-atreyee-sen/ (accessed on 8 March 2023).

Shukla, Suhag A. @SuhagAShukla on Twitter (now X). US Census. Available at: https://www.census.gov/programs-surveys/decennial-census/decade/2020/2020-census-results.htm (accessed on 27 July 2023).

Vijetha, S. N. 2014. 'Student Groups Come to Blows over Mahishasura Issue at JNU Once Again'. *The Hindu*, New Delhi, 11 October. Available at: https://www.thehindu.com/news/cities/Delhi/student-groups-come-to-blows-over-mahishasura-issue-at-jnu-once-again/article6491346.ece.

Wheaton, Oliver. 2014. '"Barbie-fication of Kali Is Wrong": Outrage at Artist's Barbie Doll of Hindu God'. 27 September. Available at: https://metro.co.uk/2014/09/27/barbie-fication-of-kali-is-wrong-outrage-at-artists-barbie-doll-of-hindu-god-4883933 (accessed on 8 March 2023).

About the Editors and Contributors

Editors

R. Mahalakshmi is Professor at the Centre for Historical Studies, Jawaharlal Nehru University, New Delhi. Her research interests include the development of state, and religious and art traditions in ancient and medieval India, Nepal, and Sri Lanka. Her book *The Making of the Goddess: Ko<u>r</u>ravai-Durga in the Tamil Traditions* (Penguin, 2011) was awarded the Professor Hiralal Gupta Prize for the Best Book by a Woman Historian by the Indian History Congress in 2013. She has also authored *The Book of Lakshmi* (Penguin, 2009), and edited *Art and History: Texts, Contexts and Visual Representations in Ancient and Early Medieval India* (Bloomsbury, 2020). She has co-edited the following: *The Economic History of India: Historiographical Issues and Perspectives-Essays in Honour of Ranabir Chakravarti*, with Suchandra Ghosh (Bloomsbury, 2023); and *Colonization: A Comparative Study of India and Korea*, with Vyjayanti Raghavan (Academic Foundation Books, 2015), in addition to contributing articles in peer-reviewed journals and books. She has been co-investigator in an international project on 'India and Korea: A Comparative Study of Colonialism', funded by the Academy of Korean Studies, Korea. She was Visiting Professor in 2018 at the Institut für Kunst-und Bildgeschichte, Humboldt University, and in 2023 at the Theologische Fakultät, Humboldt University. She has served as Secretary of the Indian History Congress for the period 2018–22. She has delivered the Presidential addresses of the Historiography Section of the Andhra Pradesh History Congress for 2018–19, and the Ancient Section of the Punjab History Conference (2019–20). She was the editor of the journal *Studies in History* (Sage), and is currently on the editorial board of *The India International Centre Quarterly*. She has been elected President of the Ancient India section, Indian History Congress (2024). She is currently working on two projects related to performative traditions in early Tamil Nadu and the history of the Cō<u>l</u>as.

Dr Malavika Binny is Assistant Professor in the Department of History at Kannur University, Kerala. She is an intersectional feminist and a gender historian who works on the theme of global medical histories. Her focus areas include Dalit histories, histories of science and religion and folklore studies. She was the recipient of the prestigious EU-Erasmus scholarship in

2015, and the Elamkulam Kunjan Pillai Young Historian Award instituted by the Kerala History Congress in 2016.

Dr Megha Yadav is Assistant Professor in the Department of History of Eswari School of Liberal Arts at SRM University, Andhra Pradesh. Her research interests include the transmission of religious traditions, Tibetan Buddhism, visual landscapes, goddess traditions and gender history in the ancient and early medieval period of the Indian subcontinent. She has made presentations and published several articles related to these themes. She is the recipient of inherit fellowship (2024–5) from the Käte Hamburger Centre for Advanced Study, *inherit, heritage in transformation*, Humboldt University, Germany, and is currently working on Thangka paintings and the visual landscape of Tibetan Buddhism.

Contributors

Dr Anisha Saxena is currently Associate Professor in the History Department at Cortland University, New York, USA. She trained as an art historian and historian of ancient and early medieval South Asia in the School of Arts and Aesthetics and the Centre for Historical Studies at JNU, respectively. Her PhD on 'Landscapes, Memory and History: Claims and Conflicts in the Constitution of Sacred Geographies in Western India' brought out important methodological and analytical frames to understand religious claims and identities. She was a Fulbright-Doctoral Fellow in 2011 at the Department of Religion, Syracuse University, New York. She has published papers on contested sacred geography and narratives of sexual assault in early South Asian literature.

Professor Arun Gupto is Director of Comparative South Asian Studies in the South Asian Foundation for Academic Research (SAFAR), Kathmandu. He is also faculty at Institute of Advanced Communication, Education, and Research (IACER). He taught for several years in the Central Department of English at Tribhuvan University, Kathmandu. His research primarily focuses on South Asia from a cultural studies perspective. He is engaged in the project 'Rethinking South Asian Studies' that critiques the existing modes of area studies as the research cuts across the conventional and hegemonic discourses of regionalism. His book *Goddesses of Kathmandu Valley: Grace, Rage, Knowledge* (Routledge, 2017) is a groundbreaking study.

He is supervising researchers to publish anthologies on Nepal-Bangladesh Memory Studies and Nepali Art: Spaciality, Texuality and Sexuality. His recently published book, *Theory and Criticism: Recent Writings from South Asia* (Routledge, 2022), focuses on a critical discourse in select South Asian English writings. He has produced three documentaries *Art of the Lake* (2011), *Art and the City* (2021) and *Anger and the Mahatma* (2023).

Dr Ashima Ahuja is an independent scholar who completed her doctoral thesis entitled 'The Contexts and Significance of the *Śilpa Śāstras* in Early India, c. 5th to 15th centuries CE', with the aim to explore the architectural typologies and to decipher the notions and social values that guided the rendering of a space, a structure or an image; this includes, urban and rural spaces, palaces, dwellings, temples, sculptures and everyday objects. She has presented papers and published in related areas.

Dolan Samanta teaches history at Vasant Valley School, New Delhi. She completed her MPhil on 'Contextualising Ūrdhvaliṅga Śiva in Central India – c. 7th–14th centuries CE' in 2022. Her research interests include social history of early India, gender and sexuality studies, and early and medieval Indian art. She has presented papers in these areas.

Dr Malini Adiga is an independent researcher specializing in the study of early medieval Karnataka, specifically on gender and family. After completing her PhD from the Jawaharlal Nehru University in 1997, she was the recipient of post-doctoral research grants from ICHR and UGC wherein she was affiliated to the Mangalore University from 1998 to 2000 and 2004 to 2009. Her thesis was published as *The Making of Southern Karnataka: Society, Polity and Culture in the Early Medieval Period (AD 400–1030)*, by Orient Longman in 2006. She has also published several papers in various edited works on gender, family and kinship as well as on state formation and economic structure in early medieval Karnataka. She presided over the Ancient India section of the Indian History Congress in its eighty-first session, held at Chennai in December 2022. Her presidential address was titled 'Contours of the Family in Early Medieval Karnataka (1000–1300 CE)'.

Navoneel Ray is a doctoral candidate at the Centre for Historical Studies in Jawaharlal Nehru University, New Delhi. After completing his graduation from the St. Stephen's College, Delhi, he specialized in ancient Indian history during his postgraduation from the Centre for Historical Studies. His research focuses on the conceptualization of Mahākāla in the Śaiva traditions. His area of interest includes various aspects of religious history, such as Tantricism, esotericism, the occult and interactions between the state and religion.

Dr Prerana Roy is Assistant Professor at Shaheed Bhagat Singh College, University of Delhi. She has submitted her PhD, titled 'Marriage, Family and Kinship in Ancient India (c. 1500 BCE–6th Century CE)', covering an array of sources such as the Vedic, Buddhist, Jaina and epic literature. Her research interests include early Indian perspectives on gender, family, households, normative and popular texts. She has presented several papers and published on these themes. Her paper 'Women and the Household in the Shadows of Marriage: The *Ṛg Veda* and *Avestan* Tradition' won the Dr. Nasreen Ahmad Memorial Prize for the Best Paper in Gender History at the eighty-second session of the Indian History Congress, 2023.

Dr Sneha Ganguly is an independent scholar who has completed her PhD from the Centre for Historical Studies, Jawaharlal Nehru University. Her Doctoral Thesis titled '*Asura, Rākṣasa* and the "Other" in the Brahmanical Tradition, c. 1500 BCE–1200 CE' is based on an examination of a wide range of literary and visual sources. For her MPhil, she has analysed the textual and visual representations of Kālī in the early medieval period. Her interest lies in the socio-religious history of ancient and early medieval India with a special focus on issues related to goddess traditions, 'othering' and visual representations. She was the recipient of the Sungum Sudhar Award for research on the *Vedas*. She has presented in national and international conferences, and published articles in journals and edited volumes. She has taught in 2022–3 at the Jesus and Mary College, University of Delhi.

Trisha is a doctoral candidate at the Centre for Historical Studies, Jawaharlal Nehru University, working on the Jaina canonical literature. Her MPhil titled 'Prognostication as Knowledge: A Contextual Analysis of the Jaina *Aṅgavijjā* (c. 1st Century BCE–6th Century CE)' focused on an important text that had not hitherto been translated, which she had undertaken in her research. She has been the recipient of Bhagwan Mahavir Fellowship for Prakrit Language from International School of Jaina Studies (ISJS), Pune, and holds a PG Diploma in Prakrit Language and Literature from Gujarat University, Ahmedabad. Her research interests include the study of esoteric traditions, socio-cultural contexts of Jaina epistemology, narrative literature and Prakrit and Sanskrit linguistics.

Dr Twinkle Siwach is Assistant Professor in the Department of Sociology at Lady Sri Ram College, University of Delhi. She completed her PhD titled 'FIR and Media: Informational Universe of Crime and Violence in Contemporary India' from the Centre for Media Studies, Jawaharlal Nehru University. She has presented several papers and published articles related to gender and law, and other aspects of contemporary society.

Index